Rod Howard is an Australian wi   ast
book *Getting Hitched* explored   nd
rituals. He has written profiles, humour, travel, parenting and sport
features for many Australian newspapers and magazines. He lives in
Melbourne with his partner Catherine and their two young children.

Louis De Rougemont, The Wide World Magazine, *1898*

The Fabulist

The Incredible Story of Louis De Rougemont

ROD HOWARD

RANDOM HOUSE AUSTRALIA

Random House Australia Pty Ltd
20 Alfred Street, Milsons Point, NSW 2061
http://www.randomhouse.com.au

Sydney New York Toronto
London Auckland Johannesburg

First published by Random House Australia 2006

National Library of Australia
Cataloguing-in-Publication Entry

Howard, Rod.
   The fabulist: the incredible story of Louis De Rougemont.

   Bibliography.
   Includes index.
   ISBN 978 1 74166 464 5.
   ISBN 1 74166 464 0.

   1. Rougemont, Louis de, 1847–1921. 2. Impostors and imposture – Biography.
I. Title.

001.95092

Front cover illustration from *The Wide World Magazine*
Back cover illustration © Hulton-Deutsch Collection/CORBIS
Cover design by Christabella Designs
Typeset in Caslon Classico 12/14 pt by Midland Typesetters, Australia
Printed and bound by Griffin Press, South Australia

10 9 8 7 6 5 4 3 2 1

for Catherine
whose wonders are beyond words

'Yamba was my advance agent and bill poster, so to say.' — De Rougemont

Preface

Louis De Rougemont is one of the most fascinating yet little-known characters in post-European Australian history. After he stormed the London headlines in the northern summer of 1898, Henry Lawson declared De Rougemont had made 'a bigger splash in three months than any other Australian writer had begun to make in a hundred years'. Lawson predicted Louis's own book, *The Adventures of Louis De Rougemont – As Told By Himself* (published in England, Europe, Australia and the United States the following year) was destined to become an Australian classic: 'one of the gospels of childhood'. But it was not to be.

I happened upon Lawson's unpublished paean to this shadowy character by chance in an archive copy of the journal of the State Library of Victoria, while researching a work on the follies of early private European expeditions to inland Australia. I had already had several accidental encounters with Louis through old newspaper clippings and had subsequently browsed the public domain version of his book at the Project Gutenberg website. The story of a French merchant's son marooned with Australian Aboriginals for thirty years seemed entirely surreal, yet it echoed accounts by other castaways and lost adventurers over the ages. De Rougemont's sudden rise to celebrity in an era of technological wonderment, when new forms of communication were shrinking the globe and revolutionising media, also seemed to have strange resonances with our own time. But who was Louis De Rougemont? Castaway or crank? My curiosity was piqued and my original purpose fell by the wayside as I became set on pursuing every lead which might help reveal the truth of this unusual man's life.

As is often the case with historical figures from nineteenth-century Australia, the real starting point was not Australia but England. In London, my quest led me to British Library Newspapers in Colindale, the UK's national archive of British and overseas newspapers, where I found thick reams of newsprint chronicling Louis's extraordinary journey to fame. While De Rougemont's original London digs near the British Museum in Bloomsbury Street had by now been radically transformed into a Radisson hotel, the Museum Reading Room, where De Rougemont had carried out his own research, was preserved much as it had been in his day, providing close insight into Louis's experience.

Contemporary newspaper accounts were equally abundant in Australia and the United States. On my return to Australia I traced Louis's descendants, hoping to gain access to diaries or letters written in the protagonist's own hand. Their assistance was freely offered but there was little to tell — when De Rougemont had deserted his young family in Australia he had been deemed the blackest of sheep, and his personal papers were destroyed soon after. Other frustrations familiar to any historical researcher also arose — enquiries at the Royal Geographical Society in London revealed that seven letters exchanged between De Rougemont's original magazine publisher and the Society regarding the authentication of his experiences had disappeared over the ensuing century. The Society's endorsement of De Rougemont had later become the focus of much controversy, but I resisted the temptation to indulge conspiracy theories.

Other explorations were more fruitful. At the height of his fame, De Rougemont was a prolific writer to popular newspapers and journals and these provide a unique record of the Fabulist's own inimitable voice. Many of his public speeches were reported verbatim at the time. Ever the publicist, De Rougemont was also in the habit of freely distributing signed copies of his book, some of which contained brief, often cryptic, letters to the recipient. One now in my possession contains a note to his landlady communicating his imminent departure for Southampton 'due to an error'. Another promises a minister in British Guiana that 'all shall be revealed soon'. Celebrity attracts company like moths to light and many of De Rougemont's contemporaries also wrote detailed accounts of their encounters with the man in books, letters and journals. These proved to be invaluable sources. However, only two previous books deal with De Rougemont's life in any real detail — a twenty-three page pamphlet entitled *The Greatest Liar on Earth* by Australian journalist Frank Clune, published in 1945, and *The Most Amazing Story A Man Ever Did Live To Tell,* a more substantial account written by Geoffrey Maslen in 1977.

Most elusive of all the leads I followed in researching this book, but eventually one of the most satisfying, was the true story of Louis

De Rougemont's fateful encounters with Charles Milward, a New Zealand Shipping Company captain who was a distant relative to the late author Bruce Chatwin. Chatwin had written of De Rougemont's meetings with Milward in his first book *In Patagonia*, but controversy has since surrounded the authenticity of his accounts. In the course of his travels, Chatwin had visited Charles Milward's daughter in Lima, Monica Milward Barnett, who permitted him to peruse the captain's journals. Without Barnett's knowledge, however, Chatwin went on to reproduce large sections of it in *In Patagonia*. A copyright wrangle ensued. Though Chatwin and Barnett later resolved their dispute and became friends, the journals had not been sighted since. As this book fast approached the printer's press, I finally traced Charles Milward's grandson, Christopher J. Barnett. Despite his mother's experience with Chatwin, Christopher very kindly offered his assistance and after a few days' search rediscovered the transcript of Milward's journal in an unmarked box in his basement. The accounts of Louis De Rougemont's encounters with Charles Milward in this book are directly based on these journal entries (Milward's original material remains copyright Monica Milward Barnett).

Bruce Chatwin's biographer Nicholas Shakespeare said of his inventive subject that he told not 'a half-truth but a truth and a half'. It is a description that could be equally applied to Louis De Rougemont. *The Fabulist* is an exploration of the life and times of a man whose talents for self-invention were unparalleled. Inevitably, the nature of such a life means that a complete documentary record is hard to establish. Some of De Rougemont's own tales were further embellished by acquaintances and reporters. Official records are no more dependable — even Louis De Rougemont's death certificate reveals posthumous amendments to his age and occupation. All newspaper, book and journal extracts reproduced herein are faithfully rendered, but on occasion I have been faced with wildly conflicting accounts of events. In a few cases, some licence has been taken in recreating conversations and events based on all available fact. My intention has been to provide a detailed portrait reflecting the many dimensions of this remarkable man.

Rod Howard
Melbourne, 2006

Table of Contents

Australian history is almost always picturesque; indeed it is so curious and strange, that it is itself the chiefest novelty the country has to offer, and so it pushes all other novelties into second and third place.

It does not read like history but like the most beautiful lies. And all of a fresh new sort, no mouldy old stale ones. It is full of surprises and adventures, and incongruities, and contradictions, and incredibilities; but they are all true, they all happened.

Mark Twain
Following the Equator, 1897

The world is travelling toward the extinction of its magic. There may come a day when every part of the earth's surface will be intimately known, when the powers will have divided up all the habitable land . . . all the mountains will have been climbed, all the deserts explored, every strange fowl and beast dissected and classified . . . There will come a day when narratives like M. de Rougemont's are the tritest commonplace and posterity will envy us our opportunities of credulity.

The Speaker
24 September, 1898

I

Strange Cargo

The real voyage of discovery consists not in seeking new
landscapes but in having new eyes.

Marcel Proust

TWO DAYS PRIOR TO his departure from New Zealand, with his
passage secured aboard the SS *Mataura*, the tramp solicited one final
forecast from the world beyond. It did not bode well. He abandoned
his duties on deck, cornered the captain and delivered his absurd
warning in a Continental slur.[1]

'I have spoken with the spirits. The ship will be wrecked but all
hands will be saved.'

Having signed him on solely for amusement, Charles Milward
surveyed the impossibly furrowed face of his new swab with fast-
fading interest.

The following day, the captain of the neighbouring SS *Waikato*,
bound for London via the Cape, visited Milward's quarters to solicit
the services of an able man. Milward told him he had none to spare,
but less than an hour before the *Mataura* was to sail, Captain Croucher
returned to his friend's cabin in desperation. He told Milward that the
Union, aware he needed a man to complete his crew, had raised
the wages a fabulous amount.

'Give me anything that wears trousers and I'll make him do.'

Milward pointed to the tramp, at that moment scrubbing his cabin
floor.

'You can take him, if you like.'

'Oh, he'll do all right,' replied Croucher.

Milward told the tramp to pack his bag and go aboard the *Waikato*.

The tramp continued to scrub without looking up.

'No,' he replied.

'Did you understand me?' said the captain. 'You will go home in the *Waikato*.'

Still the tramp did not move.

'No.'

Milward considered sending for his chief officer to put him over the side before deciding to do the job himself. He pulled the man up from the floor by the seat of the pants and the nape of the neck, hauled him from the cabin and ran him down the ship's ladder. A few rungs from the bottom he despatched the tramp's meatless rump on to the Wellington dock with a final kick. His belongings followed.

The tramp picked himself up and ran down the wharf to the nearby magistrate's office to obtain a warrant for assault. The magistrate, a friend of Milward, was eating his lunch. The warrant was not forthcoming. By the time the tramp returned, the *Mataura* had slipped her tethers and was heading out from Queen's Wharf.

The tramp ran along the dock until he was abreast of the bridge. Mounting one of the big bollards, he waved an arm to Milward and sounded his warning call.

'Captain, remember, remember! There is trouble to the Eastward.'

Spying some loose coal upon the foredeck, Milward called to his bo'sun.

'Have a shot and see if you can knock him off his perch.'

The bo'sun seized a lump and hurled it over the waters, hitting the frantically waving seer and dislodging him from his post. Undeterred, the man rose from the boards and continued along the wharf shouting his portent. When he reached wharf's end, he climbed atop the corner bollard and cried out again, 'Remember, there is trouble to the Eastward.'

Captain Milward ordered his bo'sun to take another shot but this time he missed his mark. The last Milward saw of the tramp that morning was his waving figure shrinking into the Wellington distance. As the *Mataura* slid out into Cook Strait, the captain of the *Waikato* strolled up, retrieved the black lump from the wharf and pitched it to the tramp with a smile. Negotiations were brief — all work and no pay.

Aboard the *Waikato*, the man was designated quarters in a stinking crevice of the hold. They sailed the following morning. For nigh sixty days the tramp worked twelve waking hours: seven shovelling coke into a searing furnace and five working the deck under a relentless sun. He slept five. In the remainder he filled several grimy, cotton-clothed notebooks in an elaborate scrawl, flooding their pages to the edge. He was no stranger to the life of the sea. There in the hull's depths he counted for company a colony of bilge rats. Mould grew before his eyes. He took his meals in the hold, all the while entertaining his fellows — a scrofulous, black-humoured band of stokers and way-payers — with incredible tales of adventure in the tropics. He had survived violent seas and deadly deserts, shipwreck and disaster; witnessed miraculous events and performed near-biblical feats; wrestled crocodiles and tamed snakes. It was all re-enacted with flailing limb in a performance that held his audience captive through the roaring forties and beyond. As he leapt from one astonishment to the next, his hooded, weary eyes sparked into life. The eroded face that seemed so defeated at rest joined the dance, the red-ridged flesh contorting in excitement. A voice and vocabulary too refined for a mere beggar completed an act of beguiling showmanship.

His conviction was indisputable. If the stories were true, his forti-tude, let alone his memory, was phenomenal; if false, his powers of invention equally so. The impossible events he described seemed more than enough to occupy several lifetimes, but few of his life-hungry crewmates questioned their veracity. What did it matter as long as the hypnotic tales caused one to forget the killing heat, made time evaporate and brought London drifting ever closer across the drink? Even the most leery among them stilled his tongue lest he break the spell.

To relieve the monotony and obtain some paltry reward, he also moonlighted at palmistry, demonstrating an accuracy that surprised even him. He was well connected in other worlds. Previously, in Sydney and various towns of New Zealand, he had plied the nascent trade of spirit photographer, miraculously summoning up apparitions of departed loved ones in the ill-lit background of customers' photo-graphs. In Wellington he had survived by falling in with a group of mediums attached to a travelling circus. Now his fame rose above decks, and soon sea-bored passengers were being ushered below to occupy an upturned steel trunk at the foot of the fireladder, their palms extended in anticipation. The medium chattered artfully, relaxing and drawing out his clientele, his accent exaggerated for effect. The portents were usually good — the occasional setback was thrown in only for the sake of verisimilitude. Broken hearts, catastrophe, acts of God and sudden death were bad for business. The passengers' disbelief was willingly suspended. Only a corpulent and corrupt insurance clerk would later return to complain. The medium, he said, had only reported what had already happened. But the tramp shook his head. Past and future, he said, were all the same.

'The past was the future once. It is only a different way of looking. It is best for you,' he told the gallows-bound thief, 'that I tell the past.'

The fortune-telling business earned him a few merciful guineas for his own future on English soil. At journey's end he signed off and slipped invisibly away, leaving behind nothing but a name on the ship's log.

The tramp was last to descend the plank into the first London spring morning of 1898. He clutched only a ball of torn canvas wound about with rope pilfered from the *Waikato*'s hold. It concealed a single soot-smothered vest, a stub of lead, the notebooks and a Reader's Card for the British Museum. Coal dust was baked into his skin, polished by sun and furnace to a ruddy sheen. From his wiry form hung a lattice of tweed alive with itinerant bugs, distant descendants of recent emigrants to the southern colonies.

London Dock was jammed with business under a sky fouled by smoking funnels. The thrum of steam-driven cranes, machinery and rattling chains deafened him. At the wharf's end was the port's less profitable trade — families strewn amid their thin scatterings of possessions. From their grim demeanour it was impossible to tell whether their passage had just been made or paid. At fifty yards he felt their desperation leach through his tweed coat, through the sun-cracked crust of his skin. He walked swiftly by. He did not wish to know, or tell, their fates.

He rollicked free of the port, swinging the canvas bundle, the earth in perpetual motion below sea-swaying legs. Beside him was the Thames: the same river from which the seasick Darwin had ventured on the *Beagle* to alter the course of humanity's past and future; upon which the brave explorer Livingstone's gutted, sun-dried, salt-stuffed corpse, borne lifeless out of the newfound depths of Africa, made final passage home; from which even now an expedition vessel, the *Southern*

Cross, was being readied for journey to the final frontier, the vast white wastes of Antarctica. It was the river upon which the tramp himself had some three decades earlier first set out across the seas.

He sludged from Billingsgate up through manure-ridden streets, skirting the cab-clamouring City, before being swallowed up in the riotous din of Soho. By afternoon he had secured a filthy airless boarding-house room in Frith Street, furnishing only a story as his bond. Infallible destiny had led him to lodgings inhabited by ghosts of travellers past. His very room had been host to Swift, creator of the fabulous Gulliver, explorer of imaginary lands. Soho was territory familiar to the expatriate European from his wandering youth. But his desiccated flesh now housed a different self and all seemed new once more. Here the ages collided and fused into a single continuum, the centuries of squalor, greed, misery and excess on naked parade. It emboldened him, made everything possible, fortified him with Gulliver's spirit. In Sydney, an infant city, his senses had hungered for the absent past.

Next morning, following a sleep torn by fevered dreams of fire and brine, he made his way on foot to Bloomsbury. He detoured down Great Queen Street, through the neighbourhood of the occultists and spiritualists. Clairvoyants spruiked at doorways and stairwells for custom. The futures trade. The city delivered a near inexhaustible supply of the insecure, woebegone and gullible. Opposite the Theosophists' Society he turned off Great Russell Street, up the stone steps and through the towering colonnade of the British Museum.

To either side of the entrance ran corridors leading to the great viewing halls, brimming with antiquities, treasures and relics. But he had not come to gape at the spoils of imperial conquest. Ahead in the courtyard sprouted the huge edifice of the British Museum Reading Room. The palace of the printed word, repository of more than a million works, of pages enough, laid end to end, to stretch from London to Wellington and back again. The high circular walls were crowned by a great copper dome, cloaked in grime by the city's constant effusion of smoke and char.

Entry was by possession of a Reader's Card only, an honour bestowed upon only the most serious of researchers. Thackeray, Thomas Hardy and George Bernard Shaw had all passed through these doors. He looked the Admissions Clerk in the eye and presented him with the card his brother had posted to him in Wellington. The clerk bade him sign the register and waved him through the arched doorway. The tramp's ship-soiled appearance was clearly insufficient to deny him entry. His way had already been paved by the poverty and eccentricities of his predecessors. He was not the first to appear at the entrance in rags, nor the first to gain admission under false pretences. One famous Reader's Card holder, Sherlock Holmes, did not even exist. Had the clerk cared to decipher the lavish French script in his register, he would have found that the tramp had given not the name inscribed upon the card he had shown, but instead, 'Louis De Rougemont'.

Inside the chamber, rows of oak desks radiated out from a ring of catalogues. An Inspections Officer surveyed his territory from a central wooden eyrie. Now, breathing the same dust-fouled air that had sustained Dickens and Marx, De Rougemont prepared to stake his own place in history. He laid his notebooks down on a numbered desk. His writing stub rolled slowly toward him across the surface, over wood hollowed from forty years supporting the books and heads of stale academics, godweary clergy and hallucinatory writers. The incessant rubbing of cloth, paper, skin and sweat had burnished the oak until it gleamed. Underneath the desk, heated water flowing through a copper pipe supplied warmth to De Rougemont's feet. Beyond the detection of the eagle-eyed inspector he removed his footwear — stockings and all — and the odour from his corn-crusted feet conspired with paper mould, binding glue and ink to produce a single pernicious funk.

The reading room's treasures were arrayed around the walls. Three encircling tiers of shelves, filled with over five centuries of printed works, stretched upward to the dome's inner rim. Beyond the walls lay a maze of book stacks accessible only to the dust-jacketed clerks. Huge iron ribs, like futtocks of a capsized ship's hull, curved upward to support the ceiling. Cathedral window couplets admitted pale daylight. The weak illumination left the squinting scholars below crouching over their books in the half-dark, like monks memorising scrolls in a medieval abbey. Sunrays failed to penetrate the dome's silted glass summit. In earlier times, heavy fog would force the readers to be ejected and the room closed. Now, with the miracle of electricity, arc lamps flung light from above, casting De Rougemont's narrow silhouette upon the oak.

De Rougemont left his notebook upon the desk and ascended the stairs leading to the treasures above. He crab-walked slowly along the galleys adjacent to the open shelves, circumnavigating each tier in turn and perusing the titles on offer. On the second lap he halted at the ethnographic section and scanned the worn cloth and calf spines, removing several volumes: *Among Cannibals*; Robert Louis Stevenson's *In the South Seas*; Peter Longueville's *The English Hermit*; *The Cannibal Islands*. One, an 1837 text of particular interest, boasted the longest title De Rougemont had ever encountered:

The Shipwreck of Mrs. Fraser, and the loss of the Stirling Castle, on a Coral Reef in the South Pacific Ocean. Containing an account of the hitherto unheard-of sufferings and hardships of the crew, who existed for seven days without food or water. The dreadful sufferings of Mrs. Fraser, who, with her husband, and the survivors of the ill-fated crew, are captured by the savages of New Holland, and by them stripped entirely naked, and driven into the bush. Their dreadful slavery, cruel toil, and excruciating tortures inflicted on them. The horrid death of Mr. Brown, who was roasted alive over a slow fire kindled beneath his feet. Meeting of Mr. and Mrs. Fraser, and inhuman murder of Captain Fraser in the presence of his wife. Barbarous treatment of Mrs. Fraser, who is tortured, speared, and wounded by the savages. The fortunate escape of one of the crew, to Moreton Bay, a neighbouring British settlement, by whose instrumentality, through the ingenuity of a convict, named Graham, the survivors obtain their deliverance from the savages. Their subsequent arrival in England, and appearance before the Lord Mayor of London.

At twenty-four pages long, the actual text only just outweighed the title. It told of the survival of the pregnant wife of a ship's captain, Eliza Fraser, in the company of a tribe of Aboriginals at Wide Bay in Queensland. Later, repatriated to England, she had painted up her story for profit and unashamedly presented it to public and press.

It would be half the day before De Rougemont returned to his station below. After half a lifetime in book-starved colonial wilds, he wanted to savour the menu before sitting down to the feast.

2

Chance Encounters

The web of things on every side is joined by links we cannot see.
Anonymous

HAD CAPTAIN CHARLES MILWARD heeded the tramp's grim forecast he would not have been doomed to shiver in a makeshift cabin on the glacial outskirts of Patagonia, watching from Desolation Island as the SS *Mataura* was torn apart by storm and surf in the violent western entrance to the Strait of Magellan, 4700 miles from Wellington. There had been trouble to the Eastward.

Mataura was Maori for 'survival', yet broken engines had paralysed the New Zealand Shipping Company's newest vessel, leaving it at Neptune's mercy. Milward's valiant attempt to round Cape Pilar under sail and reach the relative serenity of the strait was cut short by a pinnacle of rock that shredded the *Mataura*'s stern. From its stricken hull frozen lamb carcasses floated, legs abob, toward the uncharted Antarctic, never to grace the linen-dressed tables of the clubs of Pall Mall.

As Milward's tramp had predicted, no passengers or crew had perished. The loyal captain ferried them safely ashore in boats and remained by his vessel for two months and more, supervising the salvage of the remaining cargo. When relief finally arrived he sailed for England on the *Orellana*. After docking at Liverpool on a cold May night, Milward caught a train to London and slept in the Euston Station waiting room. After hot breakfast at the Euston Hotel he proceeded to the shipping company offices in Leadenhall Street to face the cold judgement of his masters.

Louis De Rougemont did not know of the final fate of the SS *Mataura* until he walked up from Leadenhall market that morning and met Milward alighting from a hansom cab. The newly thawed Captain froze again upon sight of the tramp. De Rougemont addressed him brightly.

'Well, Captain, was I right? Was there trouble to Eastward?'

Milward rushed past him up the steps and asked the porter at the door, a man named Mortimer, how long the tramp been standing there.

'Only about ten minutes, sir,' came the reply.

'I don't mean how long today,' Milward said, 'but how long has he been hanging around.'

'I never saw him in my life before this morning, about ten minutes ago,' Mortimer replied.

Milward returned to the pavement and grabbed Louis by the lapels.

'Tell me, how the devil did you know I was coming to England? Who told you?'

'The same what told me that there was trouble to Eastward,' replied Louis enigmatically, 'the spirits.'

Captain Milward told him to get to glory with his spirits, turned pale, turned on his heel and entered the offices. The company did not tolerate failure. When he emerged, spirit broken, he was a captain no longer. His maiden voyage at the helm was also his last. And the doomsayer was gone.

Milward later wrote in his journal:

> I cannot attempt to explain his presence, but can only state what actually happened. However, as a result of this incident, I was very much upset, which did not help me during the subsequent interview with the Manager of the New Zealand Shipping Company. A few minutes later, I left his office — sacked. Sacked! After twenty years of service with the company, on account of my ship's engines having broken down . . .

On exploratory forays from the museum, De Rougemont sought to revive his career in spirit photography. His studies there remained incomplete, but the profits of his shipboard prophecy were exhausted, compelling him to seek a new source of funds. De Rougemont's word was literally his bond, and without regular rent money, it had fast become insufficient to satisfy the Soho slumlady. He persuaded one

Great Queen Street medium to allow him a trial session, and using this man's equipment, De Rougemont demonstrated great proficiency in his craft, employing a certain alchemy with the light and emulsion to beckon forth his phantoms. But the job was also an illusion — the charlatan, new to the lurk, had only wanted to see how it could be done and offered no paying position. Even De Rougemont's mastery of the unworldly arts could not conjure cash from out of the thin London air.

The Fates had else in mind. The morning following his encounter with Milward, De Rougemont relinquished his precious post at the museum to join the throng of the dispossessed scouting for outdoor lodgings by the docks. If he was lucky, by nightfall he might find shelter in a half-rotten shipping crate or Portuguese port barrel. He left the museum forecourt, turned the corner into Bloomsbury Street and walked straight into the path of a man who had once employed him in Sydney. It was not a moment too soon. James Murphy would be his salvation.

Their acquaintance had been struck during Sydney summer at a quayside hotel where Murphy was in the habit of slaking his appetites. On this sweltering day the barmaid had shaken him from her tail by sloughing him off on an inexplicable, drinkless Frenchman bearing an umbrella at the opposite end of the bar. After exchanging the customary insults and lies, the two expatriates had made an arrangement to mutual advantage. Murphy represented the owners of a new housing estate on the Georges River, in the Sutherland area, south of the city. In order to enhance the area's attractions, they had attached romantic European names, such as Como and Sylvania, to the divisions of land. The employment of the smooth-talking Continental as salesman would help to complete the scene and lure prospective residents.

The Irishman Murphy and his new protégé had worked together over several years. The construction of a railway bridge spanning the river in 1885 assisted in enticing city-dwellers south, and Murphy had so believed in the estate's potential that he established expansive 'Pleasure Gardens' on the riverbanks at Como. He built a promenade, boatsheds, summer houses and swimming baths. He erected a band pavilion to stage dances, and the gardens soon became known as a fashionable rendezvous for courting lovers. In keeping with the European theme, Murphy even built a Swiss chalet overlooking the river for himself, but never lived there, preferring instead a one-room shed on the same property. Murphy's romanticisation of the region led to no shortage of sales prospects, but De Rougemont had grown weary of spruiking bare, stone-studded blocks of land. It held little appeal, he sulked to his employer, for a man who had traversed vast oceans and roamed unmapped deserts. Worse, the fruits of Murphy's successes had rarely been split with his sidekick. Eventually the men had parted company, though without acrimony.

Since his arrival in London, Murphy had successfully encouraged City financiers to sink perfectly good sterling into worthless West Australian goldmines. They might as well have assayed Brighton Rock. De Rougemont and his wealth of tales seemed to Murphy to present new possibilities. In honour of past debts and hope of future benefits, Murphy paid out the Frenchman's back rent and escorted him to his digs at 13 Bloomsbury Street. The rooms were directly adjacent to the British Museum and a vast improvement on Soho, the hold of the *Waikato* or a dockside rathole.

By day, De Rougemont bent his back to the bound volumes and notebooks in the museum. By night, the City prospector Murphy mined him for all he was worth, seeking to extract the seed of future ventures. It was clear to Murphy that profit might somehow obtain from the Frenchman's silver tongue, but it was not yet clear how. When he asked De Rougemont about his business at the museum the torrent of tales stuttered to a trickle, and De Rougemont resumed the cryptic mien of the below-decks clairvoyant. If pressed, the Frenchman would recline in sulky silence on the settee, his calloused unstockinged feet fishing off one end. Soon, though, he would be sitting upright again, grasping the Irishman by the singlet-straps and launching into another implausible instalment. Murphy had no choice but to bide his time and wait for matters to unfold.

De Rougemont may have been a blue-sky investment, but his wealth of stories was not his only meal ticket. Murphy liked to eat but not to cook, and the Frenchman was soon appointed *chef principal*. His specialty was not the high cuisine of France. De Rougemont told Murphy that, while pearling in the tropics, he been required to pacify the mutinous temper of a crew fed up with fish, with no more than basic rations. Then, marooned with the natives of Northern Australia, he had learnt to survive on even meaner sustenance: the ingredients found in a barren, imprisoning landscape where bread was unknown and water the utmost luxury. While Murphy contrived his next attempt to fleece the lambs of London's financial district, money ran short. They lived off a little cheap meat, flour and potatoes. Whatever De Rougemont could wrest away from other scavengers under stall-holder's feet at Leadenhall, Spitalfield and Covent Garden completed the larder. Cabbage leaves secreting verdant slime, a few wormy apples, maggot-concealing sausage. A wander along the riverbank to Billingsgate might also produce a few fish heads for soup. He once returned with an escaped Dutch eel trophied in hunting along the docks. From these he concocted an eclectic menu unfamiliar to his Irish friend.

It was sufficient to sustain De Rougemont through six weeks' toil under the great dome of the museum reading room. By now he had concluded his anthropological period; moved through the geographical; perused journals and studied myriad maps delivered from the stacks. De Rougemont's pencil ran across the page of a third notebook. One volume remained of interest to him — an Australian work entitled *A Dictionary of Dates and Men of the Time*, compiled by John Henneker Heaton. It contained a brief survey of Caucasians known to have lived in isolation with Australian Aboriginals.

Some, like the 'wild white man', William Buckley, were already familiar to De Rougemont. Convicted of receiving stolen property, the ex-soldier Buckley had been transported from England to Australia in 1803 and was among the first convicts settled at remote Sullivans Bay on the continent's south-east coast. After only a few months, he had slipped his jailers' grip, fleeing on foot with five other men, hoping to walk to Sydney. Their judgement of the distance and difficulty of such a journey was sadly awry. His fellow escapees soon decided to return to the convict settlement rather than risk starvation and the perils of an uncharted terrain, but Buckley continued alone. He followed the coast, believing that he would eventually reach his destination.

His pursuers gave him up for dead and Buckley himself would later describe the trek as 'a species of madness'. Ironically, his life was only saved by a spear. In his dire search for food, Buckley discovered the weapon impaled in a mound of dirt and appropriated it for use as a walking stick. He was observed by members of the Wautharong tribe, who were elated to see their recently interred relative's spear in the hands of a white stranger. According to their beliefs it could only mean one thing — Buckley was the reincarnated form of their dead tribesman. The 'wild white man' would spend the next thirty years in the company of the Wautharong, eventually marrying one of their number. So assimilated did he become with his hosts that when a party of explorers led by John Batman eventually came upon him they did not recognise him as one of their own.

Another story Heaton reported was that of able seaman James Murrells. In 1846, Murrells found himself the last remaining survivor of the shipwreck of his vessel, the barque *Peruvian*, on the coast of Queensland. He was taken in by people of the Bindal nation and lived with them for fourteen years. He nearly got himself shot when he finally chanced upon the first white men he had seen in decades. The shock was sufficient to send him fumbling for memory of his native tongue. 'Don't shoot me,' he famously pleaded with the frightened squatters, 'I am a British object.'

Heaton also noted one case of a white man living with Aboriginals with which De Rougemont was not familiar. It concerned a shipwrecked French cobbler's son named Narcisse Pelletier, who had become thoroughly identified with the native inhabitants of Queensland's Cape York. In 1858, the vessel *St Paul* upon which Pelletier had been a cabin boy had been torn apart by a reef in the Louisiade Archipelago of New Guinea. According to Heaton, its cargo of 350 Chinese emigrant workers survived the wreck but instead met their end in the mouths of the cannibals of Rossell Island. The *St Paul*'s captain and crew, including Pelletier, escaped on the ship's lifeboats and travelled over 600 miles to the Australian coast, landing south of Cape Direction on the Cape York Peninsula. Here Pelletier's crewmates became spooked by the presence of Aboriginals and, in their haste to escape to more accommodating refuge, left him behind. Pelletier owed his survival to the Makadamas people, who discovered him on the beach, fed him and took him in as one of their own. He spent seventeen years enjoying their hospitality and was transformed both in mind and manner. His entire body was scorched deep rouge; ochre-dyed cicatrices latticed his breast and a four-inch piece of wood swung from his right ear. He mastered the language of his and neighbouring clans, and although only a boy of fifteen when marooned, he also retained his own tongue. He hunted and fished and made sketches of the animals he encountered.

When the crew of the English brig *John Bell* came upon Pelletier in 1875, his Aboriginal 'father' tricked him into going aboard, hoping to facilitate the trade of tobacco and goods with the white men. Before the boy could return to shore, the captain of the *John Bell* ordered his crew to heave anchor and set sail, believing he had rescued him from the 'savages' — but it was not Pelletier's wish to leave. Upon being returned to France he simply vanished and was rumoured to have eventually worked his way back to Australia to rejoin his tribe. De Rougemont located Pelletier's biography, *Dix-Sept Ans Chez Les Sauvages*, published in Paris in 1876, and devoured the story in one sitting.

De Rougemont had noted mention of Heaton in another book, *Australia Twice Traversed*, the journal of fearless western desert explorer Ernest Giles. The poetic Giles dubbed Heaton 'the Imperial Member in the British Parliament for all Australians'. John Henneker Heaton had been a man of some profile in the colonies. He had quit England at the age of sixteen, swapping a privileged education at the King's College, London, for life as a jackeroo in outback New South Wales. Eventually Heaton made his way to Sydney, became a journalist, married his boss's daughter and got himself a share in ownership of *The Bulletin*. He had achieved wealth: next he sought power. He stood for election to the colonial parliament of New South Wales in the country seat of Young but fell short by a few votes. Undeterred, he returned to Britain and had himself put up for election as the Member for Canterbury. Though he had failed in the colonies, he now easily won one of the most coveted seats in the Commons. Famously gregarious, he also fast won the ear and respect of London's most influential men. Heaton believed communications to be the key to knowledge and devoted his political energies to achieving cheaper postal and cable rates between Britain and the far-flung outposts of Empire. De Rougemont consulted Murphy, his medium in matters venal, to determine how best to communicate with the man himself.

'That's easy,' Murphy laughed, 'just stand on any corner in Pall Mall and he'll run into you soon enough.'

On a clear June day in the summer of 1898, Louis De Rougemont strolled to Westminster. He observed Heaton debating penny postage from the Commons gallery. When the House rose he shadowed his quarry at a brisk gait to Pall Mall. The cab and carriage traffic in the surrounding area was phenomenal. The barrage of opening doors disgorged a stream of stout, cane-wielding, luxuriantly bearded men — *Punch* caricatures breathed life. If a man sought a position of influence, it seemed he need only take up a strategic post on the corner of St James and Pall Mall. De Rougemont watched the politician pass through the faux Doric columns of the Carlton Club on St James Street. Even Murphy, with his gilt-edged gab, had never gained entry to this exclusive conservative refuge.

Pall Mall accommodated the privileged of every persuasion. Tories had long favoured the Carlton, but when expedience required, switching political allegiance involved only a short stroll across the street to the Liberals' Reform Club. The Reform's plush environs had been graced by some of England's most gifted men: Gladstone, Thackeray and Arthur Conan Doyle. One of its most famous members, Phileas Fogg, hero of *Around the World in Eighty Days,* existed only in the imagination of Jules Verne and his readers. It was here Fogg commenced and completed his fictitious journey of more than 40,000 miles. To qualify for membership of the neighbouring Travellers' Club a man need only have ventured 500 miles from London, but it seemed some of the well-padded men who passed through its doors rarely left Pall Mall. Their weekly business simply comprised excursing between one club and another in accordance with the relative merits of their dining room menus.

Inside the Carlton, Heaton had barely felt the brandy pinch his throat when a porter appeared at his drinking elbow to whisper a message. Heaton nodded and waved him away. The porter departed muttering down the stair to permit Heaton's guest entry to the hall. He had already complained to the committee of Heaton's habit of entertaining London's least savoury dregs within club bounds.

After a brief interval, Heaton followed. At the bottom of the stair a Continental type clad in shabby tweed turned to greet him. Heaton stepped back to get proper perspective on the man. At first glance it seemed he had been subject to some artificial ageing process. The brown eyes peered out of an impossibly creased and valleyed surround; a relief map unfurled after years of neglect in a traveller's pocket. Louis De Rougemont extended a hand to Heaton and the twisted topography contracted upward into a smile.

'You must forgive me my attire. I have not long made passage from the colonies.'

De Rougemont's unlikely face had caused Heaton to entirely overlook his guest's tattered costume. Now, as he surveyed him in total, a belch of laughter filled the hall. De Rougemont smiled again and offered a shallow, theatrical bow.

'It is true. I travelled at the bottom. With the rats and roaches. But I have travelled worse. And, it is true, in worse company.'

Heaton clamped a hand on the Frenchman's shoulder and directed him into a vast coffee room off the hall. The room's occupants were lost in an obscuring plume of cigar smoke and the thunder of conversation was enormous. Together the fog and noise conspired to affect one's balance. Heaton steered De Rougemont to a pair of vacant leather armchairs in one corner. It was impossible to identify any single stream of conversation from out of the flood — De Rougemont fancied the clusters of topcoats to be dissecting the Sudan situation, or deriding Spain's folly in Cuba. Or discussing the Prince Consort's newly fractured knee.

Heaton cleared his throat and enquired of the Frenchman's business in London.

'It is as no other. My story is, I hope you will agree, quite extraordinary. I have lived like no man.'

Heaton invited De Rougemont to continue. The Frenchman transported his listener over oceans to Batavia, to the pearl-laden straits of Australia's northern coast, through tempest and disaster, to shipwreck and desolation. Heaton sat forward in his chair as the Frenchman told how he had become marooned.

'Washed up dead on a skerrick of sand. My life evaporating in the tropical sun. Two years I have lived on nothing but my wit. And if you like, divine providence. But even Crusoe had Friday. I had only a dog named Bruno. When all hope is lost, I am saved only by the natives, who appeared out of the blue as a man might one day run into another in Soho. Or Pall Mall. Out of a thousand square mile of ocean, on one tiny reef, little Bruno and I are but specks on the sand. Bugs. But they have saved us and led us home to their land. *Australie*. But not the same one you have known so well. Only I have seen it.'

The words poured forth in a ceaseless rush. For nearly an hour Heaton listened as thirty years of adventure played out. At length De Rougemont brought him back to civilisation and fell silent in the leather chair. Heaton called for more coffee and studied his spent guest.

'What is it you seek?'

'I have read Giles, of how you helped him. I never thought to be sitting here, but my story, it is, you might agree, extraordinary.'

De Rougemont pushed his third notebook, its pages covered with the pencil-scrawled detail of his remarkable account, across the table.

'I am grateful for your assistance.'

Heaton fanned through the pages before returning his gaze to the traveller opposite. Over his career he had been privy to many remarkable stories; even now he was a confidant of Mark Twain. He had known no shortage of men who had led, or claimed to lead, extraordinary lives, but even their embellished memoirs would struggle to compete with this. In the vision of decay before him, in the exhausted, crumpled flesh, Heaton saw a portrait of a man lost to the ages. He stood and thrust his thumbs into his waistcoat pockets.

'Return tomorrow at the same time. I will do what I can.'

The brown eyes shone and De Rougemont flew to his feet, resurrected. He bowed to Heaton and took his leave.

The following day Heaton met De Rougemont at the stair and offered him a visiting card.

'Take this to George Newnes Publishers in Southampton Street and they will grant you an audience.'

De Rougemont kissed Heaton on both cheeks, performed a final extravagant bow and walked out into St James Street. He flipped the card and studied Heaton's inscription:

My dear Newnes,

I am sending you the most interesting man in the world, or the biggest liar in the universe. In either case, he will be equally useful to you.

Yours,

H. H.

A few hours later the porter reappeared at Heaton's table in the Carlton Club dining room. Newnes's reply was brief.

My dear H. H.,

You have sent me an angel unawares.

Yours,

G. N.

3
The Wide World

Men of imagination and literary skill have been the new conquerors, the Corteses and Balboas of India, Africa, Australia, Japan and the isles of the southern seas.

Andrew Lang, 1891

LOUIS DE ROUGEMONT travelled directly to Southampton Street. Here, from a four-storey bluestone, George Newnes's publishing house produced the most popular magazines in the British Empire.

Newnes was a clergyman's son who had honed his pitch as a fancy-goods salesman before launching his press empire with a penny magazine of magpied articles entitled *Tit-Bits*. Newnes had been an avid collector of newspaper snippets, and his first magazine was conceived one evening after he had read out a particularly enthralling article to his wife and remarked, 'Now that is what I call an interesting tit-bit. Why doesn't someone bring out a whole paper made up of tit-bits like that?' 'Why don't *you*?' she retorted. He raised part of the capital to do so by opening a vegetarian restaurant, and, within six months, was offered £30,000 for the magazine. Seeing the enormous potential for a new style of popular press, he declined to sell.

In recent years Newnes's most successful publication, *The Strand Magazine*, had established a circulation record few thought surmountable. More than 400,000 copies a month were sold in London and beyond – ten times the circulation of the venerable *Times*. Readers weary of that paper's sober commentary rushed to imbibe the *Strand*'s heady brew of social chatter, fashion and fiction, made even more alluring by Newnes's guarantee of a picture on every page.

Like its sassy, successful New York cousin, *Harper's Monthly Magazine*, the *Strand* was revolutionising public tastes. Rising literacy and a growing female audience presented a diverse new readership whose interests went beyond the stuff of palace and parliament.

Gossip, crime and scandal were in vogue and London was exploding with popular newspapers as never before — yet still the *Strand* outstripped them all. As Newnes was proud to exclaim, a pile of all the *Strand* magazines issued from its inception in 1890 to June 1897 would equal the height of a pile of the thirty-two highest mountains in the world. Much of this success was due to the unprecedented popularity of Sir Arthur Conan Doyle's *Sherlock Holmes* serial. (When Doyle conspired with Holmes's nemesis Professor Moriarty to send the great detective plunging to his death off a precipice in the Swiss Alps in 1893, hundreds of young City men had been moved to don black armbands. Worse, 20,000 readers cancelled their subscriptions. Newnes would later insist on Holmes's resurrection, telling Doyle that, as he had been a medical man before becoming an author, this should not prove difficult.) In a note written to his editor from France, Doyle himself observed:

> Foreigners used to recognise the English by their check suits. I think they will soon learn to do it by their *Strand* magazines. Everybody on the channel boat, except the man at the wheel, was clutching one.[2]

De Rougemont came in off the street and followed a mailboy's directions to the editor's office. In the anteroom, an assistant scrutinised Heaton's card and bade the tramp wait. He took the card into the editor's office and closed the door behind him. After only moments, he re-emerged and invited De Rougemont to enter.

At thirty-one years, William Fitzgerald was around half De Rougemont's age, lean and sharp-eyed. He possessed an assured air that had commended him to Newnes as the right man to pilot his newest, boldest venture — *The Wide World Magazine*.

The *Strand*'s popularity had spawned a huge volume of unsolicited contributions cooked up by bored subscribers in parts near and far: unlikely adventure sagas, unexpurgated romances, tall tales and true. The flotsam washed up on the shores of Southampton Street and the opportunist Newnes saw riches in it. A new publication was born.

The *Wide World*, Britain's first true-life adventure magazine, was infused with the same spirit from which writers like Kipling and Haggard had conjured tale upon tale. Since mid-century, the British appetite for adventures in distant parts had grown with the government's imperial ambitions, heightened by the exploits of explorers such as Livingstone and Burton. Submarine telegraph cables and faster steamships had brought remote lands ever closer to London's door. Now sixpence spent on *Wide World* sent the man who never left the West End on a trip around the world in eighty pages. The magazine epitomised a globe rapidly shrinking through incessant exploration and revolutionary technology. It was the *Wide World* Heaton had in mind when he sent his caller, whose journeys rivalled anything he had read in fact or fiction, to Newnes.

As editor, Fitzgerald's charter was to elevate *Wide World* beyond the *Strand*'s giddy heights. To succeed he needed to unearth a phenomenon even greater than Holmes.

Fitzgerald glanced at Heaton's card and walked to his window. Since the first number of *Wide World* had fallen from the press, Newnes's associates had been responsible for making the editor's office the preferred destination of every delusional, fame-seeking fabulist in London. He determined to sweep the dust-encrusted vagrant out the door as quickly as possible and get on with the day's business. He peered out the window as he spoke, hands clasped behind him.

'How do you know my friend?'

'I was advised to seek him out upon arrival in London, that he might be interested in my little story, the life of Louis De Rougemont.'

The tramp's tone was unexpectedly formal. Fitzgerald laughed sourly.

'A life story is the one thing everybody has.'

De Rougemont was undeterred.

'I have seen what no other man has seen. I have lived near thirty years marooned in the Australian desert.' He paused before adding casually, 'As king of the cannibals.'

Fitzgerald turned from the window to face him. The Frenchman felt his deep gaze upon him. He felt him scrutinising his skin, roaming the valleyed flesh, searching for evidence of such an experience. Finally Fitzgerald returned wearily to his desk and slumped in his chair. He waved a hand in resignation.

'Tell me your story. Make it good.'

Fitzgerald tilted his head back and closed his eyes. In only four months, every conceivable permutation of every adventure story ever told had passed across his desk. The astounding tales he had published were still a hundred times more credible than the material he had rejected. His artful editing had found *Wide World* an immediate audience. Readers who had relished the like of *King Solomon's Mines* thrilled to discover such wondrous tales were now fact. The stories were rich in exotica: lost worlds, missing links, fabulous beasts, superhuman feats and terrible fates. Certain death was averted by mere inches and seconds, sometimes not at all. By sea, sand, snow and sled readers were transported to the very ends of the earth. Some tales originated, however, from much closer quarters. *Down the Perak River*, Fitzgerald told his readers, was heard first hand in the smoking room of the Sports Club, St James Square. Fitzgerald was no stranger to Pall Mall — its teeming population of politicians, captains of industry, titled idlers and would-be travellers made a rich breeding ground for eye-opening tales.

Newnes's nose for sensation knew no limits. 'Out of the Lion's Jaws' was touted as 'the most appalling true narrative on record'; 'Buried Alive by a Dead Elephant' was accompanied by a challenge to readers to judge for themselves if the claim was exaggerated. 'Bagging a Man-Eater', 'A Race Against Death', 'Nearly Eaten' — all manner of unlikely tales were served up monthly to the *Wide World* readership. For credibility's sake these were accompanied by more respectable accounts — Norwegian explorer Nansen recounted his expedition to the North Pole and Stanley summoned up visions of 'darkest Africa'. A compendium of curiosities compiled by Fitzgerald entitled 'Odds and Ends' concluded each number. Here could be found photographs of boa constrictors, maharajahs on bicycles, painted pygmies, train wrecks, stilt-walkers, giant hailstones and spewing volcanoes — yet some of Fitzgerald's most startled adjectives were reserved for a photo of an Italian woman eating a plate of snails and octopus.

At *Wide World*'s inception Fitzgerald informed his readers, 'the Magazine will be found to fascinate not merely serious men, but also women of all degrees and even the smallest children.' The magazine's photographs would be the 'most amazing ever seen' and the supply 'practically inexhaustible, thanks to the far-reaching arrangements we have made in both civilised and uncivilised countries.' Extraordinary as it seemed, *Wide World* depended for its popularity on its authenticity, but some of the tales were literally far-fetched, deriving from locations too remote to allow proper authentication.

Now, in the Southampton Street office, the tramp commenced his travelogue. After a short time, Fitzgerald's eyelids rose, but for an hour he scarcely spoke. The Frenchman's slow, controlled delivery was mesmerising, his tale breathtaking in its magnitude — even to ears accustomed to the rantings of London's best liars. On several occasions Fitzgerald thought to interrupt, to attempt to elicit even more astonishing detail, but like De Rougemont's shipboard colleagues, he refrained in case he disturb the flow. When the performance was complete, he returned to the window and looked silently into the street. Opposite, Newnes's coachman leant against his carriage stuffing plug tobacco into his pipe. Whether De Rougemont had truly experienced the incidents he had recounted or was in the grip of some fantastic confabulation, Fitzgerald had little doubt the man believed them to be fact — and would defend them to the last. He turned and looked his visitor in the eye.

'Can you vouch everything you say is true?'

De Rougemont did not blink.

'Monsieur, it is my misfortune to attest it.'

Fitzgerald returned to the desk and bent over to place his hands face down on its surface.

'Is it money you seek?'

De Rougemont slowly shook his head.

'A new suit would admit me through your door without insult. But my reward is in the telling.'

Fitzgerald motioned to the Frenchman to sit in the worn upholstered chair opposite.

'Will you follow my directions?'

'*Mon ami*, I am at your disposal.'

Fitzgerald called for his secretary to bring his credit book and letterhead. At length he pushed a paper across to De Rougemont to sign. The Frenchman obliged and the editor traded him a cashier's order and a folded note.

'Take this and go to Davies on Savile Row. Buy two plain dark suits on Newnes's account. We start at nine tomorrow.'

The editor cast a last gaze over the tramp's face and shook his head before silently setting to work on the papers at his desk. De Rougemont stood and stared down at the figures on the credit order in his hand. No longer would he need to scrounge at market stalls for sustenance. The spirits had not failed him. The secretary took him gently by the shoulder and ushered him out.

De Rougemont brushed past the doorman into the early summer afternoon. After only a few minutes Fitzgerald pushed his papers aside and followed. He roused Newnes's coachman from his pipe-sucking reverie and travelled directly to the Reform. He found the *Wide World*'s proprietor seated alone in the dining room before a dish of quivering liver and a French muscat. Newnes offered Fitzgerald a place at the table and began to summon the waiter, but the excited editor declined. He told Newnes that De Rougemont's incredible story had flowed from him 'as a man might describe a bus ride'; he was a gift from the gods, a character whose story merged the most sensational elements of contemporary fiction with revelations that would stagger men of science. Better, said Fitzgerald, his impossible tale was quite possibly true.

From *Wide World*'s inception, Newnes had known he could inflate readership beyond the *Strand*'s soaring peak if the magazine were able to promote a real-life hero, a modern day Odysseus or Gulliver, to the adventure-hungry public. The publisher was a shameless master of publicity. He had once offered £100 to the next-of-kin of any reader killed in a railway accident discovered with a copy of *Tit-Bits* on their person. Thirty-five grieving relatives had collected the windfall and what might have amounted to a small decline in readership was instead converted to a promotional success. Already Newnes could see in De Rougemont the makings of his next triumph, a gripping serial that would rapidly swell the *Wide World* audience. He rose from his meal, cast an approving arm about his editor's shoulders and directed him to ensure De Rougemont had everything he required.

Newnes's enthusiasm was fuelled by own passion for exploration. At that very moment an Antarctic expedition under his patronage was being prepared. Moored at St Katherine's Dock on the Thames was the icebreaker *Southern Cross*, soon to depart on its voyage to the frozen south, steered by a Norwegian, Carsten Borchgrevink. Investment in geographical exploration offered wealthy press barons like Newnes the opportunity not only to report, but also to make news. By delivering exclusive stories from parts never before seen, it had become possible to own, and exploit, a piece of history. Henry Morton Stanley had been despatched on his quest to find the lost missionary Livingstone in darkest Africa by the canny American proprietor of *The New York Herald*, who smelled a scoop. London's *Daily Telegraph*, which had also invested in Stanley's journey, funded an assault on Africa's Kilimanjaro. In 1896, a climbing party backed by another London paper, *The Daily Chronicle*, had claimed the first ascent of the Aconcagua, the stone sentinel of Argentina, the highest mountain in the world outside the Himalayas.

That same year, under the patronage of the same newspaper, Nansen's expedition had come within 500 miles of the North Pole. So intense had the publishers' race for glory become that Nansen was met boatless, starving and half-frozen on his fraught return journey across the Arctic by an expedition sponsored by an opposition newspaper, Alfred Harmsworth's *Daily Mail*. (This was a miraculous occurrence — Nansen had no idea where he was and the opposition expedition leader Jackson had not been looking for him. Through the mask of grease and ice camouflaging his face, Jackson recognised Nansen from a meeting three years earlier in London. Astonished, he uttered, 'By Jove, I'm damned glad to see you.')

Harmsworth was now a Newnes rival. He had got his start as a writer for Newnes's *Tit-Bits*, but resigned not long after to establish his own publication. In 1896 both master and apprentice had launched daily newspapers on the same day. Harmsworth's *Daily Mail* had flourished, but Newnes's *Courier Mail* had failed within only a few weeks.

Now, without having had to expend a single penny, Newnes had been hand-delivered the adventure story of the century. It was a coup Harmsworth's *Mail* and other competitors like *The Daily Chronicle* would be pressed to match. Newnes's commitment was unreserved.

The publicity machine was set in motion. At his employer's urging, Fitzgerald primed newspaper correspondents in the United Kingdom and Australia, painting a glowing portrait of Louis De Rougemont. At first, Fitzgerald told them, he had himself been suspicious, but the man had proved to be the genuine article.

I realised he had a remarkable story to tell. Ever since his return to civilisation, he had been trying to get people to listen to his story, but on every side he met with complete scepticism. Monsieur De Rougemont, it seems, worked his passage from Australia. Proving a gentle and amiable fellow, with a record of unique adventure, he became quite a favourite with the rest of the crew, and when he was about to quit ship, the sailors got up a subscription for him, but he

was too proud to accept it, and slipped away secretly and penni-
lessly into our vast city of London. He, who on a barren tract of
sand kept himself alive for two lonely years, came very near starvation in the heart of a great civilisation. He came to us worn out and
almost hopeless. He knew nothing of the value of his story, and
would have let us have it for a £5 note if we had wished. But the
chief of the firm gave directions he should have all the money he
required, and no time was lost putting his story into form.

In a room adjoining Fitzgerald's office, De Rougemont and the stenographer set about retrieving thirty years lost to civilisation. Fresh copy
was brought via a subeditor to Fitzgerald's desk to be moulded for
publication. In a third-floor studio, Newnes's chief illustrator Alfred
Pearse recreated the story's most compelling incidents with pencil and
ink. Pearse was a dab hand, having earlier illustrated Jules Verne's
serials for *The Boy's Own Paper*. Under Fitzgerald's interrogation, De
Rougemont presented his account in vast, scrupulous detail. Even if it
were possible, the complete verification of each and every aspect of his
story would have occupied Newnes's entire editorial staff for a year. It
was an expense and delay the company was unwilling to bear. The
effort required to disprove the castaway's raft of claims would be sufficient to deter most doubters for as long as the serial ran.

As insurance against serious sceptics, Newnes sought third-party
certification. He roused his contacts at the Royal Geographical Society
and invited their endorsement of the *Wide World* narrative. The
Society's librarian, Dr Hugh Mill, had been hired by Newnes the
previous year at generous wages to edit a major new manual of
geography. He had also been recruited to assist with preparations for
the Borchgrevink expedition. The Society's own efforts to mount an
Antarctic expedition had collapsed amid disagreement and bickering.
Enlisting the support of society secretary Dr J. Scott Keltie, Mill
consented to scrutinise De Rougemont's credentials.

An interview was conducted at the Society offices in early July.
Fitzgerald and De Rougemont came out of the clatter of iron wheels
and horns on Old Bond Street down Burlington Gardens to Savile
Row. They entered at Number One through a columned portico. To
each side of the entrance hall, gold panels honoured recipients of the
Society's Royal Medals, many of whom had made their name in

the Australian wild. Eyre, Sturt, Leichhardt, Burke, Giles, Forrest and Warburton marched by De Rougemont in a parade of colonial explorers past.

Upstairs, in the Society library, papers and journals spilt from Mill's corner desk. Tea was brought in a silver samovar and De Rougemont, Fitzgerald, Mill and Scott Keltie gathered by the empty fireplace amid a sprawl of furniture and bookshelves. Over the mantle, Darwin's *Beagle* crested a Pacific wave. Around the room's perimeter, glass cabinets preserved the spoils of expedition, artefacts from every continent, sextants and surveying instruments. Above the bookcases ran a frieze of Australian and African scenes, depicted in oils by Livingstone's Zambezi expedition artist, Thomas Baines. It was here, in 1874, that Livingstone's remains had been ceremoniously received after their procession down the Thames, before being laid to rest at Westminster Abbey. The whole room paid ostentatious tribute to Britain's glorious epoch of imperial exploration.

At the editor's cue, De Rougemont supplied an outline of his epic travels. Mill and Scott Keltie both thought the Frenchman's effortless, concise descriptions of the territory he had traversed were convincing enough. While some of his statements regarding the peoples he had encountered were confounding, from a purely geographical point of view his travels appeared plausible. On the matters of Aboriginal culture and ethnography, Mill and Scott Keltie were, like most of their Society brethren, simply not qualified to judge.

Ten years earlier there had remained 800,000 square miles of territory unexplored by Europeans in Australia's southern central and north-western regions.[3] Explorers' routes had broadly hatch-marked the great interior, but what lay between the thin lines of their desperate, water-starved journeys remained largely unknown to all but the country's original inhabitants. This was a land whose discovery and investigation had already rewritten some of western culture's most accepted fundaments of geography, anthropology and natural history. De Rougemont's tales reminded Mill of Giles's exhilaration at first setting out across the vast Australian continent. In these 'empty spaces', the desert poet had confided to his journal, there was:

> . . . room for snowy mountains, an inland sea, ancient river and palmy plain, for races of new kinds of men inhabiting a new and odorous

land, for fields of gold and Golcondas of gems, for a new flora and a new fauna, and, above all the rest combined, there was room for me![4]

Mill's endorsement was secured.

It was a warmer reception than Stanley had received after he had returned from Central Africa, having found Livingstone at Lake Tanganyika. The Royal Geographical Society had not only flatly refused to believe Stanley's story, but actively worked to disparage it. After all, Stanley was not an explorer, but merely a journalist who had been rewarded handsomely by his American newspaper to scoop the Livingstone story. It was months before the Society would finally accept the incredible truth of Stanley's effort. When he offered Livingstone's diaries as evidence, it was suggested by some they were forgeries. Even when Livingstone's son testified to the diaries' authenticity, suspicion remained that Stanley had stolen them. Mill and Scott Keltie expressed no such reservations regarding De Rougemont. Both men publicly credited De Rougemont with having experienced 'remarkable adventures in the North West region of Australia'.

Without the backing of the Royal Geographical Society, De Rougemont's adventures would remain a curiosity, an entertainment exclusive to *Wide World* readers. With it, Louis De Rougemont became worthy of serious scientific consideration, an authentic specimen for Newnes's public display.

In order to preserve his magazine's exclusive and deter rivals, Newnes needed to limit De Rougemont's public appearances until after the first instalment was published. Fitzgerald summoned the Frenchman to his office and invited him to enjoy a holiday abroad at Newnes's expense. The following week, De Rougemont was sent to Switzerland to visit his mother and widowed sister near the shores of Lake Neuchâtel, where he stayed a few days before joining his brother on holiday at Zermatt in the shadow of the Matterhorn.

In the very first issue of *Wide World*, Fitzgerald had guaranteed readers his magazine would present no fiction, but contain stories of weird adventure, 'more thrilling than any conceived by the novelist in his wildest flights'. Now he could deliver the prime example. While there were no photographs to prove De Rougemont's stories, Pearse had spared no effort in working up dramatic illustrations befitting the incredible tales. And there was always the extraordinary vision of the man himself. 'As a rule,' Fitzgerald had promised, 'the photo of each narrator will be reproduced, so that you may see for yourself what manner of man the story-teller is.' On the first Monday in August, *Wide World* readers had their chance. The photograph of the gnarled and grizzled Louis De Rougemont in his Savile Row suit, shot in the Southampton Street studio, occupied the entire left-hand page of the issue's opening feature.

Truth may have been stranger than fiction, but it was clear De Rougemont was stranger than both.

4

The Traveller's Tale

The Adventures of Louis De Rougemont

**BEING THE NARRATIVE OF THE MOST AMAZING EXPERIENCES
A MAN EVER LIVED TO TELL**

The Wide World Magazine, Volume 1, Issue 5, August 1898

We now commence what may truly be described as the most amazing story a man ever lived to tell. In all annals of geographical science there is practically but one case that can be compared for a moment with M. De Rougemont's – but in that instance the man returned to civilization a hopeless idiot, having lost his reason years before amidst his appalling surroundings. Quite apart from the world-wide interest of M. De Rougemont's narrative of adventure, it will be obvious that after his thirty years' experience as a cannibal chief in the wilds of unexplored Australia, his contribution to science will be simply above all price. He has already appeared before such eminent geographical experts as Dr. J. Scott-Keltie, and Dr. Hugh R. Mill, who have heard his story and checked it by means of their unrivalled collection of latest reports, charts, and works of travel. These well-known experts are quite satisfied that not only is M. De Rougemont's narrative perfectly accurate, but that it is of the very highest scientific value. We also have much pleasure in announcing that arrangements are being made for M. De Rougemont to read an important paper before that great scientific body, the British Association for the Advancement of Science, at their next congress, which will be held in September, at Bristol. The narrative is taken down verbatim from M. De Rougemont's lips, and apart from all outside authorities and experts, we have absolutely satisfied ourselves as to M. De Rougemont's accuracy in every particular.

William G. Fitzgerald – Editor

In the previous issue, Fitzgerald had published a photograph of the participants of an Aboriginal corroboree, accompanying an article entitled 'Savages at Play'. It described the Australian Aboriginal as 'the savagest of all savages'. Now this weary-faced figure in a starched collar was purported to have reigned over these fearsome people for nearly thirty years. Even to committed *Wide World* readers, the proposition stretched credulity. But the story began modestly enough:

> I was born in Paris, in the year 1844. My father was a fairly prosperous man of business – a wholesale shoe merchant, in fact; but when I was about ten years old, my mother, in consequence of certain domestic differences, took me to live with her at Montreux, and other places in Switzerland, where I was educated . . .
>
> When I was about nineteen however a message arrived from my father, directing me to return to France and report myself as a conscript; but against this my mother resolutely set her face . . .
>
> She and I had many talks about my future, and she advised me to take a trip to the East and see what the experience of travel would do for me. Neither of us had any definite project in view, but at length my mother gave me about 7,000 francs and I set out for Cairo . . .

As *Wide World* subscribers, impatient to read about De Rougemont's adventures in the tropics, followed him through the dusty marketplaces of Egypt and beyond, his conversational tone began to work its charm. Venturing to Singapore, the youth had an encounter that would shape the rest of his days:

> I had not been many days in that place when, chancing to make inquiries at a store kept by a Mr. Shakespeare, I was casually introduced to a Dutch pearlfisher named Peter Jensen. This was in 1863. We grew quite friendly and he told me that he had a small forty-one ton schooner at Batavia, named the 'Veielland', in which sturdy little craft he used to go on his pearling expeditions.
>
> 'I am now,' he said, 'about to organize a trip to some pearling grounds off the south of New Guinea, but I have not sufficient capital to defray the preliminary expenses.'
>
> This hint I took, and I offered to join him. He at once agreed, and we commenced our preparations without delay.

*'An octopus of enormous size seizes a man and a boat
and drags them beneath the surface.'*

After recruiting forty experienced Malay divers from the islands of the Dutch Archipelago, Jensen and his new cook De Rougemont struck out from Batavia aboard the pearler *Veielland*. Soon, an encounter with a giant octopus set the scene for the many wonders to come. A pearl diver at work near his skiff was attacked by a tentacled monster the like of which had never been seen. He scrambled back to his tiny boat but could not escape.

> The terrible creature was after him ... and to the horror of the onlookers it extended its great flexible tentacles, enveloped the entire boat, man and all, and then dragged the whole down under the crystal sea.

Battles with the warriors of New Guinea followed. By the time a single eventful season was concluded the divers' labours had netted £50,000 worth of pearls. But the greed of Captain Jensen caused the *Veielland* to linger too long in southern latitudes and doomed his crew to disaster in the cyclone-whipped waters of the Dutch Indies. On an expedition seeking the rare black pearl, the captain and his entire crew of divers became separated from the *Veielland*. De Rougemont had been left on board alone:

> The tide was favourable when he left, and I watched the little fleet of boats following in the wake of the whale boat, until they were some three miles distant from the ship, when they stopped for preparations to be made for the work of diving. I had no presentiment whatever of the catastrophe that awaited them and me.

A violent storm blew up and De Rougemont watched in horror as the boats drifted further and further away, eventually disappearing below the horizon. The storm sent walls of water crashing down upon the *Veielland*, destroying navigational equipment and wrenching off her wheel. De Rougemont and Jensen's dog Bruno, the sole surviving sailors, were left to drift rudderless through the straits. Near Melville Island in the Timor Sea, De Rougemont experienced his first encounter with Aboriginal people, when boomerangs clattered aboard the crippled boat.

Some of these curious weapons hit the sails and fell impotently upon the deck, whilst some of them returned to their throwers, who were standing on the rocks about fifty yards away . . .

The blacks kept up a terrific hubbub on shore, yelling like madmen, and hurling at me showers of barbed spears. The fact that they had boomerangs convinced me that I must be nearing the Australian mainland.

When the vessel was finally flung by tempest onto a reef and De Rougemont was dragged ashore to a tiny island by his loyal hound, his audience was hooked. One hundred and eighty years after Defoe, Robinson Crusoe had returned to life. But according to De Rougemont's account in *Wide World*, his predicament had not been the equal of Crusoe's terrible isolation. It was far, far worse.

Thank God, I did not realize at that moment that I was doomed to spend a soul-killing TWO AND A HALF YEARS on that desolate, microscopical strip of sand!

Had I done so I must have gone raving mad. It was an appalling, dreary-looking spot, without one single tree or bush growing upon it to relieve the terrible monotony. I tell you, words can never describe the horror of the agonizing months as they crawled by. 'My island' was nothing but a little sand-spit, with here and there a few tufts of grass struggling through its parched surface.

Think of it, ye who have envied the fate of the castaway on a gorgeous and fertile tropical island miles in extent! It was barely a hundred yards in length, ten yards wide, and only eight feet above sea-level at high water! There was no sign of animal life upon it, but birds were plentiful enough . . . particularly pelicans. My tour of the island occupied perhaps ten minutes . . .

De Rougemont salvaged his possessions from the stricken *Veielland*, including water, preserved vegetables, flour, maize and tinned food. Before she was completely broken up by reef and waves, De Rougemont also retrieved blankets, clothing and firewood from the well-provisioned vessel, obtaining the basic means of survival. He manufactured fire using a tomahawk, stone and wool. Then the discovery of a skull, lying next to a large circular hole in the sand, informed him he was not the first to be stranded on the isle.

Upon closer examination, I came to the conclusion that the hole must have been dug by civilized beings with spades, and I commenced scratching up the sand with my fingers at one side. I had only gone a few inches down when I came upon a quantity of human remains.

The sight struck terror to my heart, and filled me with the most dismal forebodings. 'My own bones,' I thought, 'will soon be added to the pile.' So great was my agony of mind that I had to leave the spot, and interest myself in other things; but some time afterwards, when I had got over my nervousness, I renewed my digging operations, and in an hour had unearthed no fewer than sixteen complete skeletons – fourteen adults, and two younger people, possibly women!

Determined not to join them, De Rougemont summoned every last reserve. Over the ensuing weeks he contrived a house from oyster shells to protect himself from the sun and cultivated a miraculous tropical garden in sand-filled turtle shells, fertilised with the reptiles' own blood.

'Filling the turtle-shells with blood for the propagation of corn.'

A year of solitude passed. De Rougemont tended his farm, rehearsed acrobatic routines and fashioned musical instruments. To save himself from entirely losing his faculties, he read voraciously from his only book, a French–English bible rescued from the reef, and debated theology with the remarkable dog Bruno.

> I fancied he understood every word of what I was saying. When the religious mania was upon me, I talked over all sorts of theological subjects with my Bruno and it seemed to relieve me, even although I never received any enlightenment from him upon the knotty point that was puzzling me at that particular time.

Having used the blood and shells of their dead relatives to build his garden, De Rougemont now recruited the surviving turtle population for recreation.

> I also played the part of Neptune in a very extraordinary way. I used to wade out to where the turtles were, and on catching a big six-hundred-pounder, I would calmly sit astride on his back.
>
> Away would swim the startled creature, mostly a foot or so below the surface. When he dived deeper I simply sat far back on the shell, and then he was forced to come up. I steered my queer steeds in a curious way. When I wanted my turtle to turn to the left, I simply thrust my foot into his right eye, and vice versa for the contrary direction. My two big toes placed simultaneously over both his optics caused a halt so abrupt as almost to unseat me.

Pelicans, too, were pressed into the castaway's service:

> I had deputies to fish for me; I mean the hundreds of pelicans. The birds who had little ones to feed went out in the morning, and returned in the afternoon with from three to ten pounds of delicious fresh fish in their pouches. On alighting on the island they emptied their pouches on the sand – too often, I must confess, solely for my benefit. These fish, with broiled turtle meat and tinned fruits, made quite a sumptuous repast.

'Robbing the mother pelicans of fish intended for their little ones.'

It was not the pelicans' only employment. Desperate for rescue, De Rougemont enlisted their assistance as pigeon-like messengers.

The powerful winged birds that abounded on the island one day gave me an idea. Why not hang a message around their necks and send them forth into the unknown? Possibly they might bring help – who knows? . . .

I got a number of empty condensed milk tins, and, by means of fire, separated from the cylinder the tin disc that formed the bottom. On this disc I then scratched a message with a sharp nail. In a few words I conveyed information about the wreck and my deplorable condition. I also gave the approximate bearings. These discs – I prepared several in English, French, bad Dutch, German and Italian – I then fastened around the necks of the pelicans, by means of fish-gut and shark-hide strips, and away across the ocean sped the affrighted birds, so scared by the mysterious incumbrance that they never returned to the island.

I may say here that over twenty years later, when I returned to civilization, I chanced to mention my story about the messenger birds to some old inhabitants at Fremantle, Western Australia, when, to my amazement, they replied that a pelican carrying a tin disc around its neck, bearing a message in French from a castaway, had been found many years previously by an old boatman on the beach near the mouth of the Swan River.

However, De Rougemont's only real chance to escape exile was extinguished by a disastrous mistake. Nine months were spent in the fastidious construction of a seaworthy vessel from the washed-up timbers of the *Veielland*, rendered waterfast with shark's hide. Then, on his maiden voyage, De Rougemont discovered he had built the heavy vessel on the wrong side of the island: an encircling reef prevented him from reaching the sea.

I consoled myself with the thought that, when the high tides came, they would perhaps lift the boat over that terrible barrier. I waited and waited, but, alas! only to be disappointed. My nine weary months of arduous travail and half-frantic anticipation were cruelly wasted. At no time could I get the boat out into the open sea in consequence of the rocks, and it was equally impossible for me to drag her back up the steep slope again and across the island, where she could be launched opposite an opening in the encircling reefs.

De Rougemont's despair was compounded by the periodic observation of ships, including a British man-of-war, floating heedlessly by on the horizon, oblivious to the castaway's flagpole and flagging hope. On the point of surrender to his fate, he experienced an epiphany.

I had been many, many months on that terrible little sand-spit and on the night I am describing I went to bed as usual, feeling very despondent. As I lay asleep on my hammock, I dreamed a beautiful dream. Some spiritual being seemed to come and bend over me, smiling pityingly. So extraordinarily vivid was the apparition, that I woke, tumbled out of my hammock, and went outside on a vague search. In a few minutes, however, I laughed at my own folly and turned in again.

I lay there for some little time longer, thinking about the past – for I dared not dwell on the future – when suddenly the intense stillness of the night was broken by a strangely familiar voice, which said, distinctly and articulately, and encouragingly, '*Je suis avec toi. Sois sans peur. Tu reviendras.*' ['I am with you. Don't be afraid. You will return.']

I can never hope to describe my feelings at the moment. It was not the voice of my father nor of my mother, yet it was certainly the voice of someone I knew and loved, yet was unable to identify. The night was strangely calm, and so startling was this mysterious message that instinctively I leapt out of my hammock again, went outside and called out several times, but of course, nothing happened. From that night, however, I never absolutely despaired, even when things looked their very worst.

The first instalment now approached its cliffhanging conclusion. One storm-tossed night the faithful Bruno roused De Rougemont with a tremendous barking and led his master to the water's edge.

The sea was somewhat agitated, and as it was not yet very light, I could not clearly distinguish things in the distance.

On peering seawards for the third or fourth time, however, I fancied I could make out a long, black object, which I concluded must be some kind of a boat, tossing up and down on the billows.

Then I must confess I began to share Bruno's excitement, particularly when a few minutes later I discerned a well-made catamaran, WITH SEVERAL HUMAN FIGURES LYING PROSTRATE UPON IT!

IMPORTANT NOTICE

'The Adventures of Louis De Rougemont' is not a single short story complete in this number, but a serial of unique importance, which will run for several months. You would therefore do well to order subsequent copies in advance.

Word of De Rougemont's extraordinary experiences spread and *Wide World* sales soared. Readers heeded Newnes's notice and an extra 100,000 advance copies of the September number were demanded of the printers' press. The new Crusoe was born. When De Rougemont returned to London from Switzerland he discovered he had already achieved fame. John Tussaud, son of the renowned Madame Tussaud, arranged for a portrait sitting at Marylebone and set about immortalising Louis De Rougemont's features in wax. His mannequin would stand in the main chambers alongside other great explorers of the century, including Burton, Livingstone and Stanley. De Rougemont would also join the ranks of these famous men in telling his story before the British Association Congress. It was a coup that would launch the Frenchman to unexpected heights and expose his experiences to the most vigorous scrutiny.

5

The Modern Crusoe

All these reflections are just history of a state of forced
confinement, which in my real history is represented by a
confined retreat in an island; and it is reasonable to represent
one kind of imprisonment by another, as it is to represent
anything that really exists by that which exists not.

Daniel Defoe,
Serious Reflections during the Life and Surprizing Adventures of
Robinson Crusoe, with His Vision of the Angelick World:
Written by Himself, 1720

AFTER THE PUBLICATION OF only one episode in *Wide World*, De
Rougemont's past was already transforming his future. He took new,
more capacious lodgings in Bloomsbury at Newnes's expense. It was a
remarkable rise for a man whom, if he had told his story to a person
other than Heaton, might instead have found himself installed in an
asylum. He maintained his friendship with Murphy, who could see his
own future crystallising in De Rougemont's success. A publicity item
strategically placed in Newnes's *Westminster Budget* offered a portrait
of the 'marvellous Frenchman' in his new guise as London celebrity:

The modern Robinson Crusoe (only his adventures far transcend
those of Defoe's immortal hero) is rather below the medium height,
and his face and head instantly attract attention. Indeed, so
extraordinary and distinctive is the face that it is no wonder people
stop him in the street and accost him with the query, 'Are you M. de
Rougemont, whose adventures we have read about?'

This wonderful man, then, speaks English extremely well,
though with a slight foreign accent, and gives one the impression of
being curiously shy and sensitive, but after a little while he grows
quite confidential. When one touched upon the story, however, his

expressive face changed altogether, and it is evident the subject is rather a painful one for him. 'I am a little weary,' he said, 'of people asking absurd questions – particularly ladies – and although I am overwhelmed with invitations from all parts of the Three Kingdoms, and even from the Continent and America, I am obliged to decline most of them on this account. One dear old English lady at Zermatt listened to an outline of my story, and then adjusted her glasses and looked at me sympathetically. "Dear, dear," she said, "Poor Man! How must you have suffered! But why on earth didn't you write home?"' And M. de Rougemont laughed heartily.

Now, however scepticism exists no longer, and that great and august body, the British Association, have invited M. de Rouge-mont to read two papers, one in the geographical and one in the anthropological section. He has been approached by Mme Tussaud and Sons, who will have a figure of him in their well-known exhibi-tion in order to gratify thousands of people who may not see M. de Rougemont in the flesh – although it is necessary to state that arrangements are now being made for his lectures in all parts of the Three Kingdoms, as well as in France, Switzerland, Italy and America. Already, applications are being received, literally from every part of the globe, by letter and telegram, asking about the book rights of this astounding story.

What M. de Rougemont seems to like best, however, is the supplying of scientific material, mainly of an anthropological kind, which, although of great interest to science, cannot possibly be published in a popular magazine.

'I seem to have become famous,' laughed M. de Rougemont. 'I receive dozens of letters daily asking for autographs, and only yesterday an independent gentleman came all the way from Plymouth simply to shake me by the hand. Last Sunday I went to the Albert Hall to hear the splendid music, but it gradually got whis-pered about that I was in the building and presently quite an unseemly demonstration was made among the audience, and I am sorry to say I was mobbed when I got outside. I had no umbrella and it was raining heavily. It is, as you may suppose, a very great mistake to think that I am spouting out the whole story glibly. Indeed, the connected incidents came to me only very slowly and I cannot tax my unfortunate head for more than a couple of hours at a time.'

M. de Rougemont is obviously in poor health, but he hopes to soon have another few weeks in Switzerland, which will build him up and fit him for the trying ordeals of his public appearances.

The geographical authorities are agreed that not only are M. de Rougemont's adventures entirely unprecedented, but owing to the advance of civilization it is practically certain that no other civilized man will ever again have the opportunities for going through what Louis de Rougemont has undergone.

Publication of the second instalment in *Wide World* on 1 September acted as an accelerant to De Rougemont's fast-growing fame. Readers flipped impatiently past 'Some Curiosities of Tiger Hunting' and 'How Our Baby Was Stolen by a Baboon' and read eagerly on. The miraculous catamaran that had so excited Bruno was no South Sea mirage:

My state of mind was perfectly indescribable. Here, I thought, are some poor shipwrecked creatures like myself, and I prayed to God that I might be the means of saving them. The prospect of having at length someone to converse with filled me with unutterable joy, and I could hardly restrain myself from rushing into the water and swimming out to the catamaran, which was still several hundred yards away from me.

Would it never draw near, I thought, wild with impatience. And then to my horror I saw that it was closely followed by a number of sharks, who swam round and round it expectantly. Seeing this I could contain myself no longer. Sternly commanding my dog not to follow me I waded into the waves and out to the catamaran, taking good care, however, as I swam, to make a great noise by shouting and splashing in order to frighten away the sharks. When eventually I did come up to the floating platform of logs, I found that there were four blacks upon it – a man, a woman and two boys.

The new arrivals had been swept off course by a storm from the familiar waters of their northern Australian home. After reviving their dehydrated bodies with rum and water, De Rougemont gradually overcame his guests' fear and suspicion.

They seemed not to realize what had happened or where they were until the following day, and then their surprise – mainly at the sight of me – was beyond all description. Their first symptom was one of extreme terror, and in spite of every kind action I could think of they held out for a long time against my advances, although I signed to them that I was their friend, patting them on the shoulders to inspire confidence, and trying to make them understand that I had saved them from a terrible death. I fancy they all thought they had died and were now in the presence of the mysterious Great Spirit.

The sight of the large boat De Rougemont had built floating idly in the lagoon only convinced the Aboriginals that he was indeed some kind of Supreme Spirit from another world. Over the following weeks, the sandspit's unlikely cohabitants came to rely on each other and De Rougemont formed a close attachment to the female, Yamba.

Gradually I acquired a slight acquaintance with the extraordinary language of the blacks, and had many a chat with the woman, who also picked up a few words of comical English from me. She was a woman of average height, lithe and supple, with an intelligent face and sparkling eyes. She was a very interesting companion and as I grew more proficient in her queer language of signs, and slaps and clicks, I learnt from her many wonderful things about the habits and customs of the Australian aborigines, which proved extremely useful to me in after years. Yamba, for that was her name, told me that when I rescued them they had been blown miles and miles out of their course and away from their own country by the terrible gale that had been raging about a fortnight previously . . .

It may not be anticipating too much to say here that the woman was destined to play a vitally important part in the whole of my life, and with her I went through adventures and saw sights more weird and wonderful than anything I had ever read of, even in the wildest extravagances of sensational fiction.

After several weeks, Yamba's husband indicated to De Rougemont that he was eager to return to his own land. Yamba pointed out a

'Their surprise — mainly at the sight of me — was beyond all description.'

glowing star on the horizon and told De Rougemont that it shone over
the home of her people.

After this I was convinced that the mainland could not be more than
a couple of hundred miles or so away, and I determined to accompany them on the journey thither, in the hope that this might form
one of the stepping-stones to civilization and my own kind.

With the assistance of his four companions, De Rougemont was
finally able to drag the boat over to the other side of the island. They
gathered together water and provisions and launched the vessel into

the lagoon. Experimental voyages to sea proved successful but months passed before the winds favoured an attempt on the longer journey to Australia.

> Six months had passed away from the day of the advent of my visitors, when one morning we all marched out from the hut and down to the beach, the two boys fairly yelling with joy and waving bunches of green corn plucked from my garden, whilst their mother skipped gaily hither and thither, and I myself was hardly able to control my transports of excitement and exhilaration ...
>
> I did not demolish my hut of pearl shells but left it standing exactly as it had been during the past two and a half years. Nor must I omit to mention that I buried my treasure of pearls deep in the sand at one end of the island, and in all probability it is there at the moment ...

After leaving the isle behind and sailing ten days south with only Yamba's star to guide them, the mainland was sighted. De Rougemont thought it to be Australia, but lacked the navigational aids to confirm his location.

> At the time of my shipwreck, I had little or no knowledge of Australian geography so that I was utterly at a loss to know my position. I afterwards learnt, however, that Yamba's home was on Cambridge Gulf, on the N.N.W. of the Australian continent.

After landing at a large island in the bay, Yamba and her husband lit fires and began producing smoke signals. Soon, three catamarans were seen approaching and De Rougemont grew increasingly nervous as they neared the shore.

> I viewed their approach with mixed sensations of alarm and hope. I was in the power of these people, I thought. They could tear me from limb to limb, torture me, kill and eat me, if they so pleased; I was absolutely helpless ...
>
> I knew these people to be cannibals, for, during the long talks we used to have on the island, Yamba had described to me their horrid feasts after a successful war ...

De Rougemont's fears were allayed when the three catamaran sailors came ashore to greet their returned kin.

> The new-comers, having landed, squatted down some little distance away from the man they had come to meet, and then Mr. Yamba and they gradually edged forwards towards one another, until at length each placed his nose upon the other's shoulder. This was apparently the native method of embracing. Later Mr. Yamba brought his friends to be introduced to me, and to the best of my ability I went through the same ridiculous ceremony. I must say my new friends evinced an almost uncontrollable terror at the sight of me.

More smoke signals were sent up to assure those on the mainland of the safe return of the lost family. A feast was staged and, later that day, Yamba woke Louis from his turtle-meat lulled reverie to tell him further festivities were about to commence.

> Much refreshed, I rejoined the blacks, and to their unbounded delight and amazement, entertained them for a few minutes with some of my acrobatic tricks and contortions. Some of the more emulous among them tried to imitate my feats of agility, but always came dismally to grief – a performance that created even more frantic merriment than my own.

De Rougemont's performance was followed by an all-night corroboree and the following morning more of the tribe crossed the bay on catamarans to escort him to the mainland. De Rougemont was given the honour of leading the flotilla in his homemade boat.

> As we approached the new country, I beheld a vast surging crowd of excited blacks – men, women, and children, all perfectly naked – standing on the beach. The moment we landed there was a most extraordinary rush for my boat, and everything on board her was there and then subjected to the closest scrutiny . . .
> I sat in the boat for some time, fairly bewildered and deafened by the uproarious jabberings and shrill, excited cries of amazement and wonder that filled the air all round me . . . I then learnt that the

news of my coming had been spread in every direction for many miles; hence the enormous gathering of clans on the beach.

My simple loin-cloth of crimson Japanese silk occasioned much astonishment among the blacks, but curiously enough the men were far more astonished at my footprints than any other attribute I possessed. It seems that when they themselves walk they turn their feet sideways, so that they only make a half impression, so to speak, instead of a full footprint. On the other hand, I of course planted my feet squarely down, and this imprint in the sand was followed by a crowd of blacks, who gravely peered at every footprint, slapping themselves and clicking in amazement at the wonderful thing!

Upon arrival De Rougemont was embraced by his hosts, who perceived him as a white god, invested with superhuman powers. He was offered a choice of shelters, and chose a beehive-shaped grass hut, seven foot high and ten feet in diameter with a small hole at the base through which the occupant had to crawl. The Aboriginals then lavished gifts upon De Rougemont as tribute to his visit.

Despite their generosity, De Rougemont remained determined to plan his onward journey. His hosts were equally determined their omnipotent guest should not leave.

After a time the natives began pointedly to suggest that I should stay with them. They had probably heard from Yamba about the strange things I possessed, and the occult powers I was supposed to be gifted with.

The day after his landing, the Cambridge Gulf Aboriginals executed a plan to deter De Rougemont's departure.

I was standing near my boat, still full of thoughts of escape, when two magnificent naked chiefs, decked with gaudy pigments and feather head-dresses, advanced towards me, leading between them a young dusky maiden of pleasing appearance. The three were followed by an immense crowd of natives. The interesting trio were within a few feet of me, when they halted suddenly, and one of the chiefs stepped out and offered me a murderous looking club, with a big knob on one end, which ugly weapon was known as a 'waddy'. As he presented this weapon the chief made signs that I was to knock the maiden on the head with it. Now, I confess I was struck with horror and dismay at my position for, instantly recalling what Yamba had told me, I concluded that a cannibal feast was about to be given in my honour, and that – worst horror of all – I might have to lead off with the first mouthful of that smiling girl . . .

After a tense stand-off between De Rougemont and the waddy-wielding chief, Yamba intervened, informing the Frenchman that the girl was not being offered up for his dinner but as his wife. Under her instruction, he duly tapped the girl lightly on the head with the waddy, she fell prostrate in wifely submission at his feet and the ceremony was complete. The following day, after consultation on the finer points of tribal etiquette, De Rougemont approached Yamba's husband and offered to exchange his young newlywed for his wife. His proposal was immediately accepted and De Rougemont's beloved Yamba became his constant companion. Yet still his object remained to escape exile.

I settled down to my new life in the course of a few days, but I need hardly remark I did not propose staying in that forlorn spot longer than I could help. This was my plan. I would, first of all, make myself acquainted with the habits and customs of the blacks, and pick up as much bushmanship and knowledge of the country as it was possible to acquire, in case I should have to travel inland in search of civilization instead of oversea. There was always, however, the hope that some day I might be able either to get away by sea in my boat, or else hail some passing vessel, many of which, the blacks told me, they had seen pass at a distance . . .

Meanwhile, De Rougemont remained the subject of fascination in his adopted tribe.

Everywhere I went the natives were absolutely overwhelming in their hospitality, and presents of food of all kinds were fairly showered upon me, including such delicacies as kangaroo and opossum meat, rats, snakes, tree-worms, fish, etc., which were always left outside my hut. Baked snake, I ought to mention, was a very pleasant dish indeed, but as there was no salt forthcoming, and the flesh was very tasteless, I cannot say I enjoyed this particular native dainty ... Rats were always plentiful – often so much so as to become a serious nuisance. They were of the large brown variety, and were not at all bad eating. I may say here that the women-folk were responsible for the catching of the rats, the method usually adopted being to poke in their holes with sticks, and then kill them as they rushed out. The women, by the way, were responsible for a good many things ...

There was usually a good water supply in the neighbourhood of these camps, and if it failed (as it very frequently did), the whole tribe simply moved its quarters elsewhere – perhaps a hundred miles off. The instinct of these people for finding water, however, was nothing short of miraculous. No-one would think of going down to the seashore to look for fresh water, yet they often showed me the purest and most refreshing of liquids oozing up out of the sand on the beach after the tide had receded.

Almost every evening the blacks would hold a stately corroboree, singing and chanting; the burden of their song being almost invariably myself, my belongings, and my prowess – which latter, I fear, was magnified in the most extravagant manner. I ought to mention that at first I did not accompany the men on their excursions abroad, because I was far from perfect in their language; and furthermore, I was not skilled in hunting or in bush lore. Therefore, fearful of exciting ridicule, I decided to remain behind in the camp until I was thoroughly grounded in everything there was to be learned.

Supposing, for example, I had gone out with the blacks, and had to confess myself tired after tramping several miles. Well, this kind of thing would certainly have engendered contempt; and once the mysterious white stranger was found to be full of the frailties that beset the ordinary creature, his prestige would be gone, and then life would probably become intolerable.

Thus everything I did I had to excel in, and it was absolutely necessary that I should be perpetually 'astonishing the natives', in the most literal sense of the phrase ...

The Frenchman gradually became au fait with tribal customs, including the celebrations that invariably followed the frequent wars with neighbouring tribes.

> The corroboree after a successful battle commenced with a cannibal feast off the bodies of their fallen foes, and would be kept up for several days on end, the braves lying down to sleep near the fire towards morning, and renewing the festivities about noon the following day.
>
> These men of the northwest were of magnificent stature, and possessed great personal strength. They were able to walk extraordinary distances, and their carriage was the most graceful I have ever seen. The women are not very prepossessing, and not nearly so graceful in their bearing and gait as the men. Poor creatures! they did all the hard work of the camp – building, food-hunting, waiting, and serving. Occasionally, however, the men did condescend to go out fishing, and they would also organise battues when a big supply of food was wanted.

De Rougemont also told his readers of the various methods of Aboriginal medicine, as practised by a man he identified as a native doctor.

> This functionary was called a *rui*, and he effected most of his cures with a little shell, with which he rubbed assiduously upon the affected part. Thus it will be seen that the medical treatment was a form of massage, the rubbing being done first in a downward direction and then crosswise. I must say, however, that the blacks were very rarely troubled with illness, their most frequent disorder being usually the result of excessive gorging when a particularly ample supply of food was forthcoming – say, after a big battue over a tribal preserve.
>
> In an ordinary case of overfeeding, the medicine man would rub his patient's stomach with such vigour as often to draw blood. He would also give the sufferer a kind of grass to eat, and this herb, besides clearing the system, also acted as a most marvellous appetizer.
>
> The capacity of some of my blacks, by the way, was almost beyond belief. One giant I have in my mind ate a whole kangaroo

by himself. I saw him do it. Certainly it was not an excessively big animal, but, still, it was a meal large enough for three or four stalwart men.

De Rougemont was also well catered for by his Aboriginal wife, who went to extraordinary lengths to satisfy her white husband's gastronomic desires.

> Every morning I was astir by sunrise, and – hope springing eternal – I at once searched for the faintest indication of a passing sail. Next I would bathe in a lagoon protected from sharks, drying myself by a run on the beach. Meanwhile Yamba would have gone out searching for roots for breakfast, and she seldom returned without a supply of my favourite water-lily roots. Often, in the years that followed, has that heroic creature tramped on foot a hundred miles to get me a few sprigs of saline herbs; she had heard me say I wanted salt.

But Yamba's loving sacrifices were not enough to satisfy her husband's needs. De Rougemont's own food-gathering forays were impelled by a different motive.

> The sport which I myself took up, however, was dugong hunting . . . whenever I went out after dugong, accompanied by Yamba (she was ever with me), the blacks invariably came down in crowds to watch the operation from the beach. But, you will ask, what did I want with dugong, when I had so much other food at hand? Well, my idea was to lay in a great store of dried provisions against the time when I should be ready to start for civilization in my boat.

De Rougemont's latest episode was devoured by over 400,000 readers. Though the serial had yet to reveal its most sensational incidents, the tales of exotica did not disappoint. The Frenchman's adventure seemed to include all the essential ingredients for popular interest — an unknown land, allegations of cannibalism, a white king with the power to 'astonish the natives' and his devoted native wife. *Wide World* readers who had never eaten anything more unusual than pickled eel imagined themselves gorging on kangaroo and sleeping it off under the star-strung desert sky, liberated from the irksome grind of urban life. For some, Yamba brought to mind the devotion of the beautiful native woman Foulata to Captain Good in *King Solomon's Mines*, published only thirteen years prior. While the backdrop was not the more usual darkest Africa, Australia's nor'-nor'-west was equally unfamiliar and alive with possibility.

After a century in which the earth's crust might nearly have been worn thin by the endless to and fro of European explorers, the remaining frontiers were by logic also the most remote. All journey beyond them seemed equally impossible – so impossible that anything encountered in undertaking them might just be possible. The map of exploration of the interior and west of Australia from mid-century on was marked with meandering horizontal and vertical lines. Crossing the continent from east to west, west to east or south to north had been the favoured approach. These were the feats most likely to gain financial backing and public acclaim. However, the reality of voyaging the desert regions meant it was impossible to stay to the most direct path – the exact course steered was dictated by the availability of water.

Some expedition leaders were forced by heat, illness and thirst to travel by night, returning with little to report of the features they had only seen clad in darkness. Nevertheless, the thought of deliberately deviating from the swiftest route to explore more than was visible to the horizon was rarely contemplated. In many cases it would have been tantamount to suicide.

Some set out with a specific object in mind – many still dreamt of an inland sea. In 1844, this obsessive quest had driven Captain Charles Sturt to drag a whaleboat a thousand kilometres across desert waste to within striking distance of Australia's centre. He found no water-lapped shores from which to launch his portable vessel; instead the desert sailor had 'scorched beneath a lurid sun of burning fire'.

The perpetual search for water drove explorers to map new territory, but the only other time they broadened their horizons was when they became lost. The most fruitful, if wretched, exploration of the western coast and its inhabitants had occurred in 1839 when George Grey's party, travelling by boat to the North-West Cape, became shipwrecked and had no choice but to walk 300 miles back to the Swan River Colony.

Most who suffered such a predicament would never return to tell, but Louis De Rougemont was different. He had been hopelessly lost from the outset, and thus in a position to discover things that previous explorers, hampered by considerations of survival, had not. De Rougemont's strange chronicle had the potential to reveal a country none but its original inhabitants knew. The remote regions of the continent were little understood in Australia itself and in Britain remained a total mystery to most. An Irish cleric writing in the London periodical *Leisure Hour* in 1898 observed, 'Australia, to many residents of the British Isles, is associated chiefly with thoughts of convicts, of gold-diggings, and frozen mutton.'

If De Rougemont's descriptions of life with savages were beginning to raise eyebrows in scientific circles, they tallied well enough with the public's imagining of such encounters. The lifestyle of the Australian Aboriginal was as alien to the British as that of the tribes of the Amazon, the Zulu of Africa or the legendary Wild Man of Borneo. Little had changed since the first Aboriginal, Bennelong, had been brought to London by Governor Arthur Phillip over a century earlier, done up in ruffed collars and a fancy waistcoat and presented to King George III. His travelling companion, an Aboriginal boy named Yemmerrawannie, had died before Bennelong returned home two years later. Over the next seventy years, most of the Aboriginals to visit Britain were already dead before arrival, their skulls and remains souvenired by explorers and shipped out from the colonies for scientific study and museum exhibition.

The exception was a group of thirteen Aboriginal cricketers who had travelled to England in 1868 for a sporting tour that included Lords, the game's spiritual home and bastion of the titled elite. The skilful Aboriginals, the first Australian cricket team to play in England, won as many games as they lost and nearly defeated the nation's pride, the Marylebone Cricket Club, better known as the MCC.

The tour party attracted special interest on being promoted by their manager as the 'last of their tribe'. They were touted in the press as being part of a race that was doomed to extinction. London's *Bell's Life* reported, 'They are veritable representatives of a race unknown to us until the days of Captain Cook and a race which is fast disappearing from the earth.' For most Londoners it was their first, and apparently last, opportunity to see an Australian Aboriginal in the flesh. *The Daily*

Telegraph declared that 'gold nuggets and black cricketers' were the only things of interest to come from the colonies. Despite their undoubted cricketing ability, the Aboriginal tour party remained a novelty, and they departed Britain five months later knowing substantially more of their hosts than their hosts knew of them.

Australian Aboriginal artefacts and weaponry were held in private collections and at the British Museum, but books on Aboriginal life intended for general readership were rare. Beyond academia, few works had been exclusively devoted to the subject of Aboriginal custom, and many of those had been written with little or no first-hand experience of the people themselves. After visiting the west coast of Australia in the late seventeenth century, Englishman William Dampier had famously described Australia's original inhabitants as 'the miserablest people in the world' and his attitude still seemed to hold sway two centuries later. Chauvinism was rife; in most quarters the belief in the superiority of the European races, and the primitivism of those whose lands they had usurped, went unchallenged. One ethnologist considered Australian Aboriginals to 'represent the childhood of humanity itself, revealing to us the condition of mankind . . . not long after man's first appearance on the earth'. The mature stage of humanity was understood to be represented by the nineteenth-century European.

Carl Lumholtz, a Norwegian ethnographer and explorer whose sensational book *Among Cannibals* had been published in London only ten years before De Rougemont's arrival in that city, characterised the culture of Australian Aboriginals as 'the lowest to be found among the whole genus *homo sapiens*'. Lumholtz had spent a year alone with Aboriginal people near Herbert River in Queensland and claimed not only that many were cannibals, but also that most of the tribes had 'not yet emerged from the Stone Age in the history of their development'. Lumholtz said he had been told that 'the blacks do not like to eat white people'. White flesh, he believed, gave the Aboriginals nausea, which, considering the nature of his book, was perhaps fortunate for the Norwegian.

Explorers' journals were more concerned with the physical nature of the country they travelled than with its inhabitants. Camels frequently received more detailed description than the Aboriginals the expedition parties encountered. Many only bothered to write of Indigenous people when they hindered progress or were perceived to represent a threat. Now a foreign castaway, a Frenchman no less, purported to know more of these people than even the Empire's most knowledgeable explorers and scientists.

Having returned from Switzerland to the steadily increasing heat of London, De Rougemont spent the first days of September in Fitzgerald's office preparing to face a new audience — one vastly more cynical than the *Wide World* readership.

6

The Carnival of Science

British Association

FROM OUR SPECIAL CORRESPONDENT

The Daily Chronicle, Tuesday 6 September 1898

This ancient capital of the West is preparing itself for a new feast of sensation in connection with the third visit to its midst of the British Association. Most attractive of all the sections this year and more prolific in sensations, will be that which surveys the earth [Geography], and the other [Anthropology] which surveys mankind literally from *China to Peru* . . . M. De Rougemont promises a startling paper on his thirty years' residence amongst the savages of Central Australia.

The British Association for the Advancement of Science was the paragon of scientific achievement. Its founders had coined the very word 'scientist'. Among its membership past and present could be counted the Empire's most brilliant and venerated men in every scientific field.

By staging its annual congress during holiday season, the Association seized the opportunity to make headlines while the sun shone, when newspapers sought curios to fill pages deprived of political event. Scientists took the stage to report on the results of their year's work, but with competition for grants, recognition and favour fierce, ego ran unchecked and controversy was assured. More than once, congress sessions had ended in insult, injury and even death.

Two of the more famous incidents had occurred in the Anthropological Section's program — the same section De Rougemont had been invited to address. When T. H. Huxley and Bishop Wilberforce clashed at Oxford in 1860 over Darwin's recently published *Origin of*

Species, it was reported the crowd jeered and ladies fainted. The captain of the *Beagle*, Admiral Fitzroy, thrust his Bible into the air and branded Darwin a viper. Four years later at Bath, explorer John Speke was scheduled to debate his mentor Sir Richard Burton over Speke's claim to have discovered the source of the Nile. It was cancelled due to Speke's death the day prior by his own gun, reported as a hunting accident. Burton later asserted Speke had committed suicide to 'avoid the exposure of his misstatements in regard to the Nile sources'. It would be thirteen years before Speke's claim would be officially verified.

On Tuesday 6 September, De Rougemont made the hundred-mile journey west from London to Bristol by rail in the company of Fitzgerald and his trunk of notes. On arrival, they travelled by cab to the Clifton Grand Spa and Hydro. Erected over the hot springs at Avon Gorge by none other than George Newnes, the hotel and hydropathic institution featured direct access to the curative waters, bathed in by enfeebled nobility since the seventeenth century. Newnes saw more in the springs than healing powers. His employees were now bottling the water at its source and exporting it around the globe, transforming it into clear profit.

At Fitzgerald's behest, De Rougemont relaxed in advance of the conference by familiarising himself with the credentials of the learned men in attendance. Of particular interest was the Association Head, Sir William Crookes. England's greatest living chemist, Crookes had suffered professional embarrassment thirty years earlier when he became involved with a young spirit medium named Florence Cook, who could apparently manifest apparitions of a dead woman by 'channelling'. Upon witnessing and testing Cook's powers, Crookes used a respected scientific journal he had founded to promote the validity of psychic phenomena. His more rationalist colleagues denounced his findings, describing them as impossible. Crookes was unmoved, retorting, 'I never said that it was possible, I only said that it was true.' It had been rumoured that Florence Cook's powers extended to commanding Crookes's passions, but over the long term his undisputed scientific brilliance overshadowed any real damage to his personal reputation.

Crookes also held the position of President of the Society for Psychical Research – a body whose membership included Sigmund Freud, Mark Twain and Arthur Conan Doyle – and was a member of the Ghost Club, a Cambridge-based society which met on 2 November, All Souls' Day, each year, to read the roll of its members both living and dead. (On more than one occasion deceased members were believed to have made their presence felt.) The burgeoning interest of scientists and literati in psychic phenomena reflected a parallel popular interest in the occult. The British Association took a conservative view of such matters, and had long ago dissociated itself from all consideration of the paranormal. Still, De Rougemont had clear reason to believe that, in Crookes, he had a spiritual soul mate.

De Rougemont's most formidable adversary at Bristol would be Edward Tylor. The Oxford professor was the father of anthropological science in Britain, the most knowledgeable in all of its aspects and the man who had himself appropriated the word 'culture' to define the realm of human behaviour. Fourteen years earlier he had been appointed the first president of the Association's Anthropological Section. His metier was the study of surviving ancient cultures. What was more, he had recently investigated Aboriginal societies in Central Australia, and would present his paper at Bristol on the same day as De Rougemont. Unlike Crookes, Tylor's professional standing was unimpeachable.

De Rougemont spent the early afternoon touring the attractions. Lampooned as the 'Carnival of Science' and 'Vanity Fair', the British Association Congress excelled in providing leisure pursuits for its guests. After an earlier congress in Southampton, even Charles Darwin had expressed his preference for the social over the scientific. 'We enjoyed our week beyond measure,' he had reported. 'The papers were all dull but I met so many friends and so many new acquaintances (especially some of the Irish Naturalists) and took so many pleasant excursions.'

This year, each of the two and a half thousand scientists, savants, cranks, dilettantes and their partners present at Bristol received a directory of entertainments, detailing copious excursions, dinners and theatrical events.

Britain's highest selling morning newspaper, *The Daily Chronicle*, had assigned a special correspondent to tag along with the congress attendees. He reported:

Large as the list of excursions is, they are being applied for in unprecedented numbers, and long as the list of garden parties may seem, it is doubtful whether, should the sunshine continue, all can be accommodated with invitations. But these pardonable frivolities of our idle hours only serve as contrast to a program of work all expect to be wholly useful, if not highly sensational.

Known as the 'cradle of adventurers', Bristol had been the birthplace of Ernest Giles and home to fifteenth-century Italian explorer Giovanni Caboto, better known as John Cabot. It was also the town where Daniel Defoe had supposedly first met with his inspiration for *Robinson Crusoe*, the returned castaway Alexander Selkirk, and according to some, stolen his story.

In the late afternoon De Rougemont took up an invitation to attend the official inauguration of the Cabot Tower by Lord Dufferin. The monument commemorated the Italian's voyage from Bristol to North America to discover Newfoundland four centuries earlier. A year after his return, Cabot had disappeared at sea along with four of his ships.

An exclusive banquet for 200 of the Association's most important guests was held at the Bristol Grammar School that evening. Louis De Rougemont and Fitzgerald were honoured by a position at the head table, in the company of Sir William Crookes; the Bishop of Bristol, George Browne; and the Canadian High Commissoner, Lord Strathcona. In his formal pre-dinner address, the host, Lord Dufferin, praised Cabot's achievements in providing Britain with a foothold in the Americas to counter its rival Spain. The United States was at war with the Spaniards over control of the crumbling Spanish Empire's last remaining possessions.

Dufferin's seemingly interminable speech finally gave way to a series of toasts to Queen and Empire made by the various dignitaries present. As the Canadian High Commissioner resumed his seat, De Rougemont leapt from his. Fitzgerald looked on helplessly, but to his relief, the Frenchman quickly mustered the audience's favour.

'It has been my privilege,' said De Rougemont, 'to go amongst the natives, cannibals no less, of northern Australia, as a kind of viceroy. Although I was not appointed by your Downing Street, I trust you may agree my rule was a wise one. The tribes with whom I lived for nearly thirty years, far from seeing me as a mere castaway, regarded me, or rather I led them to regard me, as a direct representative of the Great White Queen. I told them I had been sent amongst them to grant them a notion of the vastness and majesty of her mighty empire.'

It was an unexpected sentiment from a son of the French Republic. A number of De Rougemont's audience, buoyed by the spirit of patriotism, floated light applause.

'But to my dismay, the effect of my glowing descriptions of Her Majesty fell away as my audience realised that the all-powerful figure of whom I was speaking was not man, but woman.'

Laughter flashed through the hall.

'So marked was the disappointment among my brethren, that I quickly sought to reassure them, if only in the interest of self-preservation, of the Great Queen's powers. On the precipitous side of a large rock, I employed the natives' own coloured pigments to make a colossal drawing. You will excuse me if in my predicament I exaggerated Her Majesty's features for the sake of argument. Her crown I depicted as composed of feathers of the rare lyrebird, which only the most adept of hunters could obtain. Her Majesty's biceps I inflated to phenomenal size and for her sceptre, I made substitute of a mighty waddy. Lest this be insufficient to make my case, I then informed them that the British Empire embraced the whole universe.'

De Rougemont's popularity was assured. In the Sudan, British forces under Kitchener were on the brink of conflict with the territorially impertinent French. Yet here a Parisian saluted their own empire. Sections of the audience broke into loud cheers.

'Of course, I had also to inform my tribe that although the mighty ruler was a woman, she had a much beloved and powerful son, the Prince of Wales, who was a very great warrior and spearthrower. When necessary, of course, he would lead his tribes into battle and strange places where the Queen Mother could not venture. Having outdone myself I was then required to make a colossal statue of the Prince of clay, armed with many throwing spears.'

Thunderous applause accompanied the honorary native to his seat. After dinner, Association guests crowded about and Fitzgerald was compelled to assist De Rougemont's exit, spiriting him away past the reporters representing rival publications stationed in the foyer.

The success of De Rougemont's unscheduled debut guaranteed that his lectures would be the focus of great attention, but the spotlight at Bristol would not remain De Rougemont's alone. The Geographical Section program included the sixty-eight-year-old Isabella Bishop, best known as Isabella Bird. The doughty Bird, renowned for wearing holsters concealing both pistol and tea-making paraphernalia, had ventured where no western woman, and few men, had gone before. At Bristol, she would enlighten the Association membership on the subject of her expeditionary sallies into China's Yang-Tse Valley. Bird had achieved her goal, voyaging deep into Tibet, further than any white woman before her. Her courage and curiosity had previously impelled her to the summit of the world's biggest volcano; through Perak on elephant back; and, under cover of veil, to Persia's most uninviting parts. Her exploits were held in such wide-ranging respect that in 1892, under pressure from the government, the Royal Geographical Society had finally forgiven Bird her sex and admitted her as its first female member.

Henry Savage Landor, gentleman explorer, painter and amateur anthropologist — and possessor of a boundless ego — was also due to report on his recent exploits. *Alone with the Hairy Ainu*, Landor's first book of travel writing, had described his encounters with the mysterious hirsute inhabitants of the Japanese island of Hokkaido. It achieved Landor a royal audience and fame sufficient to fund a lifetime of exploration and travel. Now, under the patronage of the *Daily Mail*, the outlandish Landor had ventured deep into the wilds of Tibet. Accompanied only by native porters, he had stared down warlords, survived unthinkable tortures and beaten off murderous thieves en route. The magnitude of his daring deeds made his failure to attain his actual objective — the mysterious closed capital of Lhasa — appear of little consequence.

On Wednesday morning, however, after witnessing De Rougemont's performance at the Cabot banquet, Landor announced his surprise withdrawal from the program. He told the Royal Geographical Society he would not appear on the same bill as Louis De Rougemont, whose stories he did not believe. Before a single address had been presented and the infighting had begun in earnest, Bristol had its first casualty. Perhaps Landor was fearful that the scrutiny De Rougemont's tales would attract might be applied to his own claims.

That morning, as Landor made his retreat, De Rougemont himself attended the President's opening address, staged in Bristol's largest music hall, the People's Palace of Varieties.

Crookes began his remarks in conventional fashion, delivering a cautionary account of the diminishing supply of wheat. This was well received, and he gathered the confidence to broach his pet subject. Stating that it would be cowardice on his part to remain silent on the matter of unexplained phenomena, Crookes observed:

> Were I now introducing these inquiries for the first time to the world of science, I should choose a starting point different from that of old. It would be well to begin with telepathy, with the fundamental law, as I believe it to be, that thoughts and images may be transferred from one mind to another without the agency of the recognised organs of sense . . . It is henceforth open to science to transcend all we now think we know of matter and to gain new glimpses of a profounder science of Cosmic Law . . .

Perhaps telepathically sensing the growing scepticism of his audience, Crookes made no further reference to the paranormal, but at the conclusion of his speech De Rougemont's applause was more enthusiastic than most.

The remainder of the day and evening was passed in recreations. Formal sessions would commence on Thursday morning. Over the next seven days, fifty-one subcommittees would parade experts in every area of accepted scientific enquiry from anthropology to zoology. (The proliferation of scientific topics over which the Association presided had once led Charles Dickens to parody the body as 'The Mudfog Association for the Advancement of Everything'.)

Beyond the lecture halls, the mercury was rising and strange phenomena were observed. On Thursday, the heat was extreme. *The Daily Chronicle* would later report:

> The thermometer kicked the beam . . . so far as the present year is concerned . . . it is said the thermometer in the porch of the British Museum rose to 94½ degrees, the highest pitch to which that particular instrument has ever been known to rise. An astronomer has explained the heatwave by the fact that at the present time the sun is suffering severely from an outbreak of spots.

Meteorology was the dominant subject of the day and conference halls reached only half capacity as overheated guests sought relief elsewhere. De Rougemont remained at the spa, enjoying the comforts of Newnes's hospitality. In the evening he made a brief appearance at the Association's garden party, defending his profusely sweating brow to those who proposed that, having lived in the desert, he should hardly feel the heat. He was to deliver his first paper the following afternoon, but Friday morning's *Chronicle* turned up the heat even further.

7

'Astonishing the Natives'

'?'

BY AN AUSTRALIAN

The Daily Chronicle, Friday 9 September 1898

The marvellous tale of M. Louis de Rougemont possesses for Australian readers even a greater interest than has been shown by hundreds of thousands of people in this country, who have read in a popular magazine the first portion of his narrative.

The reason for my statement that Australasians will be more interested than Englishmen in M. de Rougemont's wonderful story is that although this gentleman has, for something like thirty years, been living among the cannibal blacks of North-Western Australia, his experiences have come as a surprise to Australians – they never knew of them until a few months ago.

Although there are some hundreds of newspapers in the five colonies, many of which are conducted with considerable ability, and take a very keen interest in the exploratory record of the country, they have not, so far as I know, heard of, or alluded to M. de Rougemont, the authenticity of whose narrative is vouched for by such high authorities as Dr. J. Scott Keltie and Dr. Hugh R. Mill. The names of these two gentlemen alone should be a guarantee of the absolute accuracy of M. de R. – more especially as the publishers of the story have checked de Rougemont's story in detail and found it to be 'perfectly accurate'.

Now, the writer of this article, with all respect to such experts and men of ability as Drs. Scott Keltie and Mill, asks them if they are absolutely satisfied of the details of M. de Rougemont's narrative so far as it has been given to us in the magazine before mentioned. If two such gentlemen can answer 'Yes' – that they are perfectly convinced of the truth of all the details of this wonderful story, then I can only state my opinion that the pearl-sheller, the Australian explorer, and the man acquainted with the Australian blacks will not be so convinced.

That there is a very considerable substratum of fact in the story, as far as the narrator's experience of the blacks of the North-West coast goes, I – and all other native born Australians – do not doubt. But it is a very serious matter for a learned society to vouch for a man's story word for word as told by him (and for that story to be accepted and believed in by the public) without the most careful investigation.

Now let us go briefly into a few details of M. de Rougemont's adventures.

He tells us, for instance, that the schooner in which he made his fateful voyage from Singapore to the pearling grounds secured £50,000 worth of pearls in one season, besides thirty tons of pearl shell. Such a record as this of one vessel has never, to my knowledge, been heard of in pearl-fishing annals. The thirty tons of pearl-shell are reasonable enough.

An octopus of enormous size seizes a man and a boat and drags them beneath the surface. During my twenty-five years' experience in Pacific seas I have never heard of an octopus weighing more than 15lb being found in shallow waters, such as pearlers would work. An octopus weighing 15lb would have tentacles about ten feet in length; but even one with tentacles of thirty feet could not take a boat under the surface. That there are some enormous creatures of this species is well known, as many a sperm whale's stomach has revealed, but I have never heard of such being discovered anywhere but in a whale's stomach or floating dead upon the surface of the sea. However, M. de Rougemont has seen one alive. His description of the anatomy and appearance of the creature is a revelation to me.

But I must hurry on; M. de Rougemont, during the lonely two years he spent on a sandbank (the latitude and longitude of which he does not give) used to amuse himself by cruising up and down the lagoon on a turtle's back. When M. de R. wanted to go to port he stuck his right big toe into the turtle's eye; when he wanted to go to starboard he stuck his left big toe into the turtle's port eye, and the turtle promptly went to starboard. Now I have caught and handled some thousands of turtle, both afloat and ashore, and I have never yet saw one which when afloat and when touched anywhere on its body, did not sink almost vertically.

Furthermore, if a turtle's eye is touched, even where he is on land, he contracts his neck and turns his head downwards and won't go for a spin even if you use spurs.

A horde of blacks assail M. de R. with boomerangs, which, after circling around his head, return to their throwers upon cliffs 200ft high. This 'detail' will be of interest to Australian readers who know exactly what can be done with a boomerang, and what cannot.

Space forbids further allusion to this wonderful story. There are many other marvels announced . . . And we Australians want to know – want to know very much. Also, we shall be deeply interested to learn of the 1500 mile voyage in a canoe, and why any of the Australian mainland blacks should make a voyage of fifteen miles, let alone 1500 – also where the voyage began.

The breakfast rooms of Bristol erupted. Had Mill and Scott Keltie been duped? Was De Rougemont a fraud? And who was 'An Australian'? De Rougemont's paper had already been keenly anticipated. Now attendance was a must. The organisers of the Anthropological Section seized the day and transferred their proceedings from the modest environs of the Catholic schoolrooms on Park Place to the more voluminous Prince's Theatre in Park Row. The rising mercury did not prevent over 1500 people filling the theatre, occupying every seat. This was Bristol's largest theatre, yet here was a crowd to match that which had queued thirty years earlier to attend the Christmas pantomime of *Robinson Crusoe*. Then, the frenzy for admission had resulted in fourteen people being crushed to death. Today, the modern Crusoe's audience took up their vantage points at the Prince's Theatre without injury, but so large was the throng that some of its number resorted to standing on ladders at the high theatre windows to see De Rougemont in action. The expectant gathering was obliged to suffer through a presidential address, five papers on folklore and Edward Tylor's treatise on the survival of Paleolithic conditions in Australia before finally, in the cloying heat of mid-afternoon, *Wide World*'s prize exhibit prepared to grace the stage.

At two o'clock, De Rougemont was introduced by Section President Mr E.W. Brabrook, who invited the audience to 'dissociate what the Frenchman now had to say from that previously reported in the popular press'. Brabrook said he felt it his duty to 'speak to the audience as a judge addresses a jury'. Already it seemed De Rougemont was on trial. Then, from the shadows of the soaring proscenium arch, below friezes of famous dramatic scenes, emerged a stooped narrow figure in a dark suit.

Those few who had not yet encountered the Frenchman in person were surprised to find him even more aged and frail in appearance than imagined. This was not the virile hero of Haggard or Verne. De Rougemont's opening remarks also provided little hint of the amazements to follow:

> The most I can say about these notes is that they are plain and simple descriptions of things that passed before my eyes daily for some twenty-eight years, during my enforced exile amongst the cannibal blacks of unexplored Australia. From this I think it is possible that I have had opportunities of observing the domestic life of tribes such as might be afforded to exploring parties passing through a given tract of country.
>
> About the year 1865 I joined a pearling expedition and was wrecked on a small sandspit in the Sea of Timor. Here I spent two and a half years and only reached the Australian coast through the instrumentality of a party of blacks, who had been blown off their course. Together then we reached the mainland of Australia in the Cambridge Gulf region, on the northern coast of the continent. Here I spent several years making various excursions, but at length I struck southwards into the interior of the continent, where I spent upwards of twenty years with the Aborigines. It is of these people and their ways I have to speak.
>
> The people are divided into tribes of which there are a great many. A tribe may consist of from 100 to 500 persons — men, women and children — the number will vary according to the nature of the country on which the food supply depends ... The people are governed by laws and regulations sanctioned by custom, and, when necessary, administered by a chief and council of headmen, composed of the older and wiser men, the chief being generally the oldest man in the tribe.

The head of the tribe has the very same food as the meanest among his people, [but] the men serve themselves first and take the best [parts]. I have seen warriors sitting down to a meal and simply hurling old fragments over their shoulders to the expectant women-folk and children behind. Intoxicating or stimulating drinks are quite unknown, but the natives chew and often swallow the leaf of a plant which causes first exhilaration, then later oblivion.

As his audience sweated silently in their seats, the speaker warmed to his task, casually reconstructing his life with the Aboriginals of uncharted Australia. The discomfort of heat was soon forgotten as De Rougemont proceeded to the subject of cannibalism.

A very mistaken idea of cannibalism generally prevails. Never once did I see any human being eaten for the sake of food. Cannibalism prevails to a very great extent, but is governed by rules. Usually it is the slain victims in battle that are eaten by the victorious side, and as the object seems to be to acquire the values and virtue of the person eaten, I endeavoured to wean the tribe in my mountain home from the practice by assuring them that if they made bracelets, anklets and necklaces out of the dead man's hair they would achieve their end equally well. When a family grows too large and the tribe are going on a walkabout or trading excursion, and the mother — being the beast of burden — has two young children, and is only able to carry one, the father orders the second child to be suffocated and eaten by the family only. Maimed and deformed children are also killed and eaten.

Women and people who die a natural death are never eaten. When a man has to be eaten there is always a great corroboree. All parts are consumed — the brain, heart and kidneys being considered special delicacies. Some of the knucklebones are used as ornaments. Often they are strung together to form necklaces, but they are chiefly made up into war belts, which rattle when the owner dances. The shin bones are used in connection with sorcery to bring about the death of enemies, and these are known as the 'death bones'. The skulls are kept and hung in trees, to commemorate the victory, but are never carried about. They may be used as drinking vessels.

Cannibalism and headhunting: the accepted hallmarks of the most savagely uncivilised beings and the stand-by of the contemporary adventure writer. Barely an issue of *Wide World Magazine* had passed without several references to these most shocking of habits. Yet it was De Rougemont's observations of other tribal matters that would provoke most discussion:

> As may be supposed, these cannibal blacks have a very primitive idea of astronomy. The leading belief is that the sky is supported by poles placed at the edges to hold it in position. The medicine men even send quantities of food and drink to the spirits who are holding up these poles. Before the spirits go to the highest heaven, which is the Milky Way, they take turns at propping up the heaven-supporting poles. The Great Spirit, they say, lives in the stars, and never dies. Every moon is supposed to be a fresh one and entirely different from the last. They know nothing whatever about the world being round, or that it revolves. They think it is flat, except for the mountains, which must nearly touch the sky.
>
> They know not a God of love, but a God of fear. They believe that after death the spirits remain about the body for some time and move about. After a period the spirit is supposed to appear again in another form, such as a kangaroo, a bird, or a tree. The soul is supposed to haunt the habitation after death; hence the burning of the home so as to destroy the possible hiding place of that soul, which, unless this is done, may frighten the people when they next come in that vicinity.
>
> Marriage is not regarded as a religious ceremony. The handing of a firestick to each party, or the exchange of white feathers between the bride and bridegroom are the only marriage ceremonies in some tribes. If a girl says to a man, 'Will you get me some food?' it is a proposal of marriage. There are of course different modes of marriage in different tribes. For example, in one tribe two upper teeth are knocked out. Wives are generally obtained by the exchange of sisters or daughters between members of different communities or tribes which are allowed to intermarry. In almost every tribe, wives are stolen with or without the tacit consent of the parents or even husband. These are more or less sporting expeditions and frequently result in a fight.
>
> Supposing that a man casts his eye upon another man's wife and determines to kidnap her. Well, he will perhaps creep early in the morning alone into the presence of the unconscious woman, armed with two spears. One of these is entwined in her hair and simultaneously the

point of the other is pressed hard against her stomach or other vital part. This is an invitation admitting of no refusal.

Should the woman refuse she is speared instantly. This event, however, is extremely rare. As a rule she immediately rises to her feet and accompanies her abductor without raising any alarm. It is, of course, open to her husband or her friends to go and fight for her, and usually they do so.

A young man avoids his mother-in-law like the plague. He believes that if he even speaks to her his hair will turn grey. In certain rare tribes, communal or group marriage prevails. Each man is the husband of all the women, and each woman is the wife of all the men. All the wives are of equal rank. As is but natural, quarrels occur among the women, usually on account of favouritism shown by the husband, or the introduction of a young and relatively beautiful woman.

De Rougemont's observations were variously received with laughter, murmurs and hushed silence. Gasps of disbelief escaped the mouths of the less scientifically minded. *The Times* would later report:

The paper was a long one and contained many extraordinary state-ments about the manners and customs of the Australian aborigines. The lecturer attributed to them many virtues with which they are not usually credited. Their children, he said, are never ill-treated or punished; reverence to the aged is an absolute virtue; the state is the landlord, and the people know not rent, rates or taxes; every man has a wife, every woman a husband; the work-house is unknown, as the strong provide for the weak. There are no millionaires and no beggars; no-one has more than he wants, and if he had it would be a trouble to him. Although these people may be considered very low down in the scale of human intelligence, and although they may display in many respects the simplicity of children, yet, said M. de Rougemont, the most civilised nations might learn something from their institutions.

Aside from their unhappy tendency to consume people, De Rouge-mont's hosts appeared to owe more to Rousseau's noble savage, Marx's socialist ideal and More's *Utopia* than was customary of traditional man-eaters. His empathy with the Aborigines' alleged behaviour, while to be expected of one who had been dependent upon their favour for survival, was at odds with the attitudes of many present.

De Rougemont next told of his rescue of two young English girls, Gladys and Blanche Rogers, who had been shipwrecked on the northwest coast and fallen captive to a neighbouring cannibal chief. De Rougemont and his wife had raised the girls as their own until, two years later, a shot at their canoe from a passing ship resulted in their unfortunate drowning. The episode lent a melodramatic touch appropriate to the matinee performance and the audience responded accordingly, voicing shock and dismay at fate's cruel hand.

In conclusion, De Rougemont indicated the location of his desert exile, on the western shore of the Cambridge Gulf, on a large map of Australia. The place had been first visited by Captain Phillip Parker King on the HMS *Mermaid* in 1819 and twenty years later by the *Beagle*, but since then had only been haphazardly explored by pearlers and prospectors. In recent times only one man, Harry Stockdale, had made a more scientific study of the region, but, as some audience members were aware, his stay had been curtailed by the cowardly mutiny of two of his party.

The Section Chairman crossed the stage to stand at De Rougemont's side and questions were invited from the floor. Edward Tylor, piqued that his own address had been upstaged, challenged the adventurer on his knowledge of tribal language. He stood with notebook and pen at the ready and asked De Rougemont to provide the native words for man and woman, sun and moon and other common concepts. This would, Tylor suggested, allow him to identify the tribes with whom De Rougemont had resided. In response, De Rougemont uttered a succession of incoherent splutters and grunts, evoking mirth from the stalls. Tylor muttered his disbelief, returned the notebook to his waistcoat pocket and slumped into his seat.

Professor Henry Forbes, a respected anthropologist and antiquary, stood to complain there was little new in De Rougemont's speech. Precedents, he said, could be found for much of what the speaker had to say. Forbes remarked upon the accuracy of the information provided by other travellers and the extraordinary points of coincidence to be found between their accounts and De Rougemont's. Contrary to the professor's intention, most in the audience took this as proof De Rougemont's narrative was soundly based in fact. That his experience appeared to confirm the many wonders revealed by past explorers only made it seem more possible.

A vote of thanks was loudly carried and the crowds departed the theatre satisfied that, at the least, they had witnessed a unique performance.

The *Daily Chronicle* correspondent tried to collar De Rougemont as he exited the stage door. The Frenchman gestured wearily to the milling crowd, shrugged and disappeared without further word into the afternoon. The reporter turned his attentions to Fitzgerald, who had been following close at De Rougemont's heel. What, he demanded of the editor, was De Rougemont's response to the letter published in the *Chronicle* that morning?

The editor said he was 'exceedingly glad' that the letter by 'An Australian' had been published. What was more, Fitzgerald said, he was certain that this Australian must be a person who knew what he was writing about. It would give De Rougemont great pleasure to meet him at a convenient hour. Everyone who had met the explorer, continued Fitzgerald, had been convinced that his experience was a 'distinct contribution to the world's history'.

'It was certainly an unusual performance,' replied the reporter sceptically. 'How do you explain his command of English? Pretty remarkable for a Frenchman stuck in the desert with the cannibals all these years, isn't it?'

Fitzgerald had anticipated the question. 'Not at all. Monsieur De Rougemont returned to civilisation a few years ago — since that time he has been in the cities of Australia and, recently, in London.'

Friday evening's aperitifs bubbled with chatter of the cannibal king. In his report the following morning, the *Chronicle* correspondent elaborated on De Rougemont's appearance:

It suited the temper of the meeting to enthrone for the moment a traveller whose singular experiences in Central Australia promised the possibility of a sensation. And all of us who know the British Association are aware how dearly they love a sensation. M. de Rougemont, I ought to explain, looked nervous and far from well. His firm, erect figure, however, together with a command of English somewhat unusual in a foreigner, even when he has not suffered a thirty-year exile, produced a very favourable impression. Questioned on this point, Mr. Fitzgerald explained that M. de Rougemont had returned from his exile some two or three years ago, since which time he had been living in your midst.

Dr Hugh Mill had spent half the previous day defending his endorsement of De Rougemont's outlandish story. Panicked by the *Chronicle*'s allegations, Mill now implored his Association colleagues to postpone the Frenchman's second paper, scheduled for Monday afternoon, but a majority of the committee, keen to capitalise on De Rougemont's sudden celebrity, rejected his request.

Henry Massingham, the thirty-eight-year-old *Daily Chronicle* editor, was monitoring the daily despatches from Bristol. Reputed to be a man of electric personality and thought to be incorruptible, the former Fabian socialist was also renowned for acting on impulse. Colleagues and friends described him as a 'detached observer of men and things' who nevertheless possessed a 'vehement dogmatic temperament'. As a young journalist, Massingham had written a book analysing London's daily papers. In it he adjudged the power of the press as being above both church and state, describing it as 'the great informer of the people'. He had served his apprenticeship on radical evening paper *The Star*, joining the *Chronicle* as a leader writer in 1891. Under Massingham's editorial guidance the *Chronicle* had become a force to be reckoned with, a liberally inclined morning paper of substantial political weight and diverse readership. Its informal style and growing audience were a direct result of Massingham's editorial influence.

Massingham himself described his paper as 'a critic at large'. Now Louis De Rougemont had fallen under its cynical gaze. The editor had lit the fire at Bristol by commissioning the recently emigrated Louis Becke, alias 'An Australian', to compose Friday morning's critique. Becke was well known in both England and the colonies for his stories of South Sea island adventure, many based on personal experience. He considered himself expert on 'native matters'. Like De Rougemont, he had survived shipwreck, once in the company of notorious Pacific Island buccaneer Bully Hayes. In 1875, he had been arrested on piracy charges and tried in Brisbane. He was acquitted, but continued to lead a nomadic life, trying his hand at goldmining, banking and South Sea trading. After marrying twice he eventually settled in Sydney and commenced writing for a living. Massingham had thought him the ideal person to take the wind out of the Frenchman's sails. He had let Becke have his head in baiting De Rougemont, though with the protection of a pseudonym. The editor had then set the *Chronicle*'s Bristol correspondent to the chase. On Saturday morning, following the previous day's performance at the Prince's Theatre, Massingham's leader, usually concerned with Westminster and international affairs, was wholly devoted to the empire's newest cause célèbre.

8

'Manners None, Customs Beastly'

Editorial

The Daily Chronicle, Saturday 10 September 1898

Our correspondent at Bristol reports today that he failed to extract
from M. de Rougemont any reply to the criticisms of 'An Australian'
which we published yesterday . . .

But surely some of the questions call for very definite answers.
We learn from the paper which M. de Rougemont read to the
British Association that his desert island is in the Sea of Timor. Is
any other voyager acquainted with the pearling grounds where
£50,000 can be picked up in one season, or with an island where the
octopus is big enough to sink a boat, and the turtle, when you sit
astride of him in a lagoon, can be navigated by gentle prodding of
the eyes with your great toes? Has anybody ever heard of natives
from the Australian mainland voyaging 1500 miles in a canoe?
What became of the two English girls rescued by M. de Rougemont
from the 'harem of a cannibal chief'?

Massingham's volley of questions continued. How was it that when
M. De Rougemont quitted his cannibals he made no communication
to the first civilised people he met? When and where did he remove his
greasepaint, don European costume and cut his hair? Were these operations performed in secret? If not, how came it that no Australian got
wind of his coming and that he reached the east coast without giving
the slightest inkling of his adventures?

Mr. Fitzgerald explains his distinguished friend's remarkable knowledge of the English language by telling us that M. de Rougemont spent some years in study after his exile. Where did he study and with whom? There is an immense gap between his mysterious departure from cannibal land, where he had so mysteriously descended, and his arrival at Sir George Newnes's office on Southampton-street. M. de Rougemont can put his finger on the map of Australia, and say 'This is where my happy cannibals lead a life which is, in many ways, ideal.' Will he give us a map of the gap? It would be much more interesting and precise.

Massingham observed that the questions put up by the professors at Bristol had not elicited much response; however, it was clear that the Aboriginals of De Rougemont's acquaintance differed markedly from the traditional stereotype. They could not, said Massingham, be treated according to the formula — 'Manners none, customs beastly' — historically used to describe 'primitive culture' in general and more specifically, the behaviour of native peoples of Africa.

They are hospitable (this does not mean that something disagreeably human is always ready for carving on the sideboard, for M. de Rougemont says that human food is not part of their regular diet). They are kind to women and children.

Life for the youngsters is a holiday, and no woman is ever without a husband. Women cannot even be divorced until fresh husbands can be found for them. Any man caught assaulting a woman is blinded. Perjury is punished with death; so (as many of our gamekeepers will be interested to learn) is poaching. But the same students will be disappointed to learn there is no primogeniture; hence the absence of county families . . . On the other hand, they are addicted to infanticide, and they eat their superfluous children. M. de Rougemont tried to break them of the cannibal habit of dining off their dead enemies by suggesting that bracelets made of the enemy's hair were as strengthening to the wearer as the enemy's liver. We can believe that he exercised a high moral influence over them, and that they have never ceased to mourn his strange and sudden disappearances. But we shall have a more respectful conception of his services, both to them and to the world at large, when he has cleared up his desert island mysteries, and enabled us to distinguish between his obligations to Defoe and his original contributions to the study of mankind.

If Massingham saw ample scope for the amusement of his readers in De Rougemont's claims, his barbed critique also had the potential to grievously wound the Frenchman's credibility. Still, De Rougemont refused to take cover, joining an Association excursion to Bath on Saturday morning. After inspecting the ruins, the hundred-strong party were entertained to luncheon in the city's Guild Hall. Following pheasant and cod, a Bath dignitary, Mr. T. Sturge-Cotterell, proposed a toast to the 'colonial and foreign guests'. Spying an opening, De Rougemont took the floor and raised his glass.

'I do not wish to appear ungrateful to the honourable gentleman's generous toast, but by his description, I feel an impostor. I may not be a Briton by birth but nor do I consider myself a foreigner. It is long ago since my country and I parted company, since I took it upon myself to represent the British Queen. Having done so, it would be unseemly for me to still claim my old nationality. Besides which, when I came back and through my own misfortune, I had forgotten my native language, I received a very cold reception by my countrymen.

'You would not, perhaps, be surprised that I had forgotten my language when I tell you that I felt it my duty to teach my wife and children English. I have been asked why I should do that, and I will now tell it publicly for the first time. It was because French would have been of little use to them or I today, and I also wanted to leave some record of my unfortunate position if a time came when civilisation reached the spot where misfortune had placed me. The wreck of my boat destroyed my nationality so far as my books and papers were concerned. I do not mean that this should be a cause for me to renounce my country, far from it, but it is simply that, as I am sorry to say, I prefer the constitution of England to that of my own country.'

De Rougemont's impromptu speech met with the approving clink of crystal.

The day's outing concluded with a visit to Claverton to observe preparations for a hot-air balloon flight. In the evening the excursion group returned to Bristol.

On Sunday De Rougemont rested in the grand surrounds of Bristol's Victoria Rooms and penned his reply to Massingham's criticisms in Saturday's *Chronicle*; but, unbeknownst to him, Fitzgerald had already taken up his defence.

On Monday morning, hotel dining rooms fell silent, tea stewed and burnt toast grew cold as engrossed congress guests absorbed Fitzgerald's letter to the *Chronicle*.

> Dear Editor,
>
> At the moment of writing M. de Rougemont is quite prostrate after the reading of his long anthropological paper before a vast audience at the Prince's Theatre. He has asked me to reply for him.
>
> He was extremely pleased to see the able article by An Australian, an article obviously written by one who knows what he is talking about. It is such men that M. de Rougemont desires to meet; and, if when he struck civilization and asked what year it was, the Australians had investigated his story instead of tapping their foreheads in derision, De Rougemont would have come among us as a hero, instead of being obliged to convince a seemingly inexhaustible supply of inquirers as to his absolute veracity . . .

Fitzgerald then openly invited *The Daily Chronicle* and 'An Australian' to put his man to the test. It was a stroke calculated to garner public support and magnify the story's exposure in the pages of *The Daily Chronicle*. Fitzgerald also issued a challenge to the *Chronicle*'s readers:

> I am not a rich man. I am a poor man. But I tell you that I will pay £500 to the man who proves De Rougemont is an impostor, who has faked the whole story . . .

It was a significant sum, but the cash was safe. If threatened, Fitzgerald's way out was in the wording — for who could prove that De Rougemont had faked *every* element of the story? Still, the staking of a reward would attract even greater publicity for the *Wide World* serial.

On Monday afternoon, a defiant De Rougemont was scheduled to deliver his follow-up performance to the Geographical Section. First, though, Scott Keltie and Mill gave their own papers on political geography and Antarctic research respectively. Mill, flying the flag for Newnes, praised his patron's Antarctic mission, and pleaded for future expeditions to 'work in harmony'. At the conclusion of Mill's lecture, the congress adjourned for the midday meal.

Following luncheon, the hall filled to capacity. Geographical Section President, Colonel G. Earl Church, introduced De Rougemont. Church, a widely travelled scholar, engineer and explorer of Central and South America, said he had read De Rougemont's paper and 'admired the calm way in which the author spoke of his travels and the light way in which he spoke of his hardships'. Describing De Rougemont's story of his time in Australia as no stranger than that of Marco Polo's sojourn in China, the Colonel commanded his audience 'listen to De Rougemont with respect'.

While Mill and Scott Keltie looked on anxiously from the wings, De Rougemont commenced his address. He explained that the preparation of his paper had not been easy, as he had had no means of recording his experiences in the Australian desert:

> It may be necessary to bear in mind that when I first landed on the Australian mainland I was absolutely destitute — without clothes, tools, or instruments of any kind, except a harpoon, a stiletto, and a steel tomahawk. I had no book, except a New Testament printed in the French and English languages; and all maps and charts had been swept away by the heavy seas that preceded the wreck. I had no writing materials whatever, so it was therefore impossible for me, even if at that time I had had the wish, to make any scientific observations, or even record my wanderings. For a time, however, I did make notes on the blank leaves and margins of the Testament, using blood for ink and a quill from a wild bird for a pen. This book was unfortunately lost after my return to civilisation in the wreck of the steamer *Mataura*, which was lost in the Strait of Magellan in the present year of 1898.

De Rougemont withheld from his audience his prophecy of the *Mataura*'s loss and his subsequent reunion with the ship's captain. Instead he described his fruitless attempts to find his way out of the Australian unknown. He claimed to have set off on one particular journey after meeting an English-speaking Aboriginal man who told him of the location of Port Darwin to the south-east, but en route, a terrible storm had struck his ramshackle vessel, and all efforts to regain the correct course failed. Eighteen months later he and his wife Yamba found themselves back where they had begun. Three years later another attempt was made, south across the continent, through the territory of other tribes. De Rougemont enlightened the gathering as to his peculiar methods of survival, including the role played by the now elderly but still athletic Bruno.

> Besides having my native wife with me, I was armed with a mystic message stick, and, best of all, I had the power of amusing the tribes by means of acrobatic performances, my steel weapons, and the tricks and even the bark of my dog, who would also go through a little performance. I emphasise these seemingly trivial things because I believe they saved my life over and over again. Strange it is that men armed to the teeth with weapons of precision should at the sight of naked savages so lose their presence of mind as to shoot them down.

Yet nor did acrobatics always suffice to pacify a disgruntled local. De Rougemont advised his audience that intruders on another's territory could also 'clap their hands to their buttocks behind and put out their tongues — these demonstrations signifying plainly that the white man's wish is respectively to sit down and eat with his hosts'. If this strategy failed, De Rougemont recommended the dancing of a jig, accompanied by whistling. This would, he assured his open-mouthed audience, cause 'the most hostile tribe to throw down their spears and practically place themselves and their knowledge at the disposal of the white stranger'.

De Rougemont then told of an unexpected encounter with four white men in the middle of the desert. As they approached, De Rougemont's tribal brothers informed him the party had previously attacked them, but De Rougemont — naked, grease-painted and sunburnt near black — rushed in excitement toward the strangers, only to be mistaken for an Aboriginal and fired upon. Said De Rougemont, 'I now know them to have been the Giles Expedition of 1874.' It was a stunning claim to make before an audience who held Giles in the deepest regard and had accorded him their Society's highest honour, the Patron's Medal. De Rougemont next reported that several weeks after the encounter, Yamba had stumbled across Giles's lost expedition member Gibson, who had become imbecile through the horrors of his lonely desert ordeal. The unfortunate man had then spent two insensible years with the Frenchman and Yamba before his eventual death.

For De Rougemont to make such claims in Bristol, Giles's own birthplace, while the bones of the brave and weary expedition leader merged with the sands of far Coolgardie seemed traitorous to an audience who regarded him as a hero.

Giles's famous account of his expeditions, *Australia Twice Traversed*, had become essential reading for the Royal Geographical Society's members and they knew the story well. In August 1873, Giles's second desert journey had begun from a waterhole near Peake Station on the Overland Telegraph Line, 450 miles north-west of Port Augusta in South Australia. His object had been to travel to the continent's west coast. With cruel irony, the expedition's commencement had been delayed for three days by a rare burst of rain. Alfred Gibson had not been a member of the original expedition team selected by Giles, but had followed his party to the Peake and begged to be included on the journey. Giles was reluctant, commenting in his journal, 'He was not a man I would have picked out of a mob, but men were scarce . . .'

The party of four men, twenty-four horses and two dogs travelled north-west to Mount Olga before crossing into West Australia. Over the border the landscape soon became menacingly difficult, the days debilitatingly hot and nights frigid. Giles observed that on some occasions the temperature dropped below freezing point, but that 'there was neither frost nor ice, because there was nothing fluid or moist to freeze'.

Weary months elapsed as Giles's party attempted to find a way across the Western Australian interior without succumbing to the terror of death by dehydration. Eventually they reached a place near the Rawlinson Range and made camp. Hoping that the mountains might signify a change in country, Gibson and Giles struck out westward from the camp on horseback, leaving two of the party behind. They took with them nine horses as water-bearers. Giles recorded in his journal a conversation that took place soon after they left camp:

As we rode away I was telling Gibson about various exploring expeditions and their fate, and he said, 'How is it that, in all these exploring expeditions, a lot of people go and die?' He said, 'I shouldn't like to die in this part of the country, anyhow.'

The water-bearing horses were set loose to find their own route home after depositing kegs of water sixty miles out. Giles and Gibson pressed on west for another sixty miles, at which point Gibson's horse died from exhaustion. Giles then insisted that Gibson take his horse, revolver and compass, retrace their tracks to the water store and continue back to their original camp. Giles would follow, making the trip of 120 miles on foot. Giles reported having 'a vague feeling, such as must have been felt by the augurs and seers of old, who trembled as they told events to come'. His last words to Gibson were, 'Whatever you do, stick to the tracks.' But after a day's travel back to the kegs, Giles discovered Gibson had turned off directly south, departing the trail and heading deep into the deadly desert.

Giles eventually reached camp and the remaining party returned to follow Gibson's tracks. They trekked 100 miles into the arid plains before turning back to save their own lives. Gibson was never seen again. Except, of course, by De Rougemont.

Despite his audience's growing incredulity, De Rougemont carried on, regaling them with ever more marvellous tales from the desert. He revealed that he had discovered regions rich in gold and stones 'of every shape and colour', the 'Golconda of gems' Giles himself had once thought possible. What a pity it was then, continued De Rougemont, that he had had no use for them save for making pots, pans and trinkets for his wife. Upon Yamba's death from influenza, he said, he had finally succeeded in escaping the desert. After setting out from camp and wandering directionless for days he had stumbled across a tree marked with the name of the explorer Forrest and then ventured south. Eventually he had come across a group of prospectors a few days north of the Mount Margaret goldfields, before making his way to Melbourne in 1895.

At this point, without warning or explanation, De Rougemont suddenly curtailed his lecture and left the stage. There was a moment of surprised silence before a rising wave of speculation and demands for the speaker's return surged from the stalls. Mill appeared from the wings and informed the audience that De Rougemont had been taken ill. Reading from the notes left abandoned on the lectern, he delivered the concluding portion of De Rougemont's paper. Upon completion, Scott Keltie rose to reaffirm his confidence in the Frenchman. He said he and Mill were thoroughly convinced of the bona fides of M. De Rougemont. They believed in his good faith but had not been shown the 'worked-up' version and had nothing to do with the way in which his story had been dressed up for public consumption. Nevertheless, Scott Keltie concluded, even some of De Rougemont's most extraordinary statements were confirmed by 'travellers of well-known repute'. Mill corroborated Scott Keltie's statement.

Other audience members rose in support. Isabella Bird declared her belief in 'the complete veracity of the reader of the paper'. Amid laughter, Bird said that if she were *Wide World*'s publisher, she would dismiss from his post the engraver of the 'wonderful illustration' of the octopus that had appeared in the magazine's version of the story. She had, however, seen one such monster in the Sandwich Islands which possessed tentacles over ten feet long and so could also attest to the likelihood of De Rougemont's story.

But the persistent Henry Forbes, who had spoken against De Rougemont at the conclusion of his previous paper, again declared his 'considerable doubt'. There had been a great deal of discredit thrown against De Rougemont, said Forbes, from the manner in which his adventures had been 'written up to catch the public'. The throng cheered, but the Section President, Colonel Church, intervened to prohibit discussion of anything other than De Rougemont's paper of that day. If every explorer was brought to trial like De Rougemont, said Church, half of the geographical publications in existence would have to be destroyed. Large sections of the audience fell quiet.

Several Australians broke the silence, voicing their own support for the absent lecturer. Frederic Bonney, a Darling River settler and Fellow of the Royal Anthropological Institute who had lived with Australian Aboriginals and learned several native languages, said there was nothing in the paper that he could not believe. He was joined by Henry Ling Roth, a widely travelled businessman and linguist who had lived in Australia and written books on the native peoples of Tasmania as well as those of Sarawak and Borneo. (Roth's *Aborigines of Tasmania*, published eight years earlier, had included a preface by Tylor, the Oxford professor who had challenged De Rougemont publicly only the day before.) Roth said he believed De Rougemont had spent a good deal of time among the Aborigines, but found a number of his statements puzzling. Australians, he said, including the country's original occupants, were 'not accustomed to elect kings or chiefs'.

In apologia for the vanishing guest, Colonel Church said De Rougemont had come down that afternoon when he ought to have been in bed and had gone home under doctor's orders. A mere seven days in the company of the British Association appeared to have succeeded in eroding the adventurer's health where thirty years in the desert had failed. As Church prepared to close the session, Fitzgerald came forward from the wings with a communiqué from De Rougemont. Church read the note aloud. De Rougemont described Professor Forbes as 'a foeman worthy of my steel' and promised to give him a future opportunity of raising any point he might desire.

There was scattered applause, but many in the audience departed the hall bemused by their experience. De Rougemont's second lecture, like the first he had delivered to the Anthropological Section, seemed to have raised as many, if not more, questions than it answered. On the surface, the Frenchman's mysterious disappearance before those questions could be put to him seemed somewhat convenient. Those who proposed the fragile-looking adventurer might simply have been temporarily overcome by 'nerves' were disappointed when he did not reappear at dinner that evening.

Nor was he seen the following morning; however, as the ill Frenchman took Newnes's curative waters at Bristol, his rebuttal to *The Daily Chronicle* was fast becoming the talk of London.

9

A War of Words

M. de Rougemont and 'The Chronicle'

HIS ANSWER TO 'AUSTRALIAN'

The Daily Chronicle, Tuesday 13 September 1898

SIR,– When a man of my position is called to appear before an august body like the British Association for the Advancement of Science, you will readily understand that at the close of such an ordeal I was not physically able to see your reporter. He says I personally referred him to Mr. Fitzgerald. Well, I take his word for this; but the statement surprises me.

In reply to my esteemed Australian friend. Let me first of all assure him that he erred grievously in stating that Dr. Scott Keltie and Dr. Hugh R. Mill had 'guaranteed' my good faith as to the story in detail, which they found to be 'perfectly accurate'. These well-known geographical experts did grant me interviews and they questioned me solely and extensively on matters geographical. They were also kind enough to state that they were satisfied I had been in the regions described by me, and there their guarantee begins and ends. They spoke in their private capacity: and I challenge Australian to produce my statement saying that the 'learned society' – presumably the Royal Geographical Society – had 'vouched for my story word by word'. How could they? Why, the thing is absurd.

When the Western Australian Government was approached on my behalf (in the matter of gold discoveries), they asked the same amusing question that 'Australian' asked. 'How is it that nothing is known of this man in Australia?' 'We have no official knowledge.'

Sir, when I struck civilisation, in the Mount Margaret region, I was still with the natives, for I always made my way from one tribe to another. Remember I was still a naked savage myself. Well, taught by bitter experience, I told one of my natives to go into a tent and get me a shirt and a pair of trousers. In fact, I instructed the native to steal these things. He got the shirt but no trousers. I strolled on to the next camp (this was in 1895). A party of diggers saw me coming and roared with laughter presumably at the queer apparition. The conversation that ensued was, as nearly as I can remember, as follows:

I said, 'Hallo, boys!' They replied, 'Hallo, where are your mates?' I said I had none, and thereupon they exchanged significant glances. The next question was, 'Have you found any gold?' I said, 'Oh, yes – plenty!' That interested them. 'How far away?' they asked. I replied I had been more than nine months on the march from the auriferous region in my mountain home. They thought me a lunatic; and when I burst out with the question I was burning to ask, 'What year is this?' they roared with laughter again, and good-humoredly offered me some tea and 'damper' as a harmless imbecile. My story was never offered to anyone in the great cities of Australia, because I fancied no one would believe it.

Beholden to no man, I took up more or less menial employment until just before Christmas 1897, when I worked my passage to London from Wellington, N.Z., on board the N.Z.S.S. Co.'s steamer Waikato. I think I gave satisfaction to Captain Croucher. I felt more alone in London than ever I had in the land of 'Never Never'.

Of my first experience and my sufferings, homeless and penniless, in your great city, I may have something to say shortly. Soon I went to see Mr. J. Henniker Heaton at the Carlton Club. I had heard of him in Sydney; and after a couple of interviews with him he gave me a letter of introduction to Mr. W. G. Fitzgerald, of the 'Wide World Magazine'. Of the value of my story I had not the faintest idea. This, then, is the bare outline of the 'gap' your leader writer mentioned.

At personal interviews I could supply far more detail. I am now convinced there are quite a number of experts, prospectors, explorers, scientists and others who are thoroughly competent to weigh and pronounce upon every statement I make. Your Australian says my narrative will not satisfy the pearl sheller, the Australian explorer (including I presume, the expert white bushman and pioneer), and the man who knows the Australian blacks. Well, let Mr. G. Skelton Streeter, of Roebuck Bay, come forward; also the pioneer, Mr. M. P. Cosgrove, of Sydney (both gentlemen are now in London, I think); and as to man acquainted with the blacks he is to be found by the dozen. I have heard of Mr. Ling Roth and I have met Mr. Frederic Bonney.

'Australian' graciously concedes a very considerable 'substratum of fact in the story'. I offer him no thanks for that. He speaks of 'careful investigation'. Ah, that is better. I court it . . .

I am practically certain that Jensen [the shipmaster of the *Veielland*] is still alive in New Guinea. The other day Mr. M. P. Cosgrove, the explorer already mentioned, came to see me, and said he had recently employed Jensen, who was trading between Cooktown and Port Moresby. He was, Mr. Cosgrove said, always trying to induce someone to promote a syndicate in Sydney to go and look for his pearls, thinking possibly that his schooner had gone down in the cyclone precisely where we left her. But I will ask Mr. Cosgrove to write and give you an account of his meeting with Peter Jensen . . .

As to the 'octopus of enormous size', I simply state what I saw with my own eyes; and I wait for other travellers of infinitely greater reputation than mine to give their experience of these monsters. The 'boat' dragged under with the Malay diver, was, I hasten to say, a mere cockleshell; and this 'Australian' will find emphasised in the story.

With regard to the turtle riding, it was one of my greatest pastimes, whilst on the little reef-protected sandspit in the Sea of Timor. I must say that when in deep water, the turtle had the advantage of me, and he often left me altogether. In most cases he would go under when I mounted him, but often I could compel him to rise again by simply leaning well back, so that his very mechanical action in swimming brought him to the surface.

But even in deep water my 'Australian' friend must know that a man can muster turtle, even if he cannot ride it. On this, as all other points, I can supply abundant detail. Admiral Moresby, who, I understand, knows these waters well, sent to the offices of the magazine a sketch showing apparently one of his own bluejackets riding a turtle, precisely as the artist has represented me in the picture published in the magazine.

With regard to the throwing of a boomerang from a cliff 200ft high and its return to the thrower, this, of course, is absurd. On the occasion alluded to, the hostile blacks were swarming everywhere, on the beach as well as up on the cliffs. I have turned to the passage and find, 'Some of these curious weapons hit the sails and fell impotently on the deck, but the remainder returned to their throwers, who were standing on the rocks about fifty yards away.'

Now, as to the two English girls rescued by me from their cannibal chief. Their story is a long one and a fearful one, and I rest confident that even after the lapse of thirty years, some relatives will come forward to hear with horror the shocking fate of those poor creatures.

I will tell you, sir, the whole story of those girls, and I will tell your Australian, and then you can tell your readers, as much or as little as you please. 'We Australians want to know very much.' They shall know, sir.

And who said that any of the 'Australian mainland blacks' made a voyage of 1,500 miles by sea in a canoe? I beg of 'Australian' to go back to the story and realise the blunder he has made. It was I who made this journey, starting with my native wife in a dugout from the shores of the Gulf of Carpentaria, south of the mouth of the Roper, firstly north and then west, until we actually reached the very spot in the Cambridge Gulf from which we had started eighteen months previously. I did not dare to confess to my wife's people that our return was involuntary. I had been groping for Somerset in the extreme north of the Cape York Peninsula, of which I had often heard the pearlers speak; and when I reached the western shore of the Gulf of Carpentaria (of the very existence of which I was unaware), from my wife's home in Cambridge Gulf, I actually thought – so great was my ignorance of Australian geography – that we had reached the Coral Sea, and that all we had to do was to strike north along the coast for the pearling settlement of Somerset!

Let you, Sir, and 'Australian' take a map and realise for yourself my monstrous blunder. Well may the R.G.S. advocate the thorough teaching of Geography in schools! But what was known of Australian geography in Switzerland forty years ago?

I am, Sir, faithfully yours,
Louis De Rougemont

The Reception Room,
Victoria Rooms,
Clifton, Bristol
Sept. 11

De Rougemont's confidence took many readers by surprise. The naive adventurer who had spent the majority of his adult life deprived of civilised company seemed to have acquired a firm grasp of the English language and was capable of using it to advantage. Cajoled by Newnes, *Wide World* magazine illustrator Alfred Pearse also took up the pen and his letter was printed alongside De Rougemont's. The Frenchman had, he said, supplied him with the minutest details, so that the drawings would be correct. What was more, he added, 'no-one who is in daily contact with him can doubt the truth of his thrilling narrative.'

As to turtle riding, Charles Darwin himself had reported some fifty years earlier that native fishermen of the Cocos Islands often captured a turtle by jumping aboard it in the water and 'clinging with both hands by the shell of its neck', holding on until the reptile was exhausted.[5]

Despite these arguments, Massingham's doubt remained. De Rougemont had risen to the bait, and the *Chronicle* would play him for as long as the readership cared. The editor responded to De Rougemont in the same issue:

M. de Rougemont has sent us a letter – this time from his own pen – in which he deals with some of the questions raised by our correspondent, 'An Australian'. We must express our regret, to begin with, that our representative at Bristol should have made what seems to have been an undue demand on the nerves of M. de Rougemont in seeking to interview him. No discourtesy whatever was intended. Our representative no doubt assumed that an intrepid traveller who had faced so many dangers, and undergone ordeals without parallel in the history of adventure, would regard his paper at

Bristol as a very trifling effort. M. de Rougemont tells us, however, that 'at the close of such an ordeal I was not physically able to see your reporter'. We are all the more indebted to him for his courtesy in so fully making amends for the little conversation that never took place.

Massingham said it was a pity De Rougemont had not offered his story to anyone in Australia before making his way to England. It would also help, said the editor, if the skipper of the pearling schooner, Captain Jensen, could be found. He reserved his greatest incredulity for the Frenchman's inability to locate white civilisation.

One rather striking circumstance about the coasting voyages is that the track always followed the most frequented parts of the pearl fisheries. Cambridge Bay, where the castaway landed, is very well known to white men, and even in the sixties there must have been diggers and pearlers constantly in the neighbourhood. M. de Rougemont was most unfortunate, and it was an evil fate that led him, after a few years in the extreme north, to undertake his journey on foot across the great sandy deserts. So far as we can make it out from the map, it is 550 miles in a straight line from Cambridge Bay to the spot where Gibson was discovered. Is it possible that tribes were found frequenting this awful wilderness? Then another 500 miles were travelled over similar country twenty years later, when M. de Rougemont struck out west, before he can have hit his tree marked 'Forrest'. The finding of two great exploring expeditions in these mighty deserts is certainly a strange coincidence.

Apart from these encounters, De Rougemont also said he had found trees marked with inscriptions he believed had been made by the lost Leichhardt. In 1848, the thirty-five-year-old German-born explorer's entire expedition had faded from the face of the earth in an attempt on the first east—west crossing of the Australian continent. Over the following decade, nine separate parties that were sent out to find him or his remains failed, but several reported the discovery of trees marked with the letter *L* in various locations, remarkably distant from one another. Even so, Massingham found it suspicious that, in his desert ramblings, De Rougemont somehow seemed to have crossed the paths of most major Australian expeditionary parties. The editor expressed regret that travels so broad had 'brought so little scientific matter to our knowledge'.

Massingham's doubts were not unreasonable. The only other Australian parallels for De Rougemont's astonishing tales were to be found in fiction. From the early 1890s on, colonial writers had begun to explore the possibilities of an Australian interior populated by races hitherto unknown. White explorers had conveniently left enough gaps in the continent's map to allow novelists' imaginations free rein, and the idea of the existence of a sort of Shangri-la set amid the auriferous sands of Australia's interior was becoming a familiar theme.

Ernest Favenc, an explorer and writer well versed in the geographical mysteries of Australia's remote regions, had written a novel two years earlier entitled *The Secret of the Australian Desert*. It described an exploration party in search of Leichhardt who discovered three of his party residing with a lost tribe of cannibals in picturesque territory littered with gold. For inspiration, Favenc owed a debt to *King Solomon's Mines*. He quickly followed up with another romance of vanished worlds entitled *Marooned in Australia*.[6] It was possible De Rougemont had read Favenc's novels and others like them.

Similar works of popular fiction explored the famous theosophist Madame Blavatsky's notion of 'Lemuria', a vast southern landmass, including Australia, where primeval throwbacks lived life as 'nature intended'. The common denominators in these works were gold, mystical occurrences and benevolent local peoples who conducted fantastic ceremonies. The books' titles reflected their utopian themes: *The Golden Lake*, *The Last Lemurian*, *The Treasure Cave of the Blue Mountains*. Their success suggested the authors had tapped a rich seam of interest in 'lost worlds', but until De Rougemont these stories had always been read as fiction, not fact. Massingham thought De Rougemont's tale nothing more than a palimpsest, his layers of fiction obscuring the faint remnants of an original truth. The editor was convinced that by methodically scraping away at the story's surface other clues might be revealed.

> There are many things to be explained, and M. de Rougemont has freely offered his help to explain them. That is, for the moment, a satisfactory pledge, and we hope to be able to assist M. de Rougemont in carrying it out.

That afternoon, Fitzgerald called his secretary by telephone from Bristol and dictated a response to Massingham. The next day, Wednesday 14 September, his letter was published:

> I am glad to hear that your own attitude 'is that of the open-minded sceptic'. Only I ask the many thousands of able, shrewd, and distinguished men who read 'The Chronicle' whether they would deduce that fact from your leader of Saturday last?
>
> A word as to myself. I am the editor of the 'Wide World Magazine', and not M. de Rougemont's 'agent'. Had de Rougemont come boastfully into my office and declared, 'I'm a wonderful fellow, and I have the most marvellous story in the world to tell,' my clerks would have shown him the door. Poor, weary de Rougemont. He came timidly to me, and said he had been told the 'Wide World' published true stories of adventure – was his of any use? He feared not, as it was not put down in black and white. I might have bought the entire story outright for a £5 note; but I did not.

Fitzgerald reconfirmed his willingness to pit De Rougemont against his detractors:

> You will notice that I speak confidently of silencing the sceptics. Why, certainly. A battle against the truth is necessarily a short one.

Already, though, one reader had spotted the gaping hole in Fitzgerald's offer of a reward, and had written to the *Chronicle* declaring:

> No-one would contend there is not a Sea of Timor, or a northwestern part of Australia, or that there is not a substratum of truth in M. de Rougemont's story. Hence, Mr. Fitzgerald's challenge counts for nothing.

Massingham was staging his own smoke and mirrors act. To date he had avoided revealing the identity of 'An Australian', and now he published letters by other unidentified writers supporting the anonymous critic's position. One letter, attributed simply to 'Another Australian Traveller', challenged De Rougemont on his knowledge of Indigenous Australian custom. The author claimed to have spent nine years with Aboriginals in the Western Australian bush, boasting knowledge of a tribe near the Champion Bay area 'notorious for cannibalism, though in comparison with M. de Rougemont's man-eaters, in a modified form'. From his experience, the medicine man, while known to Native American communities, was an unknown figure in the tribes of Australia. Also, he said, 'natives of the common variety' held no belief in reincarnation, but 'limited their belief in the transmigration of spirit to the black fellow becoming a white man'. Neither did Aboriginals believe in the 'burning of the house after death', because the only known Aboriginals built no abode, the fear of an evil spirit keeping them on the move every three days.

Other anonymous letters offered further criticisms, but some readers were wary of their origins. It was possible their writers were merely *Chronicle* stooges put up to the task of deflating De Rougemont and fanning the flames.

Wednesday's *Chronicle* did not shirk the issue. Below the headline 'De Rougemont, Is His Story True?', Massingham gave a token nod to objectivity, balancing a long inquiry by the detractor Professor Forbes with several letters in De Rougemont's favour.

Forbes asked a series of detailed questions, reiterating his disappointment with the lack of new information to be found in De Rougemont's Bristol lectures. Both papers, he said, might have been written by one who had travelled no further than the libraries of the Anthropological Institute or the Royal Geographical Society. He concluded by chiding De Rougemont for evading his enquiries at the Association congress.

De Rougemont had already found friends in higher ranks. Admiral John Moresby, who had been the first man to map the south coast of British New Guinea in 1873[7], wrote to confirm the plausibility of turtle riding. From his comfortable but dull retirement in the English countryside, Moresby boasted of his considerable experience in turtle taming.

Three things were certain, the Admiral wrote. First, that one could climb on a sleeping turtle's back; second, that by sitting far back on the shell, one could keep one's steed near the surface; and third, that it was possible to stop its career instantly by reducing it to blindness. He then presented the *Chronicle*'s readers with his credentials:

In 1871–3 I had the regulation of the pearl-shell fisheries in Torres Strait, therefore I am able to give a fairly correct opinion on the credibility of Rougemont's adventures, so far related in the pages of the 'Wide World'. I can honestly say I believe in them.

Queensland's first Governor, Sir George Bowen, also rushed to De Rougemont's defence. Bowen declared 'all who know Australian history will agree that there is nothing incredible or even improbable in his statement that he lived for a long period with one of their tribes'. There were, said Bowen, several well-authenticated precedents, including one case with which he was personally acquainted. When 'British object' James Murrells had been returned to Brisbane in 1863 after seventeen years with the Aboriginals of southern Queensland, Governor Bowen had requested to meet him:

I had several conversations with him, and found him very intelli-gent and fairly educated. So I procured him employment under the Government at Bowen (named after myself), where he was useful in communicating with the neighbouring blacks.

In conclusion, Bowen said his purpose was simply to show that there was nothing unbelievable in De Rougemont's statement that he had lived for many years among the Aboriginals of Australia.

Less than a week after De Rougemont's first lecture in Bristol, it seemed everyone in London — in all England — had taken a position. Some were adamant the Frenchman was a complete fraud; others that his remarkable tales were, at the very least, founded in fact. With neither side yet able to produce irrefutable evidence to support their arguments, the controversy intensified.

On Wednesday afternoon, Fitzgerald escorted De Rougemont to the *Chronicle*'s Fleet Street offices to face his critics. As insur-ance, Newnes also insisted his most senior editor, the *Strand*'s H. Greenough-Smith, be in attendance. The *Chronicle* had present a neutral observer, Mr Edward Clodd, author and former president of the Folklore Society, along with a stenographer to record the proceedings.

I O

The Paper Chase

De Rougemont at the 'Chronicle' Office

A LONG CROSS-EXAMINATION

The Daily Chronicle, **Thursday 15 September 1898**

We make some preliminary observations. Be his story true or false, M. de Rougemont is a remarkable man. His skin is deeply browned; he has clearly lived long under burning skies. He has a most alert, vigorous and versatile mind. He speaks English with the utmost fluency, never pausing for a reply, and expressing himself with exactness and in idiomatic phrase. Considering that he never lived in Paris than as a very young child, nor in Europe otherwise than as a stripling, and that of the fifty-four years of his life, thirty years, including the whole of his maturity, save three years, were spent with savage men, we feel a difficulty in accounting for his extreme mental alertness, his copious and refined vocabulary, and such knowledge of the topography of Paris as he has revealed to us. On the other hand we admit that he never seemed to be concocting a reply to questions which were sprung on him, and his answers were singularly direct and explicit, and that it was clear that his natural intelligence and character were of a very high order . . .

M. de Rougemont did not know what questions were to be put to him. They were surprise questions. We simply informed Mr. Fitzgerald that we desired, without investigating the main body of M. de R.'s narrative, to put some points which might lead to further light on his story. M. de Rougemont at once accepted this test.

In the *Chronicle*'s main editorial office, Massingham presided at a scuffed layout table, facing De Rougemont, Fitzgerald and Greenough-Smith. Clodd and the stenographer sat at either end.

De Rougemont thumbed the pages of the morning's *Chronicle* as the editors talked trade. Clad in his Savile Row suit and freshly groomed, he seemed at ease, displaying no lingering effects of the illness that had forced him from the stage at Bristol. There, his sudden departure had aroused suspicion of deliberate evasion, but here there was no prospect of eluding inquisition. As Massingham congratulated Fitzgerald on his magazine's precocious success, the folklorist Clodd turned to De Rougemont and smiled.

'Tell me, are you finding the natives of Britain as accommodating as those of the Australian wilds?'

De Rougemont put down the newspaper and smiled in return.

'Most accommodating, sir. And in many ways alike, particularly when confronted with things anew.'

Clodd raised a brow and the other men at the table fell silent.

'Oh, how might that be?'

'I have found their instinctive response is to elevate one, but in order to discourage the inspiration of enemies, one is expected to continue the performance of remarkable deeds. I think you would call it "astonishing the natives".'

Clodd looked at him quizzically.

'Do you have more astonishments planned for the natives of London?'

De Rougemont leant forward in his chair, holding Clodd's gaze.

'I will tell my story, sir, plain and simple. It is for others to judge whether this is remarkable or not. For me, remarkable as it may be, it is simply the past.'

Clodd sat back in his chair, hooked his thumbs in his vest pockets and shook his head. De Rougemont looked at Massingham and signalled his readiness to begin. Massingham nodded to the stenographer, glanced at his notes and commenced the interview:

— Monsieur De Rougemont, the first of the preliminary questions I propose to ask is: have you a record of the original form of your communication to Mr Fitzgerald?

De Rougemont replied in a steady voice.

— Yes; Mr Fitzgerald has it.

— As it appears, is the narrative a verbatim transcript of what you
said, Monsieur De Rougemont?

The calm fled from the Frenchman's face.

— No! No!

Fitzgerald turned and addressed De Rougemont quietly.

— Let us be absolutely clear. Corrections were made in grammar
were they not?

— Yes, corrections were made in grammar.

Fitzgerald sat back in his chair and Massingham resumed the
interview.

— Were any details added to your account?

De Rougemont appeared shocked by the possibility.

— No, everything was mine, everything!

— Were the illustrations approved by you as correct?

— Yes.

Fitzgerald raised a hand to interject.

— Except when he was in Switzerland, and the illustrations could not
be submitted to him.

Massingham's interest rose.

— What illustrations were these?

— One of them was not published; another was the destruction of a
boat by a mother whale.

De Rougemont gripped Fitzgerald by the arm.

— I described it; it was all from my descriptions.

Massingham cut the Frenchman short.

— That is immaterial. Your reply is that no detail was added, and that all alterations of your work were confined to alterations of grammar?

— Yes.

Massingham looked back down to his notes and scored a line through some words with his pen as he spoke.

— My second question I need not now ask. When I drafted it I did know how much English you spoke. I had intended to ask you what language you used to communicate with your editor. I see now it must have been English.

De Rougemont nodded.

— The third question is this: how did you acquire a knowledge of the English language?

— I spoke English well before leaving home; but I never was in England.

— Were you taught by an Englishman?

— No; I was taught by a relative of my mother, who was in England for several years.

— How were you taught?

— By speaking it. By ear first and then by book. At my school in Vevey I was in constant association with English boys, and also at Lausanne. It was for this reason I was a born fighter, and I got my best thrashings from English boys.

— What language did Jensen speak?

De Rougemont waved a hand through the air.

— I do not know. I do not know the difference between Dutch and Danish and cannot tell you.

— But he did speak English on board the *Veielland*?

— He spoke English, always English; I thought you meant what nationality was he. I do not know. They call all foreigners Dutchmen out there.

Fitzgerald and Greenough-Smith laughed. Massingham ignored them and pressed on, referring again to his notes.

— My next question is an important one. Can you put me in communication with the girls Blanche and Gladys Rogers, tell me their story and further tell me at what place they were restored to civilisation?

De Rougemont looked puzzled.

— But they did not return. They were with us only two years before they died, in circumstances most unusual and tragic—

Fitzgerald broke in to stop him.

— You must understand the details of this episode have not yet been published in our magazine. Telling them will discount their value. I can only allow Monsieur De Rougemont to give them on the condition they will not be printed in your paper.

Massingham nodded agreement and Fitzgerald asked the stenographer to make a note. He then instructed De Rougemont to supply a brief outline of the story. De Rougemont looked down into his lap as he spoke.

— I first heard of the girls from natives in King's Sound who claimed to have two women of my colour — the unfortunate victims of shipwreck — in their camp. The local tribe had speared the surviving crew but taken the girls captive. My wife Yamba arranged for me to talk to the girls and they told me they were

Gladys and Blanche Rogers, the daughters of the captain of a cargo ship called *Northumberland* or some such name. The ship was owned by their uncle and had set out from Sunderland in England for Batavia around 1868 or 1869. I managed to rescue the girls from their uncertain fate at the hands of the King's Sound tribe, and brought them up as my own until, one terrible day when they were out fishing, a shot from a passing vessel sank their little boat, beyond my aid. They both drowned.

Massingham was unmoved.

— So there is no evidence of them, no remaining article of clothing or possession?

The Frenchman did not raise his eyes.

— It is as I said.

Massingham's gaze remained upon him.

— That is unfortunate.

De Rougemont did not reply and Massingham continued to stare at his bowed head in silence. After a moment Fitzgerald cleared his throat and Massingham reluctantly returned to the questions on the page in front of him.

— Will you give me the correct names of both your parents, and their birthplace?
— Yes, Paris. My father's name was Samuel Emmanuel De Rougemont and my mother's Jeanne.
— And the location of your father's place of business?
— I can only give you Paris. I think it was in the Boulevard Haussmann, but I left there too young to remember. My father was a merchant. He sold all sorts of things but I can only remember boots.

— And when and where were you born?

— I was born on 9 November 1844. I cannot tell you where I was registered, but it might have been where I was baptised — that was at the Madeleine.

Massingham scribbled notes as De Rougemont spoke, repeating each key detail out loud. When he was finished he returned to the list.

— The next question is a rather difficult one, and if you are fatigued and want time to answer you can do so at your own leisure. Can you give me some account of your life in Australia after your return to civilisation, the names of your employers, et cetera?

— I can answer now. I was a salesman for James Murphy in Sydney. His address was 1 O'Connell Street. He is a well-known man in Sydney.

Massingham made note of the name and address.

— What did you do immediately after arriving in the Mount Margaret district?

— I did all sorts of things. I did what you call odd jobs. My first work was about Coolgardie. It was work about a house, assisting some travellers to come. Yes, it was about an hotel.

Massingham held his pencil poised in anticipation of further information, but De Rougemont did not elaborate.

— As a waiter, perhaps?

— No, not waiter, it was lower than that. I have cleaned boots. I have cleaned knives.

Again there was a pause. Massingham dug further.

— Would they know you there?

— Yes, they would remember me there.

— What was the name of the hotel, or its owner perhaps?

— I do not remember. They did not know me as De Rougemont.
I was called Louis.

Massingham leant back and laughed in disbelief, shaking his head.

— Did anyone know you as De Rougemont?

The Frenchman was unfazed.

— Yes, Mr Murphy of Sydney did know me as De Rougemont. He is
in London now. He is the first friend I met here. Mr Murphy was
manager of the Southern Estate in Sydney, and let the land in
small plots on lease at low rental, also helping the purchaser to
build a house so I could easily induce people to buy.

— Did you go anywhere else?

— Yes, I was in Brisbane for some time. I worked for a tea merchant.
I cannot remember his name.

— You spoke English to all these people?

— Yes.

— When you met the Mount Margaret party you called to them,
'Hallo, boys!'

De Rougemont nodded.

— How did you remember your English all that time — for thirty
years?

— I spoke English to my wife and children. I taught them English.

— Why not French, your native language?

De Rougemont leaned forward, rested his elbows on the table and
clasped his hands beneath his chin.

— That is rather an extraordinary circumstance. It was first because the natives grasped English better than French. Then when I was in the centre of Australia with my children I knew that some day civilisation would meet them. I knew therefore that English would be of some use to them. It would show that a white man had been there and it might be an Englishman. As a memorial I could leave behind my English-speaking children.

Massingham pushed his notes away in frustration and pursued a different line.

— Did you not consider it strange that you did not meet any white people?

De Rougemont leant back in his chair.

— I did not say I did not meet white people.
— Did you make any efforts to return to civilisation during the thirty years?
— Many times.

Massingham glanced back to his notes.

— I believe there were white settlers near Cambridge Gulf? That ships visit there for fresh water from time to time?

De Rougemont inhaled deeply.

— No, there were no people, nor ships. I would like you to grasp the situation please. I have learned since that the nearest settlement in those days was called De Grey, belonging to a party called Grant and something. I cannot tell you anything more. It was about 1500 miles away, west-south-west.

For the first time, De Rougemont seemed ill at ease. Sensing it, the newspaperman increased the pace of his inquiry. Fitzgerald shifted anxiously in his chair — he himself had not subjected the Frenchman to such aggressive scrutiny.

— Surely Darwin was closer? Why did you not try for it instead?

— I tried to reach Port Darwin with the girls but gave it up. It might have been five or six hundred miles away. I did not know where Port Darwin was.

— Could the blacks not tell you? Surely they had heard of it?

— No, they couldn't tell me. They pointed out a direction, but it was north-east; it was really, I believe, north. Long years before Port Darwin, there was a settlement called Port Essington. But we were in such a vast territory they gave you confused directions.

While De Rougemont's grasp of remote Australian geography seemed shaky, Massingham's was even worse and he returned to the prepared list.

— Where did you travel after finally meeting the miners at Mount Margaret?

— To Coolgardie and then Fremantle. I then worked my way to Melbourne.

— On a ship? Do you remember the steamer line?

— No, I do not.

— Where else did you travel?

— I have been in Brisbane, in Wellington, in Perth. I was only in Perth one day and in Brisbane for some time, where I worked for a tea dealer, as I told you earlier. In Wellington I canvassed for someone.

Massingham picked up his pencil once more.

— I would like to check these. Are there any names you could give me?

— No, I do not recall any names.

De Rougemont seemed to be tiring. Fitzgerald pointedly took out his watch, but Massingham ignored him and maintained the pace, attempting to trip the Frenchman by going back over old ground.

— To return to the language question: you had always learned English not from Englishmen, but from foreigners?

— Yes. But I associated with English boys at school.

— Did the miners whom you met at Mount Margaret take you for English?

— Well, I should not like to say they took me for a countryman. They might have taken me for a lunatic. My skin showed marks of the clay and grease. I looked like a half-caste. My hair was cut. I cut my hair with a very sharp stiletto I had. I gave it to the natives as a memento. It was softer and finer and longer than theirs. They were glad to have it.

Fitzgerald was unsure if De Rougemont's rambling was intentional or simply a sign of fatigue, but it appeared to temporarily distract Massingham, sending him fumbling through his notes for his next question.

— Have you heard anything from Professor Tylor as to those words he took down from your mouth?

— I wrote to Professor Tylor offering to compile a whole dictionary. But I have something more to say. If Professor Tylor came to me tomorrow and asked me to do it I would refuse. I will tell you why. A syndicate has been formed to go to the parts of Australia where I was, and they have wired me not to divulge a word of the language until they have taken up their land. If Professor Tylor came to me tomorrow I would say, 'Not yet'. I would ask him to wait until the syndicate had given me leave. Why? Because if you had the words of language, you would have the tribe, and if you had the tribe, you would have the location.

— I was going to ask you if you would write down phonetically in the Australian with which you are familiar the equivalent of a number of English words.

— I cannot do so. I will give absolutely none.

Massingham looked to Fitzgerald.

— I would not publish them. What I proposed doing was to submit them to Professor Tylor, who would report on them privately.

Fitzgerald shrugged his shoulders and De Rougemont was unmoved.

— I will not give them now. Later, perhaps.
— But, Monsieur De Rougemont, you have pointed out the region on a map at the British Association. How could the words lead to the identification of the spot more closely?
— The language would easily lead to its identification. You cannot go from tribe to tribe without spotting the difference. It is the truest of all guides. Take a map and I will point it out again. But I will give no words. The syndicate have wired me to keep my mouth absolutely sealed.

Massingham held up a piece of paper.

— I have a list of forty words here.

De Rougemont shook his head resolutely.

— I will not give you ten; not five, not one.
— If you can get the permission of the syndicate to give certain words, will you do so?
— Certainly.

Massingham began to gather up his notes from the table. De Rouge-mont took the cue to rise but Massingham stopped him by proffering his pencil.

— Perhaps we could contact your syndicate ourselves? Will you give me James Murphy's address in London?

De Rougemont took the pencil without argument and wrote down the address. Massingham was discouraged: the rogue's willingness to oblige made it was clear there was nothing to gain by pursuing his Irish friend. As De Rougemont, Fitzgerald and Greenough-Smith prepared to leave, Massingham made them an offer. He revealed that the letter-writer 'An Australian' was in fact Louis Becke, and invited De Rougemont to confront his challenger the following day. After some consultation the invitation was accepted, on the proviso that Becke, who had never travelled extensively in the Australian desert, confined his enquiries exclusively to De Rougemont's sea voyages.

What perplexed Massingham most was not De Rougemont's account, but the nature of the man himself. Was he simply a serial plagiarist who had lifted various incidents from other travellers' journals? As Forbes had asserted at Bristol, there were enough points of coincidence between De Rougemont's narrative and others' reports to suggest this was possible, but these similarities were equally sufficient to suggest their truth. Or was he an impostor who had stolen his whole experience lock, stock and barrel from the life of some other colonial frontiersman? If neither, could it all be pure invention? It would seem to require a man of singular genius, a Swift or Defoe, to have imagined all De Rougemont claimed — and a virtuoso actor possessing unyielding nerve to carry it off in the face of expert interrogation.

In 1719, when Daniel Defoe's *The Life and Strange Surprizing Adventures of Robinson Crusoe* was first published, many readers refused to believe it could be fiction. They thought the fantastical tale simply too detailed to be capable of invention, the narrative too realistic and heartfelt to be mere literary vanity. The book's immediate popularity was phenomenal. The initial print run of a thousand copies sold out in a fortnight. Four editions were published in four months, followed by its appearance in serial form in a London newspaper. Within a year, *Crusoe* had been published in four languages and two sequels followed in rapid succession. George Newnes had in it good precedent for the commercial success of his own venture. Like *The Adventures of Louis De Rougemont*, Defoe's *Crusoe* was accompanied into print by a portrait of the protagonist, but Robinson Crusoe was depicted standing on the shores of his island home garbed in goatskins and brandishing a pair of long-barrelled guns — a far cry from the starched-collared, hood-eyed oddity of *Wide World* fame.

Defoe had also had good precedent. In the year previous to *Crusoe*'s publication, there had appeared in reprint a factual account of the rescue of a castaway, Alexander Selkirk. His saviour, Captain Woodes Rogers, had been part of a fleet that discovered the Scottish sailor marooned upon the Pacific island of Juan Fernandez, 400 miles west of Chile.

Selkirk had been a ship's master on a privateering mission to the South Americas led by William Dampier in 1704. He requested he be put ashore after quarrelling with his captain, Thomas Stradling, over fears his worm-eaten galley, the *Cinque Ports*, would sink. The captain accused him of mutiny. When his crewmates declined to join him Selkirk changed his mind, but Stradling refused to let him return aboard and the vessel departed without him.

Selkirk's isle was some thirty-six miles around and blessed with a subtropical climate, abundant sea life, food and fresh water. A large family of goats roamed the lush hills and savannah, distant descendants of a small herd landed by the island's eponymous discoverer more than a century before. Compared to De Rougemont's 1000-yard-square 'microscopical strip of sand', it was a vast Eden. Rogers reported Selkirk had taken with him 'his clothes and bedding, with a firelock, some powder, bullets, and tobacco, a hatchet, a knife, a kettle, a Bible, some practical pieces, and his mathematical instruments and books'.[8] The spiteful Stradling had left him only enough sustenance — a meagre ploughman's lunch of quince marmalade and cheese — for one day.

Yet Selkirk had survived on the island in isolation for four years and four months — a notion utterly unthinkable to readers of the day. Like De Rougemont, 'he diverted and provided for himself as well as he could', but for the first eight months 'had much ado to bear up against Melancholy, and the Terror of being left alone in such a desolate place'.

When Rogers came upon Selkirk he observed 'a Man cloth'd in Goat-Skins, who look'd wilder than the first Owners of them'. While he had preserved sanity by reading the Bible and singing psalms, his capacity for spoken language was vastly reduced. In the absence of human companionship, Selkirk, like De Rougemont, had recruited the island's wild beasts — goats, cats and even rats — for recreation. Juan Fernandez was also home to turtles, but unlike his latter-day counterpart, Selkirk neither rode them for pleasure nor made farms of their shells, preferring instead to simply dine on their flesh.

As time proved, Selkirk's survival was more likely on the island than at sea. His fear that the outfit's leaking vessel was doomed was vindicated when the *Cinque Ports* sank off Barbacora in Peru, sending all but seven men to their deaths below.[9] Four years later Woodes Rogers happened upon Selkirk on his island and returned him to England. Over the decade following his salvation, Selkirk's story was popularised by the essayist Sir Richard Steele, whom some would later claim was the real author of *Crusoe*.

The Selkirk accounts primed Defoe's audience to accept the possibility of such a miraculous feat of survival. The parallels with Crusoe's predicament led many to believe that Defoe had actually met Selkirk soon after his return and based his novel directly upon the sailor's experience. Later, this evolved into the more heinous allegation that Defoe had in fact stolen Selkirk's draft manuscript, embellishing it and publishing it in his own name. Selkirk's survival, without a Friday or even cannibals for company, was in some respects more remarkable than even that of Defoe's romantic hero. Familiarity with Selkirk's saga, coupled with Defoe's own imaginative powers, was enough to persuade many of his audience that *Crusoe* was indeed a true account.

Defoe was no stranger to writing in the guise of another. He frequently employed a variety of pen names including 'Heliostrapolis, secretary to the Emperor of the Moon'. But he never claimed *Robinson Crusoe* was true. The notion that Crusoe actually existed was only a fantasy manufactured by his audience. Now, like Defoe's true believers, certain members of De Rougemont's readership were reluctant to perceive his astounding adventures as anything but fact. The parallels to *Crusoe*, and even Selkirk's story, only encouraged these readers, and to Newnes's and Fitzgerald's delight, propelled *Wide World*'s circulation beyond that of every other newspaper and magazine in England. Even the hero's name had resonance in 'Defoe'. Might the son of a Paris shoe-peddler, like the butcher's son Daniel Foe, have gentrified his name for literary purposes?

Crusoe had strongly shaped perceptions of remote lands. Some early emigrants to Australia were disappointed to discover their new home was not the idyll of Defoe's dreaming, but a landscape in which mere survival was the greatest challenge. In 1790, one young convict transported to New South Wales complained in a letter to a friend in London that 'to give a just description of the hardships that the meanest of us endure, and the anxieties suffered by the rest, is more than I can pretend to do. In all the Crusoe-like adventures I ever read or heard of, I do not recollect anything like it.'[10]

The island continent certainly wasn't populated by wild goats, or even ten-foot tall hermaphrodites, as conceived by French writer Gabriel De Foigny in his 1676 work *La Terre Australe Connue*.[11] (This was fortunate for Louis De Rougemont, as De Foigny's mythical giants had a penchant for murdering shipwrecked visitors to their shores.) But many British readers, courtesy of Defoe and his fellow writers, still pictured the Antipodes as home to monstrous beasts, cannibals and savages. De Rougemont had not let them down.

If he was simply a liar, Massingham thought, he was one to surpass Sir John Mandeville, the fourteenth-century knight who had brilliantly welded outrageous fictions to known geographic fact to construct imaginary lands in Europe and Asia populated by one-eyed giants, dog-headed men and dragons. These tales were related in his book *Mandeville's Travels*. Half a millennium later, Mandeville was still considered 'the greatest liar of all time'. Proper exploration had exploded the truth of his claims, but doubt over his true identity remained even in Massingham's day. While debate over the credibility of De Rougemont's experiences was growing, the editor thought the real key to solving the riddle lay in establishing the man's identity.

If little else, the interview in the *Chronicle* office had provided him with some useful clues. After his guests had departed, Massingham contacted his Paris correspondent by wire and sent him sifting through registry books at the Madeleine, seeking confirmation of De Rougemont's birth details.

11

Mercury Rising

I am free as Nature first made man,
Ere the base laws of servitude began,
When wild in woods the noble savage ran.
John Dryden, *Conquest of Granada*, 1670

IN DE ROUGEMONT'S ADOPTIVE Swiss homeland, anarchists looking to make their own headlines had assassinated the Empress of Austria in the streets of Zurich. In Fashoda, a town on the White Nile in Sudan, a territorial dispute between the British and the French escalated, raising the possibility of war. In Paris, the Dreyfus affair — in which a Jewish military officer had been wrongly imprisoned as a spy, sparking a bitter divide between supporters of the Republic, the army and the Catholic hierarchy — was reaching its climax. Vesuvius was once more hurling fire and molten rock at the gods and a hurricane had destroyed Barbados. But in London's newspapers, Louis De Rougemont commanded pride of place.

The heatwave that had dampened brows and emptied halls at Bristol continued. As the thermometer on the porch of the British Museum rose, London came to a standstill. So hot was it that it made news halfway around the world. *The Sydney Morning Herald* commented:

> People accustomed to sunnier climes will find it difficult to realise what a few days of brilliant untempered sunshine means to the average Londoner accustomed to the damp and fog and the smoke-laden atmosphere of the great city . . . the most hardworking Englishmen find it difficult, and in not a few cases, impossible, to get through their day's work at a temperature of this sort . . . nobody can eat, few can sleep well, and deaths from sunstroke and heat apoplexy are reported from all quarters.[12]

Despite the heat and the magnitude of international events, the De Rougemont affair now occupied more than a quarter of the *Chronicle*'s total editorial territory each day. De Rougemont had become a mystery to be solved — a case worthy of Holmes. Not since the terrors of the Ripper a decade before had a story so gripped public and press. Each new doubt raised seemed to double the correspondence received at the *Chronicle* offices. Mail clerks, resentful at having to work at all in the suffocating heat, sifted through a new mountain of envelopes each morning. Such was the outpouring of interest the editor was obliged to publish an advisory note:

TO OUR CORRESPONDENTS

We are overwhelmed with correspondence on this subject and can only overtake it by degrees. We shall endeavour to give all views, friendly or hostile, impartiality.

The Times, no friend to the left-leaning *Chronicle*, continued to offer its support to the Frenchman. In its leader of Thursday 15 September, it was commented 'M. de Rougemont must not take it amiss that his statements have met with a certain amount of hesitation.' Turning to history, the paper found ample precedent for De Rougemont's predicament:

> Such in old times was the fate of Bruce, and also in our day of Du Chaillu, and we hope that, as in these cases, our latest traveller will before long find that what he tells us will receive ample corroboration from independent sources.

James Bruce, a well-to-do, red-haired son of Scotland, the former British Consul to Algiers, had set out in 1768 to reveal the source of the Nile. Over six years he travelled through Northern Africa, from Cairo to Abyssinia and back. Upon his return to Britain, Bruce's meticulous accounts of life in the King of Abyssinia's court in Gondar were roundly denounced as fraud. Counted among the critics was Dr Samuel Johnson, author of a romance of Abyssinia that Bruce's accounts supposedly contradicted.[13] Other travellers would later verify Bruce's reports of ancient kingdoms, bizarre natural phenomena and strange beasts in the region of the Nile.

New Orleans–born Paul Du Chaillu's exploits in Africa were the very stuff of which *Wide World Magazine* was made. At the age of only twenty, unaccompanied by other white men, Du Chaillu had travelled over 6000 miles into equatorial Africa by foot. Du Chaillu was the first white man to witness and record the behaviour of gorillas; he was also the first to report the existence of West African pygmies. He claimed to have escaped poisoning by a homicidal tribal cook, witnessed ritual beheadings and been brought down by 'African fever' no less than fifty times. Some aspects of his stories, such as his coronation as the 'King of the Apingi', seemed to have distinct echoes in De Rougemont's tales. He had taken with him no camera or other means of recording his journeys, beyond pen and paper. He kept a daily journal, which he said 'involved more painful care' than he liked 'even to think of', but upon his return, these journals would cause him even more pain. The vivid language he had employed and the thrilling nature of his travels led many to believe them to be fiction. In the United States and England, Du Chaillu was met with general derision and mocked as 'Mr Gorilla'. He was later vindicated when other African explorers, including Stanley and Burton, verified his observations of cannibals, pygmies and gorillas.

Recalling the disdain with which Du Chaillu's 'chimpanzee and dwarf stories' were greeted in England, the *Chronicle* admitted that these were no longer matters of faith but accepted history. Still, the fact that one suspected fake had been proved genuine did not mean De Rougemont was telling the truth. However, the editor was willing to concede De Rougemont the upper hand over Du Chaillu in the matter of etiquette, reporting that at one learned society meeting the chairman's incredulity had so exasperated the African explorer that he spat in his face.

In seeking to counter *The Times*'s defence of De Rougemont, Massingham might have done well to invoke an even earlier case. In 1704, *An Historical and Geographical Description of Formosa* had appeared under the authorship of 'George Psalmanazar, a native of the said island, now in London'.[14] On Psalmanazar's Formosa, cannibalism, polygamy and infanticide were everyday affairs. The book described in detail the society, culture and habits of the residents of a remote, little-known land. Like the *Wide World* serial, the tales were enhanced by lavish illustrations depicting everything from native costume to human sacrifice. Psalmanazar had even appended a complete chart of the Formosan alphabet, unlike De Rougemont, who would not divulge a single word of his tribal language. Though his blonde hair and blue eyes prevented him looking in the least part Oriental, both man and book gained immediate celebrity, and Psalmanazar was absorbed holus-bolus into London's social whirl. Over the next ten years, his travel guide went through several editions and was translated into French and German. Like De Rougemont, Psalmanazar was invited to address the Empire's scientific experts at the Royal Society, where he got the best of astronomer Sir Edmund Halley in a debate over the position of the sun in Formosa. Oxford University even proposed to offer a course in Psalmanazar's Formosan language.

Psalmanazar's success was in no small part due to the extremes to which he would go to prove he was indeed a Formosan. He insisted at all times on doing things as he claimed the natives did there, eating his meat raw and going without sleep. To complete the charade he would forego his bed for an easy chair and leave a candle burning in his study so that neighbours might think he studied throughout the night. Psalmanazar's introduction to the second edition of his book could have flowed from De Rougemont's own pen. In answer to those critics who accused him of being a fraud, Psalmanazar wrote:

> You do me more honour than you are aware of, for then you must think that I forg'd the whole story out of my own brain . . . he must be a man of prodigious parts who can invent the description of a Country, contrive a religion, frame laws and customs, make a language, and letters, etc., and these different from all other parts of the world; he must also have more than a human memory that is always ready to vindicate so many feigned particulars, and that without ere so much as once contradicting himself.

During his lifetime, Psalmanazar never publicly conceded that he might not be all he said he was, but in his memoirs, published a year after his death, he disavowed his earlier book as 'a scandalous imposition on the public,' and a 'monstrous romance'. He claimed that the secret of his success had been that whatever he had once affirmed in conversation, 'tho' to ever so few people, and tho' ever so improbable, or even absurd, should never be amended or contradicted'. Psalmanazar also found himself to have a facility for answering questions for which he was not prepared, saying 'I seldom found myself at a loss for a quick answer, which, if satisfactory, I stored up in my retentive memory.'

Though Psalmanazar ultimately admitted to his hoax, he did not reveal his true identity. His success was so complete that nearly 200 years later, as the nineteenth century drew to a close, the mystery still remained. There was no doubt Psalmanazar's achievement was at least partially due to the lengths he was willing to go to maintain his charade. His audience were willing to accept his fraud for as long as it remained an entertainment. So it also appeared De Rougemont's readers would swallow the more well-spiced elements of his story, providing they were palatably presented.

De Rougemont had already persuaded many to take his part; he had even managed to convince the dignified *Times* that the act of poking out a tongue while gripping one's buttocks might 'prove useful to any future explorers visiting the remote desert country'.

Now a further editorial in the broadsheet quoted the seventeenth-century poet Dryden to illustrate its support of De Rougemont:

> Conditionally, at all events, we claim the privilege of endeavouring to believe him, and of allowing him to transport us in imagination to the time '*when wild in woods the noble savage ran*'.

A distinct part of the appeal of De Rougemont's stories seemed to be the idyllic way of life he attributed to the tribe with whom he had lived. *The Times* said it was:

> ... gratified to find that many of the virtues of which poets have attributed to the human race as its indefeasible heritage are actually existing, and in full working order, among tribes whose refinement has not arrived at the use of clothing, but who seem to be generous, just, hospitable, and friendly.

They were virtues it seemed *The Times* was also keen to demonstrate to De Rougemont.

Displaying a rare paternal interest in the welfare of native Australians, *The Times* invited the Colonial Office to do 'what is in their power to prevent these simple and kindly people from being demoralised by the temptations which the pioneers of civilization are too apt to bring in their train'. De Rougemont's protectors were worthy of 'the care which is too often expended upon persons of infinitely smaller desert and promise'.

If nothing else, De Rougemont had inspired a rare flurry of concern for the treatment of the Australian Aboriginal. Via the vast columns of correspondence now filling the *Chronicle* and other newspapers, the public were also obtaining unprecedented insight into some of the more obscure traits of Australian tribes. Self-appointed experts, including ex-miners, pearlers and the Agent-General for Western Australia, debated numerous aspects of De Rougemont's observations, from wife-swapping to weaponry. But most could only offer unsubstantiated 'personal experience' to support their arguments.

Reports from the remaining days of the British Association Congress had now been relegated to the *Chronicle*'s back pages. Despite the other scientific subjects of import discussed at Bristol, including Marconi's revolutionary demonstrations of the wireless telegraph, De Rougemont's lecture appearances were hailed as 'the most striking event of the meeting'. The wayward balloon flight of a Professor Bacon and his eventual safe descent in Claverton received some attention; otherwise the event had been completely appropriated by the French adventurer. *The Times* said:

> The general impression is that M. De Rougemont is telling the simple truth; that some of his ethnographical information is of considerable scientific value; and that he is hardly to blame for the sensational style in which his adventures have been served up to the public.

The end of the British Association conference did nothing to still the controversy fomented by newspaper reports in London. On Friday afternoon, De Rougemont and Fitzgerald returned to the *Chronicle* offices.

Unhappy with the rival paper's version of the first interview, Fitzgerald had demanded the attendance of a *Wide World* stenographer. Massingham and Clodd were again present, along with De Rougemont's original adversary, Louis Becke.

12

The Last Pirate

You are now in London town,
Louis Becke,
Keeping up your old renown,
Writing yarns of women brown,
Getting yellow money down,
Or a cheque.

Victor Daley,
Wrecked Illusions (dedicated to Louis Becke), 1898

SPORTING PANAMA HAT and linen suit, tall and tanned of skin, Becke already had a reputation in London as the very model of the colonial adventurer. Beside him, De Rougemont seemed trivial. Upon his arrival from Australia in 1896, the *Daily News* had reported that Becke had hands 'strong enough to crush a coconut or a skull'. The reporter was obviously smitten:

> When roused I should say that he is well able to take care of himself . . . I thought I detected just a faint smell of the sea, but it was soon absorbed by blue clouds of that black plug tobacco the hard-headed ones love to smoke.

Becke's romantic repute had only been enhanced by reports he had deserted his wife Bessie in Sydney and sailed abroad with his paramour, Fanny Long. That town's newspapers remained in his thrall, the *Daily Telegraph* correspondent describing him as 'looking the picture of bronzed integrity'. *The South Australian Register* dubbed him the 'Rudyard Kipling of Australia'. Ironically, the suntanned South Sea adventurer found it difficult to cope with London in the heat. Describing it as 'a gigantic brick-kiln twelve miles long by twelve miles wide', Becke wrote, 'those who can, run away, those who cannot stay, swear, suffer and swill'. Becke stayed and made it his business to impress the men of influence in Pall Mall.

Becke's collections of short stories and novels had been well received, and on arrival he had immediately been welcomed into the London literati. He had made the acquaintance of Twain; Doyle had him put up for the Authors' Club and Massingham, the Devonshire. Rudyard Kipling was a neighbour and friend. Such was the regard in which Becke was held that, despite having never been an explorer, he was to become the first Australian accepted as a member of the Royal Geographical Society. Another collection of short stories had just been published and November would see a new biography of Governor Phillip.

Like James Murphy, Becke was also keen to trade on the City's slight knowledge of affairs south of the equator through the creation of new South Sea investment syndicates. His American writer pal Harold Frederic introduced him at the Liberal Club as 'the last genuine pirate'. Becke had himself been at the centre of a famous plagiarism case, in which he was represented by the Australian lawyer poet A. B. 'Banjo' Paterson. Becke had charged the writer Rolf Boldrewood (alias Thomas Browne) with using Becke's own auto-biographical notes verbatim and unattributed as the basis for a novel, *A Modern Buccaneer*, and won the case.

Becke was already seated at the table with Massingham and Clodd when De Rougemont and his *Wide World* entourage were shown into the *Chronicle* office. At Massingham's invitation the party sat down, but on this occasion no small talk ensued between the editors. Massingham immediately addressed De Rougemont in French, asking him if he would say certain words in that language.

De Rougemont looked surprised, then answered the editor in English.

— Monsieur, I cannot any longer hold a conversation *en français*; however, I can answer any question you might like to put in that language.

De Rougemont paused and laughed at himself.

— At least I think I can.

Massingham expressed no amusement. He spoke to De Rougemont again in French, asking him once more where he was born, in what year and where he was baptised. As requested, Rougemont responded in simple French, providing the same answers he had the previous day. Finally, Massingham asked whether his father Samuel Emmanuel was a Jew or a Christian. To this, De Rougemont replied in English.

— Monsieur, I do not know if he was Jew or Christian and I'm afraid I do not see the point of your question in French or English. I have already given you this information yesterday afternoon.

Massingham made no acknowledgement of De Rougemont's protest but returned to questioning him in English.

— You said that one of your employers in Sydney was a James Murphy, and that this gentleman was now in London?

De Rougemont sighed in exasperation.

— *Oui, monsieur.*

— When in his employment, did you mention to him that you had found gold and precious stones in the course of your explorations?

— I did.

— What did he say?

— As near as I can recall, he said 'I wish you had come sooner, as owing to the fact the banks have smashed us up, it would be difficult now for me to do anything. No-one would go into such an undertaking at the present moment.'

Fitzgerald put a hand up to Massingham and addressed De Rougemont.

— Had not Mr Murphy lost money in the Australian bank smash?

— I do not know; you must ask him that.

Massingham resumed.

— Did you put to him the question of whether a syndicate should be formed to exploit these lands?

— No, I put no such question, I simply stated the fact.

— His reply was that he could not enter into it?

— That was his reply in effect.

— Did you mention the pearls to him?

— I think so, I feel sure so.

— And suggest that an attempt should be made to recover them?

— No, I mentioned to him the fact of them. I made no attempt at asking him to spend a penny for me in any shape or form, except for my daily work for him. I simply stated facts and he could please himself what he did.

— Why did you leave the pearls on the island? They would have been a small bundle?

— Very small. That's quite right.

— May I ask why it did not occur to you to take them, place them around your neck or make a parcel of them around your body and keep them?

— It did not occur to me to take them away for the simple reason that I knew I would return for the shells, and consequently for the pearls.

— Why not take them with you?

— My dear sir, I was simply going, I knew, among uncivilised people, and how long I was to be with them in my boat I did not know.

— After your return to Australia, did you make any attempt to recover the pearls?

— Yes, several.

— Alone?

De Rougemont appeared puzzled.

— What do you mean by 'an attempt'? Would it be an attempt if
I asked someone to assist me in recovering the pearls?

— Yes. Did you seek assistance?

— Certainly I did.

— Whose assistance did you seek?

— Some pearlers'.

Massingham's pencil appeared once more.

— Can you give me names?

— I am a bad hand at remembering names. Mr Murphy introduced
me to a man. A man well known in Australia.

Massingham put the pencil to the page.

— Can I have his name?

— No.

The editor sat back in his chair and thought for a moment.

— With regard to Murphy. You came to England and you were
practically destitute?

— Yes.

— Did you communicate with your employer?

— No.

— Subsequently Mr Murphy comes to England and appears as the
promoter of your syndicate?

— That's wrong. You say Mr Murphy came subsequently. I say
nothing of the kind. I simply met Mr Murphy accidentally in the
street. He came before me to England.

— The following question is a delicate one which you may refuse to answer if you so desire. Did Mr Murphy suggest putting together the syndicate to exploit the riches you discovered in your wanderings?

— I can answer: yes, he did and I agreed. It is the only way I could think of returning to those parts.

— You stated yesterday that Murphy knew you as De Rougemont in Australia. Is there anyone else who knew you by that name?

— No. It was not necessary. If I was working as a salesman for someone I would simply travel under the name of their company.

Massingham appeared bemused, so De Rougemont explained further.

— When I was working for Murphy on the Sutherland Estate I used his name as his representative. If I had been travelling for, say, a tea-merchant called Murphy, that would also have been my name at the time.

Massingham and Becke exchanged a glance. The notion seemed unlikely but alone it proved nothing. Massingham told De Rougemont that as he had no more questions, Becke would now take up the interview.

Before Becke had a chance to speak, De Rougemont fired his first shot.

— I would also like the opportunity to question Mr Becke, in particular regarding his authority to speak on maritime matters.

The slur irritated the Australian, who had commenced ocean travel at the age of fourteen and held a substantial opinion of his own sea-worthiness.

— You can ask me what you like, but it is not my authority in question here.

Becke's obvious annoyance encouraged De Rougemont.

— I have something of interest to tell you. I was delighted to read in the paper this morning, not the *Chronicle* I am afraid, that a shipment of live turtles has just arrived at London Dock. As you have an interest in the subject, I wonder if you would like to accompany me to a bath and I can show you how the riding is done? I thought perhaps you might like to try it?

Fitzgerald stifled a laugh and Becke bristled.

— I'm afraid I am not so venturesome.

De Rougemont smiled.

— That is too bad. Nevertheless, I want to ask you a question before you ask me. There are certain things with which I am not at all satisfied . . . I should like to settle that point. Now do you know anything about turtles?

— Yes, I do.

— Have you ever got on the back of one?

— Yes, but never afloat.

— Oh, never afloat? As you have never been on the back of a turtle afloat, how is it you contradict me? You represent yourself as an expert, and you have never ridden a turtle about in the water.

— I say this is absolutely impossible.

— Now, do you not think Admiral Moresby is a better judge than you?

— No, I do not think so.

— Do you think that Admiral Moresby made a misstatement when he wrote that letter? Do you mean to say that he would make that misstatement by hearsay?

— No, it is perfectly feasible to get on a turtle's back in shallow water.

— You absolutely admit that. In shallow water?

— Yes.

— Did I say in deep water? In the magazine I said shallow water. But I have been in deep water, and it was today I wished to show you how to go in deep water. Many a time the turtle has left me in deep water.

Massingham broke in.

— I think Mr Becke would concede that he is not an expert on turtles. He has observed many, perhaps hundreds, in their native home, that is all. Perhaps we should proceed.

De Rougemont laughed.

— Indeed we should proceed. From turtles to octopus, or perhaps squid as Mr Becke calls them. Tell me, Mr Becke, what is the largest squid you have ever seen?

— The largest I have seen was dead. In pieces floating on the water.

— How large were these pieces?

— I would say the tentacles were around four feet in length and eight or nine inches in diameter at the thickest part.

— I see. How many tentacles would you say an octopus, or squid, has?

— Six or eight. The ordinary squid in shallow water has six. But I have never seen a squid exceeding ten feet.

Becke's best was still sixty-five feet short of equalling De Rougemont's boat-breaking monster. De Rougemont shrugged.

— I am quite willing to accept that as fact.

He paused for a moment before leaning forward and speaking very softly, almost in a whisper, to Becke alone.

— I shall not contradict you Mr Becke, because I am a Frenchman . . . and you know what that means.

Becke gave a nervous laugh. What was it De Rougemont meant to imply? That a duel might be required? It seemed ridiculous, but the scoundrel appeared completely serious. Massingham sought to relieve the tension by inviting Becke to ask the questions he had prepared for De Rougemont.

De Rougemont whispered with Fitzgerald as Becke arranged his notes. Finally Becke resumed the interview with a series of questions relating to the storm-crippled *Veielland*.

— When the great sea broke on board the schooner, when it was riding at anchor, it carried away the bulwarks?

— The bulwarks had been more or less carried away before.

— Then how did you slip your cable and let the anchor run out?

— As soon as I had my chain very taut, when it was at its greatest tension, I had a big axe and gave it a violent blow and it parted.

— Where was this axe usually stowed? Was it not the axe used in the galley?

— Yes.

— Was not this axe washed away?

— No. It was stowed away below.

— When this big sea broke aboard and carried away the companion way, part of the bulwarks and the wheel, and after you cut the anchor cable, you rigged a jury-rudder? One with sweeps perhaps?

It seemed to De Rougemont that Becke simply wished to flaunt his knowledge of sailing. He turned to Massingham and Fitzgerald and begged their relief.

— Does Monsieur Becke have a point to all this? We all know he has been aboard a boat. Several that were wrecked, I believe.

Becke raised his voice.

— My point, Monsieur De Rougemont, is how you were able to handle the boat alone. Assisted only by your dog.

— It had been Jensen's dog.

— An Australian dog, I think you said. How did you know it was Australian? Did it bite you?

De Rougemont ignored the insult.

— It had been given to Captain Jensen by an Australian pearler — Cadell, I think, was his name. He was well known in those parts.

Becke agreed he had heard of a former riverboat runner by the name of Francis Cadell, who had also been involved in pearling and was later murdered by a member of his own crew off the New Guinea coast. He returned his attention to De Rougemont's voyage.

— How did you build your raft when you struck the reef?

— From the hatches of the *Veielland*.

Massingham watched impatiently. However great Becke's expertise as a sailor and writer, his interview skills seemed sadly lacking. Several more questions relating to the *Veielland* followed before at last, exasperated, Becke enquired of De Rougemont if it was possible that errors may have crept into his narrative.

— It is, of course, possible. When I made my statements, I was not the man I am today.

Becke was done, but Massingham would not allow De Rougemont to escape without one final assault. It seemed self-evident to the editor that as De Rougemont had spent most of his time near naked, his body should have become as tanned as his face. The revelation of a pale arm or torso would also expose a lie.

— There is another question: a delicate question you may object to answer.

— Tell me the question.

— Do you mind showing your bare arm?

— I have not the slightest objection to do so, but I think it is an impertinent question. I will do so if you press it.

— If you consider it a personal indignity I will withdraw it.

— I do.

— Very well, I will not press it.

The interview concluded and Fitzgerald and De Rougemont stood to go. As they were leaving the office, De Rougemont suddenly turned and addressed Becke.

— I have no objection to showing *you* my arm, Mr Becke, at the appropriate hour.

He resumed his exit without waiting for a reply. Afterward, Becke wondered if the offended Frenchman had meant to suggest the possibility of fisticuffs. Legend had it that when Samuel Johnson exposed the writer James Macpherson as a literary forger, the Scot had threatened to assault him. Perhaps De Rougemont had the same in mind. Johnson had reportedly responded by buying a massive truncheon with which to defend himself, but the Frenchman would need to contend with Becke's celebrated skull-crushing hands.

13

Dinner with the Cannibal King

Life itself was meat. Life lived on life. There were the
eaters and the eaten.

Jack London, *White Fang*, 1906

LOUIS DE ROUGEMONT HAD arrived at the height of his fame. In London, he was as feted by believers as assailed by critics, and his frequent public forays were accompanied by a clamour of curious onlookers. Fitzgerald had aborted his efforts to constrain the ebullient author. Newnes's cash advances allowed De Rougemont to fully indulge his fame, entertaining new friends at restaurants that would once have had him swept into the gutter. Those who encountered him at close quarters were struck first by his unique appearance and then by his unexpectedly eloquent, ethereal charm.

One Londoner described to the *Chronicle* his chance mid-September meeting with De Rougemont in an Italian restaurant:

> De Rougemont had just dined. He was drinking lager and smoking a cigarette. He smoked with great daintiness, merely touching his lips with the cigarette, and laying it down after each whiff in the saucer of his beer glass. He was no less dainty in his drinking. There is indeed reason to believe that he is very temperate in alcoholic matters.

The observer was less impressed with his face. Judging it as disappointing to those who had seen his photograph, the man reported that it was:

> ... broken up with lines and furrows which the photographer has not reproduced; the hair on the face has a coarser, more grizzled and

bristly appearance, the cheeks are more haggard, the rather ape-like wrinkles on the forehead more pronounced, the broadness of the nostrils more noticeable, and the shell-like ear with its indented rim more protruding than the man in the photograph. I have heard a lady say it was no wonder the cannibals did not eat him.

De Rougemont's countenance had left its usual impression. The broad and bulging forehead, fine-textured hair springing upright and curling at the tips, heavy-lidded eyes, emphatic nose and long thin face culminating in the goatee beard had suggested to the Londoner a nervous force and intellectual power. 'It strikes you at once,' he said, 'as the face of a man who has spent his energies in the sphere of thought and emotion, rather than in physical effort.'

It was also, he said, the face of:

... a man who has been misunderstood, who has met severe mental disappointments, of a man who has dreamt dreams, never to be realised, who has never been able to march in step with his fellows, who has throughout life been his own enemy.

In conversation, the face becomes animated and expressive. It, so to speak, seems to dilate and loses its shrunken appearance. You may then fancy you are in the presence of an enthusiast, an idealist – if you like, a crank. It is difficult to talk with the man and set him down as coarse and brutal; it is almost equally difficult to give him credit for being needlessly honest, candid, self-sacrificing, or magnanimous.

According to this London gentleman, De Rougemont spoke like a man accustomed to holding forth to great or small audiences. What surprised him most was a certain intellectual refinement that appeared in his manner and conversation.

The Frenchman also had a peculiar susceptibility to suggestion. Invited to join the table, the loquacious De Rougemont had told his new friend of his return to civilisation. Hats and boots, he said, had been his chief troubles. Asked whether the soles of his feet had become thickened during the years he had gone without foot covering, he replied they had changed a good deal. One of the diners remarked that he supposed the entire sole would swell and form a soft pad about half an inch thick, like the sole of an indiarubber shoe. De Rougemont said that this was indeed the case with his feet. It was then suggested that the sole of the foot might become in time coated with a horny growth like a corn. De Rougemont, not apparently seeing anything incompatible in the two suggestions, also adopted the second, and said the soles of his feet were like an enormous corn; that was the reason why boots were at first so uncomfortable to him.

De Rougemont's hands, reported the man, were not of the kind to be expected of a person who had spent thirty years among the cannibals. The nails were long and spotlessly clean, the fingers delicate and tapering, the palms soft as a woman's, and on the back the blue veins showed through transparent white skin.

Everything about De Rougemont's descriptions of his life with the savages, he said, was vague in detail, but full of emotional force:

> The atmosphere is that of *The Boy's Own Magazine* and Dr. Watts' poetry.[15] M. De Rougemont's savages are nobler than Rousseau's; his cannibals are actuated by a higher altruism than our own amiable vegetarians. They remind you of the characters in a tragedy upon a Greek subject, written by an eighteenth-century French poet. The personages are full of the noble and most approved sentiments, and conduct themselves in a strikingly well bred manner . . .

De Rougemont had explained to these new acquaintances the effect he meant to have upon a gathering when he lectured. He would tell audience members that the first child Yamba had by him she had killed and eaten, because he thought this story would provoke a certain sensation. The table emphatically agreed that it would. But the greater effect would be produced, De Rougemont had said, when he explained why she had done this. She had done it to save his life. He had been ill at the time and Yamba was giving him suck from her breast. His listeners in the restaurant understood him to mean that he had required exclusive access to his wife's milk, giving her no choice but to kill the child or let it starve.

One member of the dinner party asked what disease he was suffering from at the time. The question did not seem to have previously occurred to De Rougemont. He hesitated. His interrogator suggested fever. He immediately adopted the suggestion: yes, he must have been suffering from fever at the time.

Surprisingly, the table agreed that in the circumstances his wife had taken the correct course in killing the child. But why, it was asked, did she eat it? Were there not other methods of disposing of the body? De Rougemont would not hear of alternatives.

'With us,' said De Rougemont, 'the women always eat their first children. They marry very young, at the age of fourteen. The first child is usually sickly and so the mother eats it.'

Cannibalism then consumed the conversation. Someone asked De Rougemont whether human flesh had a distinctive flavour of its own. He answered no, that it was very much like other meat, beef or mutton, but his questioner was offended to think that anyone could eat him, without giving him credit for excelling sheep or oxen as an article of diet. Human flesh, he contended, when properly roasted, might compare more than favourably with pork.

De Rougemont assuaged the gentleman's wounded feelings by agreeing that human flesh, when skilfully prepared, might be superior to pig. This defender of the edibility of his fellows then asked whether a man, when roasted, had a crackling like pig. 'No, no crackling,' De Rougemont replied, but this also caused offence, and the questioner said he was convinced that if a healthy human being were brought up like a pig — that is, with a view to a culinary ending — he would undoubtedly develop crackling when adequately roasted. Anxious to satisfy, De Rougemont conceded that a well-roasted man had a kind of crackling, qualifying his reply only by saying that it differed in some respects from the crackling of a pig.

The diners then quizzed their guest over his performance at the British Association. There were times, De Rougemont told them, when he had felt almost inspired, standing on the stage before such an eager throng. It was strange, he said, how this power came and went. He had been awkward at first, but in a short time the words seemed to rise to his lips of their own accord. For over two hours he had talked and talked and the people had listened breathlessly. Those denied entry had set ladders against the walls outside and listened at the windows. Not a stir, not a whisper among the crowded audience! They had listened spellbound. And at the remembrance he laughed aloud.

Following dinner, the man reported, De Rougemont had presented a kind of impromptu performance upon a small stage in the rear of the restaurant.

> The Enlightener stood, his back to the footlights. His hat was on his head, his double-breasted coat of a dark slatey colour was buttoned over his breast and clung tightly to his spare form. His hands were thrust open into the side pockets of his coat. And these were the words, as nearly as it is possible to transcribe them, that he spoke.
>
> 'You Christians have an impersonal God, of whom, you say yourselves, you know nothing. Your religion is in books. We savages have a Father whom we know. How do we know him? By the messengers he sends us. What messengers? The spirits of our dead people. No, not dead, for there is no death. We savages know there is no death. How do we know? Because the messengers the Father sends us tell us there is no death. They tell us of the place to which they have gone, of the things they do there, of the life they lead.'

As long as M. De Rougemont kept to generalities, the man said, everything was plain sailing. But De Rougemont continued on as though possessed and his speech became stranger and stranger. His thesis was a curious melange of native superstition, theosophy and modern spiritualism. He spoke of naked cannibals seated in circles holding spiritualistic seances; of savages, not dead, but merely digested, appearing before the eyes of those who had dined off them a little previously. Ultimately, De Rougemont's dining companion was unconvinced:

> If you can conceive yourself uncanny enough to continue in this strain indefinitely, and with every outward sign of a sincere inward belief in the appalling gibberish you are talking, you will then have a faithful picture of a man who has lectured before the British Association discoursing upon the divine truths revealed to him and his cannibals. You refuse to believe it? So should I in your place. It's true all the same. Absolutely!

14

Tinned Milk and Savages

> It is an old maxim of mine that when you have excluded the impossible, whatever remains, however improbable, must be the truth.
>
> Sherlock Holmes,
> in Sir Arthur Conan Doyle's
> 'The Adventure of the Beryl Coronet',
> *The Strand Magazine*, 1892

THE DAILY CHRONICLE, with its boasts of exclusive interviews with the new Crusoe splashed across newspaper placards throughout the West End, could now claim ownership of the escalating De Rougemont saga. It was the only paper now investing resources in tracing the tale to its source. *The Times* persevered with its cautious defence, maintaining a conservative distance from the anonymous attacks beloved of its rival. The London *Figaro* was first to lampoon De Rougemont's tale, publishing 'The Preposterous Adventures of George Washington Munchausen de Spoof', substituting shrimps for pearls and a winkle for the giant octopus. In place of remote Australia, the adventures commenced off Southend.

Word of De Rougemont had already crossed the Atlantic. Cabled stories were now appearing regularly in *The Chicago Tribune*, *The Los Angeles Times* and *The San Francisco Chronicle*. *The Washington Post* erroneously referred to De Rougemont as 'the French Scientist'. *The New York Times* had run reports under the headline 'The Australian Cannibals'. As the controversy grew, Louis Becke's pal Harry Frederic kept stateside readers alerted to the latest revelations.

Many North American readers were familiar with the case of the 'Tichborne Claimant', in which a well-larded Australian butcher from Wagga Wagga had made a fraudulent claim upon the fortune of the Tichborne estate in England. It had become the subject of one of the longest running legal actions in British history. The claimant, known in Australia as Thomas Castro, posed as the long-lost heir Roger Tichborne. Despite initially convincing even the man's mother and generating significant public support, Castro was eventually exposed as the English-born Arthur Orton, convicted of perjury and sentenced to fourteen years' imprisonment. After his release he declined into poverty, dying on April Fools' Day 1898, one month after Louis De Rougemont's arrival at London Docks. His likeness now stood at Tussaud's, proximate to that of the modern Crusoe. Reporting for *The New York Times*, Frederic saw parallels between Orton's case and that of De Rougemont.

Louis De Rougemont, he declared:

> ... is fast becoming a Second Claimant, and though there are no landed Tichborne estates to play for here, yet the stakes seem pretty high. So much money is pouring in from the public that it will have a new sensation.
>
> Parties are forming, as in Orton's days, one holding that Rougemont is a genuine king of wild men, the other frankly labelling him a well-drilled impostor. Midway, a certain number of plain people hold the strange creature's narrative to be of the snowball order. Inside there may be a hard foundation of truth, but he has rolled it with such success that the amount of fact bears but a modest proportion to the huge volume of accredited fiction.

In order to keep the snowball rolling following the conclusion of the British Association Congress, Newnes had supplemented the *Chronicle*'s coverage with advertising for *Wide World*'s upcoming issue. On the same day De Rougemont jousted with Becke at the *Chronicle* offices, the publicity-hungry Newnes placed a page-high advertisement in the paper. The advertising revenue alone was sufficient to justify Massingham's continued pursuit of De Rougemont. In effect, the publishers were colluding to derive maximum profit from the story.

Under a banner shouting 'The Most Gigantic Sensation Of Modern Times', Newnes's advertising department used every superlative at its disposal to tout the wonders of Louis De Rougemont:

> Even momentous events in the world of international politics are forgotten in the unparalleled sensation created by 'The Adventures

of Louis De Rougemont', being the most amazing story a man ever lived to tell.

This astounding narrative, which is the talk of all Great Britain, and which is attracting such keen attention from the greatest living scientists, appears solely and exclusively in the WIDE WORLD magazine. To which world-renowned Journal belongs the honour of discovering this marvellous man and giving his story to the world.

The advertisement then telegraphed Newnes's next move:

The expedition to the wilds of New Guinea to bring back Peter Jensen starts immediately and the whole world will wait breathlessly for a glimpse of M. De Rougemont's pearling partner.

Look out for startling and romantic developments in this absorbing story. Peter Jensen will be brought back from New Guinea by the WIDE WORLD magazine. And the story of an amazing escape will also be narrated.

Alongside ran a page of letters dissecting the De Rougemont phenomenon. From the Savage Club in the Strand came a contribution from an Australian signing himself only as 'Sundowner'. He suggested De Rougemont might have been a lost member of Leichhardt's ill-fated expedition, rumoured to be living among Aborigines in central Australia. Another, mysteriously styling himself 'X', contended it was impossible for the average Englishman to understand De Rougemont. The experiences of men who stay at home in England, he said, must of necessity be different from the experiences of a man who had passed a number of years amid the 'savages of Australia'.

And certainly different from those in the midst of the Savage Club. The club had been formed at the Crown Tavern in 1857 to accommodate 'gentlemen connected with literature and the fine arts, and warmly interested in the promotion of knowledge, and the sale of exciseable liquors'. While several explorers, including Nansen, had addressed the club's membership, it was associated more with wild parties than the wilds of the Antipodes. However, at least some of the *Chronicle*'s correspondents were, in Massingham's words, 'men who had knowledge of Australia or had been explorers themselves'.

Albert Calvert, a polymath goldmining engineer, property owner and journalist who at the age of twenty had written a book on Western Australian Aboriginals, took De Rougemont to task on the powers of jig-dancing.[16] In a letter to the *Chronicle*, he wrote:

> This would have satisfied the natives of Western Australia and Central Australia, but would not have insured a friendly reception from the natives in the Far North of Australia, and especially those about the Alligator River, where the jig commenced in the open air, would, in my opinion, be completed in the interior of the natives it was intended to conciliate.

Calvert had more authority than most: he had written several books on Australian exploration and in 1894 authored the first single volume history of Western Australia. In his letter he also defended Ernest Giles from accusations of firing upon Aboriginal people:

> The members of [Giles's] party were noted for their inoffensive atti-tudes towards the natives, and had [De Rougemont] thrown down his weapons and walked open handed towards them he most certainly would have been received and accorded a hearing. Two of the four men that he met on that occasion I knew personally, and can unhesitatingly answer for. One can only conclude . . . that Mr Rougemont did not show the same ingenuity in approaching white men as he did when making overtures to the blacks. In describing his rebuff by Giles's party, he says that he 'was repulsed in this way more than once'. My own involuntary comment is – impossible! But things that would seem to be impossible anywhere else have been known to happen in the great Australian interior.

Calvert's own explorations had been lambasted for their lack of imagina-tion. A London exploration company had financed his 1891 North Western Exploring Expedition, and his transport was not camels but a second-hand buggy hired from Roebourne. A letter to *The Western Mail* described it as 'accomplishing the unprecedented feat of travelling the enormous distance of 500 miles through settled and well-known country'. The journey ended when the party was 'obliged to return to Roebourne, in consequence of, as reported, its supply of tinned milk having become exhausted'. Calvert was known thereafter in *The Gerald-ton Express* as 'the Tinned Milk Explorer of W. A.' In 1896, Calvert had financed an even more disastrous expedition from Geraldton to the Kimberley on which two of the party had died and all mineral specimens collected had been abandoned. For this he was still paying the price and, in September 1898, even as his letters to the *Chronicle* were published, his estate was in the process of being declared bankrupt.

Still, no matter their extent or success, Calvert's experiences had fostered in him a sympathy for Aboriginal people. In his book *The Aborigines of Western Australia* he expressed the view that British colonisation had done much to destroy the Aborigines. Observing that their 'degrading customs and brutal crimes' had been argued as justifi-cation for their speedy extinction he asked:

> If degradation alone be held to justify extinction, how many subjects of Her Majesty might well be wiped off the face of the earth within a four mile radius of the British Museum?
>
> There are those that flatter themselves that they belong to a higher order of created beings than the Western Australian abori-gines, who have been represented as mere baboons possessing an innate deficiency of intellect, which renders them incapable of instruction or civilization. It will be well for such persons to reflect that a similar opinion was one time held by the cultured Romans concerning the aborigines of Great Britain.

Massingham interrupted the flow of correspondence from British readers to recall two of the most famous incidents involving white men living with Australian Aboriginals, stories familiar to De Rougemont from his museum studies. Musing on whether a man could really lose the facility of speaking his native tongue, Massingham observed that William Buckley had suffered that exact experience when confronted by white men for the first time in three decades. Perhaps De Rouge-mont's own native tongue had simply evaporated in the desert. The *Chronicle* editor published a further account that appeared to lend weight to De Rougemont's claim that Giles's party might not have been able to distinguish him from the Aboriginals. Twenty years after joining with the Wautharong people, Buckley had sighted a ship close to shore and later gave this account:

... a boat put off from the side, and steered away two or three miles farther up the beach towards a small island, where they landed. Seeing this to be a chance opening up for me, I followed as fast as I could run. Before I could reach the spot, they had shoved off, only laughing at my unintelligible cries, little thinking who I was, or that I was any other than I appeared to be in my native dress. Forgetting all this, I reproached them to myself very bitterly, thinking them worse than savages thus to leave me in my misery. Instead of their having been guilty of inhumanity, I should have remembered the possibility, and probability, of them firing on me.

According to some *Chronicle* correspondents, De Rougemont's salvation should have been the Overland Telegraph wire. Tracing the route of John McDouall Stuart's pioneering continental crossing from Adelaide to Port Darwin, the telegraph had saved more than one stray adventurer from peril in its twenty-five year existence. Only a year earlier, in 1897, a French cyclist, Jerome Murif, had completed the first south–north crossing of Australia on two wheels by closely tracking the line. When Murif damaged a wheel, he promptly summoned assistance by cutting the wire and waiting for the repairman to arrive.

Why De Rougemont had not stumbled upon the wire in his travels perplexed one writer. After all, if he had reached the telegraph line he had only to follow it a comparatively short distance in order to arrive at a line-repairer's station. The telegraph, connecting the rest of Australia to the submarine cable which ran from Darwin to Java, and from there on to Europe and England, was remarkable in its effect, permitting communication with London in a matter of hours, rather than the previous minimum of forty-five days by sea. De Rougemont may never have sighted it, but over the past week that crucial cross-continental strand had sped some brow-raising stories about him from London to the Australian press.

Now, reports of Australians' growing incredulity were beginning to speed back across the searing desert and illimitable seas to London.

15
Tales of the Century

> Miss Josephine Kipling, the eldest child of Rudyard Kipling,
> was whipped for telling a fib and went to bed sobbing
> rebelliously: 'My pa writes great big whoppers, and everybody
> thinks they're lovely, while I told just a tiny little story, and
> gets whipped and sent to bed!'
>
> *The Daily Telegraph*, Sydney, 2 November 1898

As DE ROUGEMONT DINED out on his meteoric celebrity in London, Australians were slowly becoming aware of the sensation across the seas. The first reports appeared in *The Home News*, a publication purporting to offer 'a summary of European intelligence' for readers in the British colonies. The newspaper's man in Bristol described De Rougemont as the lion of the British Association meeting, characterising his tale as 'the most remarkable story ever told of personal experience'. De Rougemont, he said, had successfully withstood the ordeal of cross-examination. 'If he were an impostor,' he wrote, 'then it could only be said that he has an imagination which out-Haggards Haggard.'

> In dramatic interest there can be no doubt that his narrative wholly
> eclipses that of Selkirk . . . how comes it, we are asked, that the
> Australian press, which is very much alive to its business, failed to
> discover him and run him for all he was worth?

Sydney's *Daily Telegraph* had initially reported De Rougemont's British Association appearance without resort to its trademark cynicism, but as details of the second lecture trickled back the tide began to turn. Below the heading 'Robinson Crusoe the Second' and alongside an ink sketch of the *Wide World*'s studio photograph, the *Telegraph*'s London correspondent relayed the surge of popular interest.

Whether viewed as a tale-of-the-century Robinson Crusoe, or simply as an extra special, gilt-edged copper-bottomed liar of unique capabilities, M. de Rougemont, it must be confessed, is a phenomenon. How Australian editors, not to mention Mr. Henneker Heaton, who saw him first, came to overlook such treasure trove in the way of 'copy', I can't imagine. Perhaps Mr. Heaton may have been struck, as I was when beginning the story, with the similarity to those of 'Robinson Crusoe'. A reader of that romance, and of Herman Melville's 'Typee' and 'Omoo' might possibly have, with some personal experiences, vamped those opening chapters up. If so, the work has been capitally done, for the wealth of detail is remarkable.

Sydney's *Evening News* was indignant, branding De Rougemont's tales 'a series of astounding adventures that will undoubtedly open the eyes of Australian readers with regard to places in Australia of which Australians humbly thought they had a fair knowledge'. They were likely, forecast the editor, to amuse Australians but 'not in the way the editor of the *Wide World* magazine seems to anticipate'. *The Sydney Mail* reported the story would only reconfirm what Australians already knew, 'that the British public is one of the most gullible in the world'. The ease with which worthless Western Australian mining shares had been dumped on the British market was evidence enough.[17] The *Mail* commented, 'Men who profess to have personal experience will tell you that it was easier to float an out and out West Australian wild cat in London than a genuine mine in any other colony.'

In the south, Melbourne's *Argus* suggested that by exporting his adventures to England, De Rougemont had escaped the more rigorous scrutiny he might have experienced in Australia:

Many eminent travellers have had to endure ridicule, scorn, and contempt before they won confidence for their narratives. This has been their hard lot from Marco Polo down to Abyssinian Bruce. Much more fortunate is Louis De Rougemont, who has found a warm welcome in England ... the whole episode is, indeed, a triumphant reply to those who declare that this is an age of unbelief.

The paper also hinted at a commercial motive, alleging:

... no company promoter could have drawn up a prospectus with more flowing pen than could De Rougemont ... in the meantime we may expect to be charged in London with a cynical incredulity, and there may be an imputation that there is a jealous envy here because the thrilling narrative has slipped through the hands of the Australian press.

Meanwhile the South Australian chapter of the Royal Geographical Society had received a letter from William Fitzgerald. The *Wide World* editor was undertaking his own exploratory mission, seeking photographs of Giles and his expedition party of 1873.
'We have startling information,' wrote Fitzgerald:

... about Gibson, who was found dying and demented by a Frenchman, having been a castaway among blacks for two years. Half an hour before death, Gibson became sane, and gave his saviour full details.

Fitzgerald informed the Society he wished to use the photographs to accompany a future instalment of De Rougemont's story in *Wide World*. The Royal Geographical Society's London headquarters was also much interested in seeing those photographs.

Upon learning of Fitzgerald's request, *The Argus* recalled other attempts to solve the mystery of Gibson's death. The Elder expedition of 1891 had been asked to search for traces of Giles's missing companion in the Victoria Desert but found none. The following year, Giles's second-in-command, William Tietkens, has been called to the Liverpool Benevolent Asylum in New South Wales to interview an inmate who claimed to be the lost explorer, but the man did not resemble in any way Tietken's colleague.

The Royal Geographical Society treasurer wrote to Tietkens asking if he could supply the requested photograph. Tietkens replied that no such thing existed. He added that those who knew the habits of the Australian Aboriginals considered it possible that Gibson, who had been lost while attempting to return to camp on horseback, might have been received into some tribe. Tietkens himself considered this unlikely, arguing 'their boundaries are clearly defined and trespassing is a crime'. In any case, he could not see how Gibson could possibly have made the 1000-mile journey from the Great Victoria Desert to anywhere near the north coast.

Public interest was growing. The August number of *Wide World* had now completed its leisurely journey to Australia by sea and transcripts of the British Association lectures were appearing in the colonial newspapers.

A former West Australian resident, Charles Fenwick, had read of the marooned De Rougemont's attempts to contact civilisation by attaching messages to the necks of pelicans. He reported a similar tin disc attached to a bird's neck had been discovered by a boy at the mouth of the Swan River in Fremantle. The bird was an albatross rather than a pelican, but the message it carried was written in French and its writer purported to be shipwrecked. The only problem was that the disc had been found only ten years previously and the bearings the castaway provided were for the Crozet Islands in the southern Indian Ocean, over 4000 miles from the West Australian coast. The event had been well reported and officially communicated to the Home Office; the tin disc was later taken to Perth Museum. In all probability, said Fenwick, it would 'now be looked at with renewed interest as it may be the means of testing the accuracy of the strange story, or, of confirming a still more remarkable coincidence'.

Meanwhile in London, Henry Massingham was tenaciously pursuing the scant leads De Rougemont had provided about his background. The Frenchman had given his birth date as 9 November 1844, but exhaustive investigations of birth records held at the Madeleine, the Palace of Justice and the archives of the Seine in Paris revealed no child born under the name Louis De Rougemont between 1840 and 1849. A child of that name had been born in Paris in 1859, but the parents' names differed from those given by De Rougemont. Furthermore the *Chronicle*'s reference library had revealed that De Rougemont's father's shop could not have been located in the Boulevard Haussmann, as he had stated. Napoleon III's city planner Baron Haussmann, for whom the street was named, had not commenced his major work in modernising Paris until 1853, nine years after De Rougemont's birth and only a year prior to his departure to Switzerland. For the majority of the time young De Rougemont had lived in Paris, the Boulevard Haussmann had simply not existed. Massingham also remained puzzled by the Frenchman's facility for

English over his own native language. De Rougemont's ancestry appeared more baffling than ever.

Massingham's enquiries had turned up no evidence to support the account of the rescue of the two shipwrecked English girls. Searches of Lloyd's Register of Shipping showed a vessel named the *Northumberland* had been lost in Australian waters in 1868, but on the south-west coast of Australia near Albany. All crew had been saved. It was too much of a stretch to imagine this as the same vessel that had carried Gladys and Blanche Rogers. A reporter sent to Sunderland to ascertain the origins of the girls, the doomed ship and its captain spent two days interviewing numerous locals and examining port shipping records without result. Concluded the editor:

> . . . the story is unconfirmed, and no ship named the *Northumberland* or the *Sunderland,* and no Captain or owner named Rogers have thus far been identified with M. de Rougemont's story.

Overall, he said, 'our opinion is that the verdict of men who base their conclusions on reason cannot, on the evidence that has been given, declare itself in M. de Rougemont's favour'.

Louis Becke, stung by De Rougemont's handling of the interview at the *Chronicle* offices, ventured once more into print. In De Rougemont's favour, said Becke, he had appeared to be a man who 'courted investigation and was eager to reply to sensible questions'. It was only the answers Becke had found wanting, particularly those relating to the Frenchman's solo sailing efforts aboard the *Veielland*. At the time of the shipwreck, Becke reminded readers, De Rougemont had been a raw youth fresh from Switzerland with only a few months' experience at sea. How was it that he had single-handedly been able to survive treacherous seas in a broken vessel designed for an experienced crew? Even Bruno came under the affronted adventure writer's fire. Becke 'doubted exceedingly' that any dog, even an Australian one, could have had strength enough to tow De Rougemont ashore to his islet through open ocean by means of his tail.

To a public whose knowledge of the intricacies of sailing was limited and whose love of a shaggy dog story was well evidenced, Becke's grievances seemed petty. Becke knew there were many who felt De Rougemont was suffering undue criticism, particularly at the hands of jealous authors whose own books had not sold a tenth of the *Wide World*'s current print run. Lest anyone think he was conducting a vendetta against De Rougemont or was commercially motivated to impugn his publisher Newnes, Becke added that he had visited Fitzgerald at Southampton Street to further explain his position.

> I desired him to assure M. de Rougemont that, beyond [my first] article in *The Daily Chronicle*, [. . .] I had not written, nor suggested to anyone else to write, any article, paragraph, or comment upon M. de Rougemont's narrative. I have heard, casually, that I am believed to be the person to have either written or inspired to be written, many attacks upon M. de Rougemont in various newspapers.

Becke told readers his motive was not to prove M. De Rougemont a liar. 'I wanted him to convince me of the veracity of that portion of the narrative upon which I felt I could criticise his statements.' Nonetheless, concluded Becke, 'speaking impartially and for myself only . . . I am not convinced'.

Becke's uncertain stance prompted De Rougemont to go on the attack. In a letter to the *Chronicle* editor he re-floated the turtle story, taunting Becke over his claims to be an expert who had handled 'thousands of turtles'.

> It is perhaps only just to Mr. Becke to say that when he wrote the article he was under the impression that he really had handled thousands of turtles afloat and ashore. But when he met me and was invited for a ride he suddenly remembered that he had never been on one afloat. Possible but hardly probable. If so I am ready to accept his apology.
>
> It is only fair to assume that Mr. Becke's knowledge of seamanship is equal to his knowledge of turtles, a subject upon which he writes, and your readers will therefore understand why I do not try to follow him through columns of his laboured details, but leave his report to the judgement of the public. I am sorry to have to humiliate him, but he has gone out of his way to look for it, and as an author and expert he should have reckoned it up when he started out on the apparently safe pastime of anonymously 'hammering' a strange brother who did him no harm.

The public feud had become embarrassing. Becke, fast losing face, refused to reply. Now a tale started up in Pall Mall alleging that on the day Becke had visited Fitzgerald at Southampton Street, the editor had made him a proposition. Seeing an opportunity to convert an enemy into an ally, Fitzgerald had invited Becke to submit his own stories of true adventure for publication in *Wide World*. Appealing to Becke's readily inflated ego, Fitzgerald commissioned three stories, which he told the author were to be 'absolutely veracious'. Becke agreed and later submitted his material, but Fitzgerald was dissatisfied and told the author his stories were not up to form. 'Can't you remember some livelier incidents?' enquired Fitzgerald. Becke replied that, as the editor had insisted on the truth, he could not. 'Quite so,' said Fitzgerald, 'still I think you might — if I may use the word — *titivate* these narratives a trifle.' Becke refused, preferring to withdraw his stories altogether.

Becke confirmed the rumour's truth, but defended himself. 'It wouldn't have mattered if the stories had been invented. I would have titivated them then to his heart's content. But to embroider on genuine facts, well known to half Australia, and all the islands, would have given me away as the basest of Ananiases. I had to think of my reputation.' (Ananias was a disciple of Jesus who, having defrauded the church in Jerusalem, was rebuked by the Apostle Peter and fell dead.)

If Becke, the man who had been described as the 'last pirate', had been persuaded to launch his assault on De Rougemont by the lure of gold, he was to be disappointed. Later, he complained in a letter to a friend that while *Wide World* had accused him of being retained by Massingham to expose De Rougemont, the *Chronicle* had only paid him his usual word rate. Becke's 'bronzed integrity' had somewhat paled. He made no further public comment; however, his last sally was to send a private letter to De Rougemont asking if, in fulfilment of his promise, he would show his arm. There was no reply.

Events were now beyond even Newnes's artful choreography. The affair had already upstaged his planned British Antarctic Expedition. For several weeks now, the icebreaker *Southern Cross* had been under preparation at St Katherine's Dock near London Bridge and its explorers' equipment on display at Pall Mall. Few had bothered to inspect either. Becke, now writing for Sydney's *Daily Telegraph*, gleefully reported on the indifference displayed toward the departure of Newnes's expedition, his spite spilling out on to the page.

Not one tithe of the interest displayed in the Jackson–Harmsworth Expedition or Nansen's trip to the North Pole has ever been evinced in the Newnes–Borchgrevink venture. To bring the *Southern Cross* within the reach of every Londoner and country tripper in the height of the dull season seemed an admirable idea and one expected the vessel to be visited by tens of thousands. But, as a matter of fact, I question whether a couple of thousand people all told took the trouble to look over the ship, and the 'crowd' which gathered at St Katherine's on Monday to bid the exploring party Good-Rid, I mean Goodbye, numbered hundreds only.

De Rougemont's diversions had consumed vast tracts of column space that might instead have promoted the century's last great exploratory quest.

The *Chronicle*'s attacks continued, but De Rougemont's supporters still defended their man. *The Speaker*, a journal more often given to political commentary and foreign affairs, denounced the *Chronicle*'s righteous campaign:

> Every great traveller, from the days of Marco Polo and Sir John Mandeville, has been suspected of romance. This sceptical attitude is natural to people who stay at home, and who do not reflect that a description of a day in Cheapside would seem just as incredible to a denizen of Terra del Fuego as some aboriginal practices to the cautious reader of the morning paper . . .

The Speaker upheld the right of the adventurer to tell his tale in whichever manner proved most entertaining, saying 'no traveller of recent times has excited so much interest'. It argued that while cynics might scoff at De Rougemont's story, future generations would 'sigh for the improbability which is still the spice of adventure in strange oceans and unfrequented continents'.

> When the world empires are all parcelled out, the wildest parts of the globe will gradually be brought under the levelling, petrifying influence of 'order'. Order is the ideal of administrators and the direct enemy of romance. When order literally reigns in the heart of Africa the writer of adventure stories will be driven to bookkeeping.

Worse still, no book of travel will find a market, for all the traveller's tales will have been told . . . It is this saddening prospect no doubt which disposes some people to be indulgent to the traveller who tells the unlikeliest yarn. Why should he be lured into newspaper offices and cross-examined by inquisitorial editors? Why strive to spoil the pleasure of the man who rides on nothing wilder than an omnibus, and would like to believe that some nautical expert has saddled the sea serpent?

It seemed the autobiographical author of true adventure was permitted, if not obliged, to employ a measure of flair, a certain elan. Even those who professed an authentic purpose were granted unspoken licence to 'spice' their journals with a touch of romance here and there. The general readership had an expectation, long encouraged by fiction writers like Haggard and Verne, that their hero would come dashing through the wilds unbridled, not trudging desperately through endless miles of sand dunes and spinifex. What was the purpose of frontier travel if not to unlock the many mysteries that lay beyond and emerge with stories of outlandish wonder? And if danger, or even death, be the price, then all the better.

Henry Savage Landor was one author-adventurer who made the most of the latitude afforded him by an eager public. He was, of course, the same man who had withdrawn from the British Association Congress in protest at De Rougemont's inclusion. Landor's journal, *In the Forbidden Land*, was published shortly after the congress had ended. In it, he took liberties that De Rougemont might have paled at. He had ascended the Himalayas without climbing boots, reaching further into Tibet than any European before him. He had been taken captive by aggrieved locals and survived bouts of torture by whip, rack, red-hot poker and iron-spiked saddle. His final reprieve from death by beheading only came by virtue of some unexplained mystic power he had wielded over a sword-swinging lama. These ordeals were simply de rigueur for the swashbuckler at large. *The Home News* described his book as an 'exhaustive, thrilling and valuable account'. There was little outcry from learned quarters. Nor did the *Chronicle* launch an investigation into his bona fides.

Landor came from aristocratic literary stock. His grandfather Walter had been one of the most respected poets of the century past, standing alongside Byron and Shelley. Fabrication ran in the family. Walter Savage Landor's most famous works were his numerous volumes entitled *Imaginary Conversations*, comprising invented discussions between real historical figures. Those reviewers who suspected his grandson to be laying it on a bit thick in Tibet still celebrated his gall. Said one:

> Even the ever-present suspicion that the author puts in highlights with a somewhat lavish hand, and his almost naïve delight in his own pose as the central figure in the panorama, cannot detract from the charm of a book without a dull page, and crowded with illustration.[18]

One critic who dared to doubt Landor's *Boy's Own* mountaineering exploits was Douglas Freshfield, an experienced climber who had previously conquered the highest mountain in the Caucasus and would soon become the first Englishman to explore India's sacred Kangchenjunga, the world's third-highest peak. Freshfield questioned Landor's extraordinary climbing speed in the absence of safety equipment and also his assertion of the existence of several mountains not marked on any map. He met with savage treatment in *The Times*. Landor responded to his criticisms with a personal attack, labelling Freshfield's statements 'inaccurate beyond belief'. Where their accounts of Tibet differed, this was attributed to his critic's own ignorance of climbing in the region.

If Landor's pedigree and charm earned his book the benefit of the doubt, many 'real' explorers' journals were no more reliable. In 1863, the ill-fated John Speke, former friend and now bitter rival of Sir Richard Burton, returned to England having located the head of the Nile at Lake Victoria. His journeys had been made under the patronage of the Royal Geographical Society but his own publisher had labelled his journal 'unpublishable'. Having won the rights to Speke's work on promise of a £2000 advance, John Blackwood had been dismayed to find the first chapters of his diary 'written in such an abominable, childish, unintelligible way that it is impossible to say what anybody could make of them'.[19] What was more, Speke's accounts of life with African people were more candid than was to be expected of a respectable explorer. Still, Blackwood remained convinced that out of Speke's raw material, 'a most quaint, interesting Robinson Crusoe like narrative may be made'.[20] A pro-Empire ghostwriter, respected Scottish historian John Hill Burton, who had never set foot on the African continent, was duly hired and given the charter of 'unravelling Speke'.[21] Like De Rougemont, the explorer was interviewed on every aspect of his adventures and the results written up in his name. Speke was persuaded to reside with the ghostwriter and within a mere two months they had cranked out 200,000 words appropriately dressed for public view. The result was the *Journal of the Discovery of the Source of Nile*, a seamless blend of fact and fiction strongly advocating the establishment of British Imperial government in 'darkest Africa'. Speke's sympathetic view of the people he had met was reworked to portray the African male as a godless man who 'works his wife, sells his children, enslaves all he can lay hands upon, and, unless fighting for the property of others, contents himself with drinking, singing, and dancing like a baboon to drive dull care away.'[22] Blackwood told *The Times*:

> We have done nothing to his text except by questioning him, and correcting him where he was likely to prove unintelligible. So the book is entirely in his own quaint language, and a more genuine one was never published.

None attacked Speke's ghosted book for its embellishments. One critic said reading it was 'like travelling with an excessively good-humoured, genial, and amusing companion'.

It appeared one of Louis De Rougemont's failings might have been his readiness to defend the truth of even the smallest detail of his account. By simply claiming the licence due the gentleman explorer, he might have evaded any real damage to his reputation. De Rougemont and his editor Fitzgerald seemed too ready to take on every challenger. It was strategically impossible to win a war fought on so many fronts, and the battle Fitzgerald promised would be 'a short one' had now become a protracted campaign.

Landor and Speke, unlike De Rougemont, knew better than to offer themselves up for inspection at the British Association Congress. And as good-humoured, amusing and genial a travel companion as De Rougemont was, he could not claim Speke's record of achievement nor Landor's lineage. Without blue British blood in his veins the critics were unlikely to afford him the same indulgence.

16

Last of the Explorers

It behoves a man who wants to see wonders to sometimes go
out of his way.
                    Sir John Mandeville, *Mandeville's Travels*, 1371

IN JANUARY 1898, just three months before De Rougemont would
materialise on London Dock, another man had sailed up the Thames
fresh from his colonial exploits. Twenty-seven-year-old Scot David
Carnegie, bairn of the ninth Earl of Southesk, returned home seeking
reward for five years' labour in the remote interior of Western Australia.

Having squandered his schooling and professional prospects, the
Earl's profligate son had been banished from Kinnaird Castle at
twenty-two to grow tea in Ceylon, but the young man saw no future in
the leaves. Only weeks after he had arrived in Ceylon, he deserted the
plantation and set off for Australia with his chum Lord Percy, son of
the Marquess of Queensberry. Carnegie and Percy landed in Albany,
milked funds from a passing Scottish acquaintance in Perth and rode
out east on shiny new steeds to seek their fortune on the booming
goldfields of Coolgardie. They found their path crowded with herds of
ex-prospectors travelling in the reverse direction, running the few
wells dry. Having failed to find gold, the miners now fought for mere
water. By the time Carnegie sighted the first dirt heaps of Coolgardie,
the boom was near bust, their horses near dead from thirst and the
sun had stained their fair skin red. After three weeks, Percy retreated
west to wire home for more finances. Carnegie remained, and finally
managed to turn profit from a gold syndicate at Lake Darlot, but
eking out an anonymous existence under a relentless sun was not the
destiny of a son of Southesk. He soon tired of life on the sand and
turned his attentions to more thrilling ventures.

A new syndicate was got up to seek out pastoral plains and
gemfields to the north. For two years, Carnegie vainly searched for

gold and green on the desert horizon, each time venturing a little further into the unknown. From his labours were born grander aspirations. Might the vast stretch of continent beyond conceal riches? At Lake Darlot, his makeshift bookshelf filled with the deeds of the colonial explorers. In the great nameless voids of their continental maps Carnegie saw history awaiting his imprint. No white explorer had yet attempted the south–north crossing of the Western Australian interior. The vision entered his head and refused to leave. A trek from Coolgardie to Halls Creek in the Kimberley would bisect the routes taken by both Ernest Giles and the colony's governor, Sir John Forrest. This was territory neither had seen profit in. According to both Giles and Forrest, it was not a question of what was there, but what was not. Carnegie thought differently.

Using funds obtained from the sale of his Lake Darlot lease, Carnegie began to fit out the expedition. In July 1896, accompanied by nine camels, three men, an Aboriginal lad and a fox terrier, the virgin explorer set out north. The camels were laden with supplies but still the journey became torturous, a continual battle with thirst. Carnegie's band was diminished when itinerant miner Charles Stansmore accidentally shot and killed himself while hunting kangaroo. Weeks elapsed in which they located no water and local Aboriginals recruited at gunpoint declined to reveal their hidden sources. Yet somehow the remaining party survived both to reach Halls Creek in the Kimberley and to return to Coolgardie thirteen months later, having surveyed more than 3000 miles of spinifex and sand. Carnegie bitterly reported the far interior of the colony to be worthless. The hope of riches had been a mirage. Carnegie's great discovery had been an endless plain of inarable, nugget-less nothingness.

Back in Perth, Carnegie drew up his precious expeditionary map and went to Governor Forrest to claim his due. Forrest himself had been the beneficiary of land and cash when he returned from exploring the desert in 1874. A year later, Giles had ridden into town to hallelujahs and garlands. The brass band at Perth Town Hall struck up 'See! The Conquering Hero Comes'. Balls and banquets were thrown in his honour. The West Australian government had offered to pay Giles's expenses and the colony was drunk dry of champagne.

Carnegie received naught. To the Scot's chagrin, his efforts won scant attention in Australia. The age of exploration was over. Seven years before Carnegie's folly, Giles had dubbed himself the 'last of the Australian explorers'. On the eastern seaboard, few knew or cared about some Scottish heir's ramblings in the bald backblocks of the west. Furthermore, Carnegie came under attack for his treatment of the Aboriginals he had tried to coerce.

He sought solace for his injured pride in the company of his Perth landlord's daughters and a comely local barmaid. A visit to a fortune teller promised great things to come, if only he would guard against his worst enemy, alcohol. Carnegie reported that the woman told him, 'You have been surrounded by temptations to drink and at one time, being cursed with a love for it, you nearly went under to it and wrecked your life.' She also averred that he was in discussions with the government over payments he did not expect to receive. Nonetheless, Carnegie continued to cultivate his contacts, made an ally of the Surveyor-General and even played tennis with the Governor's wife, but by the time of his departure aboard the SS *China* on 3 November 1897, his solicitations had yielded nothing. From a second-class cabin Carnegie wrote to his sister 'If I could buy myself at others' valuation and sell myself at my own I should make a fair profit.'[23] But there were no willing purchasers.

Carnegie's passage home was tedious and uneventful, but his reception was warmer than in Perth. In London, his name bought greater respect than in the colonies and his feats attracted the recognition of the Royal Geographical Society. In February 1898, he was invited to speak and delivered an expedition paper as long, dry and featureless as the desert he had travelled. So uninspired was his audience that the only question asked at the paper's conclusion was whether the sand was soft or hard. At a public lecture in Edinburgh, applause was reserved for tales of Carnegie's canine companion, Val the fox terrier. The lecture circuit would clearly pay no dividends.

Backed by the Royal Geographical Society, Carnegie sought a position on an upcoming expedition from Cape Town to Cairo, but he refused to consider any role but leader. He planned his own journey to the Nile and pressed the Society to throw its weight behind it. He fantasised over a quest to the South Pole. It all came to nothing. With no other immediate prospects, he sought publication for his Australian expedition journal. There was little support. From Kinnaird Castle came word his father thought he was motivated by vanity alone, had nothing to tell and no prospect of a publisher. Nevertheless, Carnegie eventually managed to wheedle a deal with C. A. Pearson in London and proceeded to prepare his manuscript.

In early August, at tea with Scott Keltie in Savile Row, Carnegie learnt of the publication of De Rougemont's story in *The Wide World Magazine*. As Scott Keltie spelt out the extraordinary tale, Carnegie became enraged. After all the indignities he had suffered, it seemed his account of his years of hardship would be eclipsed by De Rougemont's extravagantly sensational opus. What were Scott Keltie and Mill thinking giving the Society's imprimatur to a sixpenny magazine editor and his puppet? He later told *Chronicle* readers:

> When . . . I heard from Dr. Scott Keltie of M. de Rougemont's story I was much interested as he claimed to have spent a number of years in the region mapped out by me.
>
> After listening to the tale I expressed my disbelief to Dr. Keltie in it, adding that I should like to meet M. de Rougemont. Through the instrumentality of my friend Mr. George S. Streeter (the owner of a pearling fleet at Broome, N.W. Australia, and of a cable-station in the neighbourhood) and through the courtesy of Mr. Fitzgerald and M. de Rougemont, a meeting was arranged and took place in Mr. Streeter's house at York Street on the 3rd of August (or within a day or so of that date).

George Streeter was a member of a well-known London family who had made their money in jewels. He had returned to England from Broome after his efforts to establish Australia's first cultured pearl industry at Roebuck Bay had failed. (Broome itself had been settled by Streeter's father, who had developed the town as a pearl lugger's port. Streeter had later assumed ownership of the new telegraph cable station established in 1889 to link north-western Australia direct with England, via Singapore, India and Egypt.) Streeter's accumulated knowledge of Australia's Kimberley regions rivalled even the young Scot's.

Carnegie's meeting with De Rougemont had taken place over a month prior to the British Association lectures. When his guests first arrived at Streeter's home, Carnegie noted that De Rougemont was limping and clinging to Fitzgerald's shoulder for support. The editor explained that De Rougemont had been involved in an omnibus accident, was greatly shaken and therefore unwilling to be closely questioned. They sat down together in a spacious drawing room, in which were displayed an extensive collection of Aboriginal curios, implements and weapons procured in Australia by Streeter and his family.

While the hobbled Frenchman nodded approval, Fitzgerald outlined the key events of De Rougemont's narrative. When he had finished, De Rougemont consented to answer a few questions. Carnegie spread out his beloved map on the table before them and asked De Rougemont to identify the location of his adopted home in Australia.

De Rougemont pointed to an area of the Kimberley, north-western Australia, in the hilly region between the ocean on the north and west and the Fitzroy, Margaret and Ord Rivers to the south and east.

Carnegie then invited De Rougemont to indicate the exact route of his desert wanderings on the map. He was unable to do so, telling Carnegie he was 'not a man of science' and found it impossible to know in which direction he travelled. Accepting that this would be difficult without a compass, Carnegie pressed De Rougemont to describe the desert country he had traversed. The Frenchman described the landscape accurately – undulating sands studded with pincushions of prickly grass, the despised spinifex – yet Carnegie remained unconvinced. De Rougemont was only as well acquainted with the general characteristics of the land as 'anyone might be who studied the maps of the explorers of the region'. His descriptions might aptly explain any part of the interior between Coolgardie and the Kimberley. It was the question of water, though, that most vexed Carnegie.

What was the source of De Rougemont's unfailing supply? The Scot had detoured mile upon mile off course only to find waterholes dried up and brimming with the detritus of drought – the stripped bones and carcasses of dead lizards and birds – but rarely water. It was the common experience of every Australian desert explorer from Eyre forward. The bone-dry interior had extracted the life from such resilient men as Leichhardt, Burke and Wills in mere months.

De Rougemont explained his tribe's method of scraping away sand to uncover reservoirs of precious water lying only a few feet below the surface. Carnegie's calm evaporated. It was impossible. He and his company had never once found water by simply 'scraping sand'. The mere proposition tested credulity. Over a period of some nine months spent negotiating one single stretch of desert they had encountered thirty native wells, all sunk to a depth of fifteen to twenty feet, and all near dry. Hours, sometimes days and nights on end, had to be spent in digging them out. There was rarely found any substantial source of water, even when they press-ganged the aid of Aboriginals as guides and kept them on short rations to spur their desire.

Carnegie then revealed his motive for staging the interview at Streeter's home. He took two wooden artefacts from the surrounding collection and placed them on the table. They were, he told De Rougemont and Fitzgerald, items used by Kimberley Aboriginals. He challenged De Rougemont to tell him what they were.

De Rougemont correctly identified the first as a boomerang, but Carnegie knew it to be a boomerang of peculiar shape, used for killing fish in shallow water. He would later sneer, 'This he knew nothing about, beyond the fact that it was a *boomerang*.'

The second was a flat square piece of wood with a wooden spike at either end. De Rougemont inspected it carefully and pronounced it to be a 'cooking utensil'. Before his visitors' arrival, Streeter had assured Carnegie the item was used by the Aboriginals around his station for manufacturing string from hair. Puzzled as to how it could possibly be used for culinary purposes, Carnegie interrogated De Rougemont further.

'Was it used for roasting meat, perhaps?'

'Yes, for roasting,' agreed De Rougemont immediately.

'Does not the fire burn the wood?'

'Ah! We use it for other purposes too,' replied De Rougemont.

Satisfied of De Rougemont's ignorance, Carnegie then exhibited a number of spearheads. They were, said Carnegie, of a particular type chipped out of quartz, and since the advent of the white man, out of glass. But De Rougemont was also unfamiliar with their origin or use.

Carnegie returned to the map, inviting De Rougemont to indicate the location where he had encountered Gibson in the desert. De Rougemont traced a line with his finger and stopped at the point where Giles had turned back after losing Gibson's tracks. De Rougemont said he had been so desperately anxious to see again his fellow man that he had 'nearly taken leave of his senses from excess of joy' when he happened upon the dying Gibson. Surely then, argued Carnegie, it would have been natural to track Gibson back to his starting point — an easy matter for any of his natives — and make himself known to Gibson's companions.

De Rougemont shook his head.

'Alas! No! Before, when we had approached their camp, Giles and his men came out on horseback and, mistaking me in my condition for a native, levelled their guns at us and fired, several times. We had no choice but to retreat.'

Carnegie snorted derisively.

'Could you not have returned with Gibson?'

'No, it was many days later before we found that unfortunate soul, and his tracks did not lead us to the remainder of the party. He was too insensible to help us find them.'

Carnegie took his map from the table and stood.

'Monsieur, I'm afraid I simply cannot believe you. It is impossible.'

De Rougemont laughed.

'As you know, Monsieur, the desert is large and things happen there of which most are not aware.'

As the conversation at York Street threatened to degenerate into conflict, Fitzgerald brought the meeting to a close, pleading De Rougemont's ill health.

Shortly after the men had parted company a message arrived at Streeter's house by courier:

M. De Rougemont is very anxious to know if Mr. Carnegie ever used his rifle or revolver on his travels in Australia?

17

The Hunter and the Hatter

They sought it with thimbles, they sought it with care;
They pursued it with forks and hope;
They threatened its life with a railway-share;
They charmed it with smiles and soap.

Lewis Carroll,
The Hunting of the Snark: an agony in eight fits, 1876

FOLLOWING THE ENCOUNTER with De Rougemont, Carnegie retired to the family seat by the river Southesk at Brechin in Scotland. He read manuscript proofs and corrected maps in anticipation of the autumn publication of *Spinifex and Sand.* Unable to convince the Royal Geographical Society to back an expedition under his leadership and devoid of funds to mount his own, there was little to do but bide his time until royalties began to flow from his book.

Determined that his colonial experiences should not be seen in the same light as those claimed by the ludicrous De Rougemont, Carnegie opened *Spinifex and Sand* with a dry, but pointed, preface:

> The following pages profess to be no more than a faithful narrative of five years spent on the goldfields and in the far interior of Western Australia. Anyone looking for stirring adventures, hairbreadth escapes from wild animals and men will be disappointed. In the Australian bush, the traveller has only Nature to war against, over him hangs always the chance of death from thirst, and sometimes from the attacks of hostile aboriginals; he has no spice of adventure, no record heads of rare game, no exciting escapades with wild beasts, to spur him on.

Carnegie's Australia was, unlike De Rougemont's, a harsh, unrewarding place populated by an even harsher people. His Aboriginals were impediments at best, murderers at worst. They were, according to the prospector turned explorer, only fit to be treated as animals. Of the settlers' habit of kidnapping and keeping Aboriginal boys for work, Carnegie had written, 'the most useful, contented and best-behaved boys I have seen are those that receive treatment similar to that a highly valued sporting dog gets from a just master'.

Privately, Carnegie still fumed over the meeting with De Rougemont and the note that had followed enquiring into his use of guns in Australia. It had seemed a thinly veiled threat, a clumsy attempt to ensure his silence: a suggestion that De Rougemont possessed evidence that he had fired upon Aboriginals. His displeasure intensified when Louis De Rougemont addressed the British Association on 9 September. It was an invitation that had not been extended to Carnegie. He watched on as, shortly after, the public frenzy surrounding the self-styled explorer and his unbelievable tales began in earnest. With his book yet unpublished, Carnegie could contain his frustration no longer. On 22 September, a fortnight after De Rougemont had first astonished the crowds at Bristol, the spurned laird went public.

He wrote to the *Chronicle*:

So long as Louis de Rougemont confined the narrative of his adventures to the pages of a magazine for the delectation of the public it is of little moment whether that narrative be true or false. When, however, M. de Rougemont appears before a scientific meeting for the purpose of speaking knowledge, I think it is right for anyone who has reasonable doubts to cast on his statements to do so.

Carnegie shared with readers a full account of his interview with De Rougemont conducted at Streeter's house more than a month earlier. De Rougemont's lectures to the British Association had now provided him with even more ammunition.

Carnegie reported that he had started the interview by inviting De Rougemont to identify the location of his adopted home in Australia, and in response, the Frenchman had pointed out a region of the Kimberley in the north-west. When speaking in Bristol, though, he had indicated that his mountain home lay near the centre of the continent — many hundreds of miles away.

'How does M. de Rougemont explain this?' Carnegie asked.

For the sake of argument, let us assume that the position of the mountain home was in the Kimberley. M. de Rougemont told us that from his camp in the mountains he made periodical trips into the desert – vain attempts to reach civilization, which in spite of his entire ignorance of Australian geography, he knew to exist in the south. Before the name of Coolgardie brought West Australia to the fore, how many people in this country could have stated the position of settled country in that colony? Very few I am sure. I therefore am surprised that a Swiss boy should be aware of the position of the localities inhabited by white men in the little known land of Australia.

Carnegie next took issue with De Rougemont's account of his meeting with Giles's party, and the hostile reception he received.

Now let me tell M. de Rougemont that it is not the custom of any white men, explorers or prospectors, to fire upon unoffending blacks. Several times M. de Rougemont tells us he was fired upon, but in this case, he made a direct accusation, viz, that explorers Giles and his party fired at unoffending natives for no cause whatever. Now Giles poor fellow is dead, and so is Gibson; therefore M. de Rougemont is comparatively safe to make this accusation. However Tietkens, Giles' first officer on that and all other expeditions, still lives, I am glad to say. He will, I know, indignantly deny such a charge, for brave men do not shoot natives without cause . . .

Carnegie finally shared with his readers the cryptic message sent by De Rougemont after their meeting's conclusion, which, he said, implied that he himself had fired upon Aboriginal people.

Now what did that letter mean? Was it meant as a threat? Does M. de Rougemont think that the knowledge of the numberless natives' deaths at my hands will seal my lips? Does he wish to accuse me of having fired at him? Let me assure M. de Rougemont that I never had occasion to use either rifle or revolver or gun against any aboriginal, nor has any man in any of my expeditions taken the life of a native. I repeat it is not the custom of bushmen or prospectors to fire upon natives as if they were rabbits, as

M. de Rougemont would have us believe. Natives are shot in the bush for stealing from camps, attacks on men, or the spearing of horses, cattle or camels. If M. de Rougemont was shot at, what cause did he give his persecutor?

Carnegie appeared the blueblood upbraiding an insolent servant. Still, there was little doubt that, gun or no gun, he had blasted some holes in De Rougemont's tale. And the words 'to be continued' appended to the letter left readers in no doubt his business with the Frenchman was unfinished.

The furore over the Frenchman's bona fides had monopolised London newspaper editorial since early September, yet only now, several weeks on, had Carnegie elected to come forward with his revelations. De Rougemont's supporters had reason to be suspicious. Carnegie's attack seemed strategically timed to elevate his own profile prior to the publication of his book.

The following day, as promised, Carnegie resumed his assault. Referencing his trusty maps, his library of explorers' journals and first-hand knowledge of the Kimberley region, he deduced that the location De Rougemont had provided for his 'mountain home' was far from isolated. The Kimberley gold rush in 1888 had sent thousands of men traipsing across the mountains from Halls Creek, and pastoral lands in the area had earlier been identified by the explorer Forrest. Dray roads had been cut through the foothills and a telegraph line constructed from Derby to Halls Creek and on to Wyndham. Carnegie could find little room between these points for 'remote tribal lands'.

For what reason would a man, after twenty-odd years of exile, a man pining for the sight of another white face, choose a desert march (which he had already attempted in vain) of at least 1100 miles if he went in a beeline, in preference to a well worn cart-road and a telegraph line? Can anyone believe that such a course of action is possible? I do not.

Was it my party that de Rougemont met? No. What were the names of the members of this party? I know most of the West Australian prospectors that have made any lengthy journeys. On his return to civilisation, what steps did he take to give publicity to his story? Did he tell no-one of his adventures? He thinks that in

Australia no-one will believe him, and on that one point M. de Rougemont and I are as one.

Carnegie then took direct aim at Murphy's syndicate. Murphy had received Massingham's letter requesting that De Rougemont be permitted to provide a few words in his tribe's language for analysis and, on Fitzgerald's advice, declined the request. Murphy told the *Chronicle* he had consulted with other unnamed members of the syndicate and regretted that due to legal advice they could not grant the permission sought. They would, however, be able to do so once the lands relating to De Rougemont's gold and mineral discoveries had been legally secured. Grasping the opportunity to spruik the syndicate's worth, Murphy had said it would apply to the government for:

> . . . the usual rewards for the discovery of three separate gold fields, and to take up a large area of the richest mining lands before making known the localities, and we believe that these will surpass anything yet discovered in Australia.

The object of the syndicate, Murphy said, would be entirely defeated if the location was revealed to an Australian audience, which might be done through the cables. The language was the key to the tribe, the tribe the key to the gold deposits. But the cable had already telegraphed Murphy's manoeuvres to Australia, stirring up further speculation as to De Rougemont's motives.

Carnegie was incredulous. De Rougemont, he said, spoke of nuggets of gold so large he had made cooking pots out of them, but the Scot had heard dozens of similar stories from 'half-daft *hatters* in the bush'. A hatter, he explained, was a man who, preferring his own company to that of anyone else, travels and lives alone, although sometimes accompanied by one or more 'gins' or Aboriginal women. Years of this solitary life, said Carnegie, 'softened the brain', and hatters raved at length about their wonderful finds of gold. No-one, however, paid any attention:

> Stories of enormous gold discoveries meet with no credence in Australia, for the simple reason that any man finding a rich patch has only to stick a stout post at each corner of his claim and apply

for the ground. Therefore though in this country [England] it sounds very grand to be in 'negotiations with the Government for concessions', the fact of the matter is that most such transactions never take place for the reason above stated.

Carnegie would not relinquish the spotlight. The following day, 24 September, he resumed his exhaustive study of the location of De Rougemont's supposed mountain home. If it was assumed that this was not situated in the Kimberley but toward the centre of the continent as British Association audiences had been told, what possibilities remained? Certainly not the interior of Western Australia, where Carnegie's own investigations had revealed no suitable ranges. The Alfred and Marie Range was 'merely a long chain of isolated barren sandstone hills, not capable of supporting a dingo'. The Rawlinson and Petermann ranges were no better suited to the task. According to Carnegie, the only mountainous part of the entire Australian interior properly equipped to sustain a tribe was the MacDonnell Ranges. In which case, he said, 'De Rougemont lived as a savage for the best part of thirty years within easy distance of numerous horse and cattle stations.' Upon considering the possibilities, the Scot baldly declared that he did not believe De Rougemont's story.

Mr. Fitzgerald, I feel confident, believed in M. de Rougemont at the time of our interview, and possibly still does so. I would not suggest for a moment that that gentleman was knowingly imposing upon the public, but I do think that before publishing the narrative as true, Mr. Fitzgerald should have taken some steps to verify some part of it.

We are told in Wide World that Dr. Keltie and Dr. Mill have verified De Rougemont's adventure. May we know how they did so? Are we to understand that Dr. Keltie or Dr. Mill will guarantee the growing of corn in turtle shells? For my part I do not believe that those gentlemen had much idea of what adventures were to follow, and merely gave it as their opinion that a man might have run with the blacks, and that this particular man's account of the interior tallied with that of authentic explorers; and surely it would be no hard task to study the maps of a country so thoroughly that one might pass a critical examination. I do not doubt but that Dr. Keltie, for instance, could give as detailed an account of Africa or that he could, if he was so minded, make anyone believe that he had traversed it from end to end.

Carnegie shifted his sights to De Rougemont's knowledge of Aboriginal customs; in particular, his claims of cannibalism.

> The natives of the Nor' West are said to be mild cannibals. I may be wrong in this, but I should say that no authentic case of cannibalism has been proved in the region. In Kimberley the natives are not cannibals. I have questioned numerous prospectors, bushmen, police etc on this point . . . In the interior the natives are not cannibals; this I state on the authority of Joseph Bresden, one of my companions in the desert, who was born and bred in Central Australia. Where, therefore, are M. de Rougemont's loathsome eaters of human flesh to be found?

Carnegie's attacks on De Rougemont stirred writers to rise in his defence. Yet now it was the Frenchman's supporters, perhaps fearful of future embarrassment, who sought the shelter of anonymity. A reader identifying himself only as 'Anglo-Australian' wrote to beg readers not to take the discrediting of De Rougemont seriously. Australia, he said, was a big country:

> If one or two of your correspondents know anything worth telling from personal observation, it will refer to only a very limited area, and in no sense to the portions visited by M. de Rougemont, which remain almost unexplored.

Those who criticised De Rougemont's portrayal of the Aboriginals because they did not accord with their own observations in other parts of the country 'might as well deny that tall and fair people live in Sweden because he had not gone further north than Italy'. 'Anglo-Australian' concluded:

> Just one word on the matter of facts. I trust many an Englishman's cheeks have tingled, as mine have, in reading the treatment this forlorn Australian adventurer has received from the critics. It reminds one that when a dog is to be beaten any stick is good enough for the purpose.

18

Flight of the Wombats

Come and meet me, O my dusky,
When the wombats homeward fly,
And the kangaroo grows husky
As he carols in the sky
                    'The Cannibal Chief to His Love',
                    Punch, October, 1898

KEEN TO CAPITALISE on the extraordinary attention, Newnes rushed the October number of *Wide World*, incorporating the third instalment of 'The Adventures of Louis De Rougemont', into print. It was prefaced by a note from Fitzgerald reassuring readers as to the truth of the tale and apologising that De Rougemont had been unable to respond to 'even a tithe of the correspondence' received at the *Wide World* offices. He was, Fitzgerald said, 'busy working up his scientific material for the learned societies, tracing his relations in Paris and Lausanne, etc.'

The narrative proceeded from where De Rougemont had left off in September. While much of its most startling detail had already been revealed at Bristol, it contained the adventurer's most incredible claim to date. While camped with the Aboriginals near Cambridge Bay, De Rougemont had decided to explore the nearby islands, searching for wombats from whose skins to make sandals. 'I knew that wombats haunted the islands in countless thousands,' said De Rougemont, 'because I had seen them, rising in clouds every evening at dusk.'

Even in London, this remarkable feat of flight would not go unchallenged. On the first day of publication, a reader wrote to the *Chronicle* aghast:

How could his editor allow such an absurd statement to appear? The wombat is a species of marsupial, of the genus Phascolomys.

It is about the size of a badger, being about three feet in length, having moderately long, very coarse fur, mottled with black and white. It is a burrowing animal, a root feeder, and far from active – yet M. de Rougemont has 'seen them rising in clouds'. His adventures are indeed amazing.

What was it De Rougemont had seen? Some family of fruit bats or flying foxes ascending into the air? Or were the clouds a mirage; a tropically induced hallucination? It was astonishing no-one had discovered the error before the magazine went to press. Perhaps Newnes, in his desire to seize the day, had been too keen to hasten publication, precluding proper editing. In other circumstances, the flight of the wombats could have been forgiven as an error any foreign traveller might make, but after Carnegie's attack, it was simply more ammunition for De Rougemont's critics.

Historian J. S. Laurie, whose own book *The Story of Australasia* had been criticised by Mark Twain as 'intemperate', came to De Rougemont's defence. Calling De Rougemont the 'worst heckled man of the present hour', Laurie said he found 'a kind of satisfaction in defending him against too literal an interpretation of his wonderful story, whether real or fictitious'. De Rougemont did not claim to be a skilled naturalist and had probably mixed up some names, for instance 'wombat for bat or flying fox'.

Sensing the growing absurdity of the affair, London's *Evening News* put its carping into verse:

The wombats, rising quickly into view
Soar to the summits of the forest trees
Where, in her nest, the gentle kangaroo
Guardeth the eggs her nimble foes would seize

The Frenchman's foes were mounting. From St James Square to Southesk, De Rougemont hunting was fine sport. While readers debated the mysteries of marsupial aviation and kangaroo tales, Massingham announced that the *Chronicle*'s investigation of the De Rougemont mystery was practically concluded, saying, 'We hope to close the controversy by the end of the week.' Goaded by Carnegie, Scott Keltie and Mill also released a public statement protesting that they had not attempted to verify any of De Rougemont's adventures in the manner they were published in by the *Wide World*.

> He answered all our questions readily, and his replies were in the main accordant with the published statements of reputed Australian travellers. The variations we were able to detect seemed to us no greater than are to be expected when an honest man speaks from memory of events spread over a period exceeding a quarter of a century, and of which he had no made no exact observations, and kept no record. We considered it impossible that M. de Rougemont had obtained his information from books, or in any other way, except from direct experience.

Mill and Scott Keltie complained, however, that the form in which their opinion on the matter had been worded by Fitzgerald was not submitted to them for approval before publication.

> Had we been aware of the sensational manner in which the narrative was to be written, illustrated and advertised, our names would never have appeared, and it is due to the publishers to say that on our pointing this out our names were immediately withdrawn.

Massingham's Paris correspondent had exhausted all avenues in France and then extended his investigations into Switzerland. But enquiries of families bearing the name of De Rougemont in Neuchâtel, Vevey and Lausanne had led nowhere. Perhaps, he suggested, De Rougemont could remember his mother's maiden name? Or the details of his parents' deaths? Neither were forthcoming. Instead, De Rougemont wrote to the *Chronicle* denouncing Massingham's use of 'so-called experts' to undermine him. Ignoring Carnegie's most recent attack, De Rougemont chose critics Forbes and Becke as the focus of his derision. As these were examples of the style of experts he was expected to defend himself against, said De Rougemont, he had decided not to allow further questioning of this type. Under Massingham's heading 'Withdraws from Controversy', De Rougemont wrote:

> I am advised by my friends that the British public would not take any notice of any opinion manufactured by such experts ...

I therefore will have nothing more to do with your experts but leave my case to the open minded judgement of the public, with every confidence that, as a stranger coming amongst them, they will see that I receive fair play.

De Rougemont added a postscript informing readers that he would 'find time to attend to Mr. David Carnegie in a day or two'.

Looking to shore up public support, Newnes and Fitzgerald announced they had arranged through the London Lecture Agency for De Rougemont to deliver an address at St James Hall in Piccadilly on Monday 3 October. Fitzgerald also attempted to arrange lectures beyond London. Anyone interested in booking De Rougemont was informed that his fee would be 'in the realm of Nansen'. When pressed for a figure, the agency stipulated fifty to a hundred guineas. Fitzgerald also submitted a letter to Massingham in his man's defence, telling his rival that the *Chronicle*'s reportage was so biased that he did not consider its opinion of any value. The paper, he said, had constituted itself a high court of justice. The attacks on De Rougemont over the flying wombats demonstrated that the *Chronicle* had 'no sense of proportion as to the importance of evidence in this case. A recent letter writer had been quite within his rights in denying that wombats rise in clouds', he said, but nevertheless:

De Rougemont meant flying squirrels, and the error is of slight importance in the discussion . . . he has not been treated over fairly either, for while the half of his critics complain that his inventions verge on the impossible, the other half maintain that he records little that has not been published by other travellers.

Fitzgerald also took issue with the continuing requests by Louis Becke and the *Chronicle* for De Rougemont to reveal his bared arm. Some, he said, had attributed the Frenchman's reluctance to the fact he was an ex-convict from New Caledonia, claiming the telltale brand would be found upon his arm.

M. de Rougemont however, volunteered in this office to show both his arms, and stripped to the waist before three members of our staff, and there is not a scintilla of a sign of any kind of any such mark as there would be had he come from New Caledonia. For a highly sensitive man such as M. de Rougemont, the submission to this indignity caused him considerable pain but he voluntarily went through it.

Judging from the many columns you have given to Mr. David Carnegie, you regard him as M. de Rougemont's most formidable assailant ... you are further aware that M. de Rougemont commences appearing before the public on Monday next, where he will further unfold his life's history, and we fail to see how a promise to reply to his principal assailant in the Press, and to appear at an open public meeting in a few days is withdrawing from the controversy; and you know that it is not. You gave Mr. Carnegie his own time, and it is only fair that M. de Rougemont should have a reasonable period in which to prepare his reply, as the length of the letters is such that it will require considerable care to condense the rejoinder into reasonable space; and further, M. de Rougemont is very much engaged now over preparing his lectures and in other ways. Our words of admonition ... are these: In your persistent attempts to discredit M. de Rougemont we recommend you not to discredit the 'Daily Chronicle'.

Massingham duly published Fitzgerald's letter in the *Chronicle*, accompanied by his own curt response. It was unfortunate, he said, that 'neither Messrs. Newnes nor M. de Rougemont seem able to conduct a controversy without impertinence'. While it was true that De Rougemont had promised to reply to Carnegie's critique over following days, 'there have been so many failures to fulfil pledges made by him that we may be forgiven for failing to attach too deep a significance to the latest of these promises'.

Furthermore said Massingham, more evidence was to hand regarding Giles and his party. After Carnegie had reported that Tietkens was still alive and living in Australia, Massingham had contacted his colleagues on *The Sydney Morning Herald* by cable:

Kindly ask Tietkens Lands Department whether Giles Expedition he accompanied ever fired inoffensive blacks. Rougemont alleges.

No matter the truth, Tietkens was unlikely to admit to such an act. The *Herald* editor responded immediately:

Tietkens denies.

It was, said Massingham, another instance in which a test had been applied with a result unfavourable to De Rougemont.

On 29 September, De Rougemont delivered on his promise to attend to Carnegie. From the outset, it was clear he would not be browbeaten by the Scot.

Under the pretext of criticising my work, Mr. Carnegie of Kinnaird Castle, Brechin, appears to be bringing out a new serial in your paper. I have tried to spell through Parts 1, 2 and 3 of the work, which appears to be a history of his travels and exploits in distant parts. From so much of the book as you have published, it would appear that although it may be doubtful whether he is the actual discoverer of Australia, he has explored more of it than all the Australian travellers ever heard of. He has penetrated deserts, where all other explorers have left their bones, and has done all this in such quick time as will make the railways look to their records. He personally knows all the prospectors seeking gold in an area of 1000 miles square. Truly, Jack the Giant Killer will have to stand down, for here is the Explorer General.

I have not time to follow him in all his magnificent exploits, but as he has alluded to me occasionally in a familiar and jocular way, and exercised his brilliant wit on my work, I hope you will not deny me a little latitude in the same direction as (for the greater part of his work) it is difficult to take him seriously. Hon. David Carnegie is a very young gentleman, as may be readily understood from the mixture which he has ladled out to overflow your paper. He is an explorer, as I understand, from the Piccadilly Desert territory.

The brave explorer started out to criticise me with a tomahawk, but after letting himself loose and floundering blindly about in your paper, he tangled himself up and got 'bushed', and frantically implored anybody and everybody for Heaven's sake to help him . . .

The lavender water explorer says, 'I know enough of practical astronomy to enable me to find my latitude, with a sextant or a theodolite, with the help of a nautical almanac and numerous tables: even with such facilities it is not altogether a simple job.' The explorer ridicules me for being able to find latitude without his camel load of travelling observatory apparatus. In your paper of 26th last, Mr. Arthur H. Baker, B. A. of Board School, Lavender-Hill, shows that two of his schoolboys found their latitude, 'with no apparatus than a pair of compasses'. Could Mr. Baker find room in his class for the celebrated explorer of Kinnaird Castle? . . .

In regard to my statements that we were fired upon. The intrepid explorer says 'It is not the custom of white men to fire upon unoffending blacks.' Now every Australian traveller knows that the blacks are often fired upon to 'cow them', make them afraid of the whites, to show them water, and every real explorer and bushman is aware that the most frequent trouble is caused by the whites interfering with the women. Of course, the whites are always quite indignant when such a suggestion is made in the papers.

It is also well known that the blacks are fired upon, as Mr. Carnegie admits, for stealing from camp. This often means the great crime of taking a pannikin, knife, belt, pipe, etc. For these trifles the kings of the forest are 'laid out', 'put to sleep', etc.

The explorer says that he could not find water by my method. No one accused him of it. I said this is how the blacks find it. Now I ask any Australian, is it likely that the natives in a dry country will show the water to a strange party of whites with a string of camels which would empty their little wells (especially if they did not know it was the Explorer General in person)? The dauntless explorer says that he camped for a long time on the shores of a lake. This shows commendable caution on the part of one so young. There is no safer place for an explorer in dry country than by a lake.

It is not good for an explorer to get out of the sight of water, especially one of the lavender water variety, because it gives such facilities for exploring the country around the lake for a distance of at least five miles in every direction, while the bushman in charge winks the other eye at his mates. This is the stamp of explorer that the Australian boys like – no work, stick near water and something funny to laugh at.

The daring explorer tells us that in nine months he crossed and re-crossed country about 1500 miles long and 1000 miles wide. Does this include the months he was paddling about in the lakes? It does not matter, a trifle like this can make no difference to an explorer of this stamp. He says, 'We left no very large portion of the interior untraversed.' Why, this could not be done in a lifetime by real bushmen.

I ask Australians, what is the point of trying to answer such stuff as this? Every Australian explorer and traveller knows that a large area of the interior is still unexplored. The desert has baffled and turned back all the real old Australian 'ironback' explorers, men afraid of nothing, of unconquerable courage and resolution, and yet we have this youth telling the English people how he waltzed through it . . .

The unexplored country in question will never be made access-ible unless explorers make friends with the headmen, not only of one tribe, but of every tribe whose territory is traversed. This is the only means by which they can make sure of getting water, which however can be obtained if they know how to make friends with them, and will try to do so. The explorer says, 'I know most of the West Australian prospectors who have made lengthy journeys,' amongst thousands of the most adventurous men from all parts of the world, in the wild rush for gold across a large continent on the other side of the globe. This young man 'knows most of them' – this is the critic that doubts the veracity of others.

I had almost forgotten my interview with the explorer, to which he refers. The stick he showed me, as I said at the time, is similar to those used by the blacks for turning large joints of meat, and also for beating the seeds out of the native grass from which they make flour.

The daring explorer says that the water stuck to his copper boilers and was an awful bore. He can't understand how I managed my kettle. I did not suspect that he did. All the little things that he doesn't know would make a big book. The next time he risks his life in venturing to explore a five mile desert around a lake I will tell him what to do with his salt. His readers will want to take the whole of it to season his exploring yarns.

In his dangerous expedition across the Hyde Park district, he might be able to see all the hills in that area, but it would hardly be safe for any other explorers to tell even Londoners that in one trip across and back he minutely examined the whole of the physical features in a territory of 1000 miles square; yet this is what the lavender water explorer did. The explorer filled columns of the 'Chronicle' day after day in the endeavour to prove that if I had been bottled up there in my mountain home he must have trampled on us in that one trip.

He subsequently gives himself a little more rope, ties himself up in a series of knots, wobbles and gropes about all over the 'Chronicle', and finally admits what he has been for weeks vainly trying to deny in these important words, 'Although between our upgoing and return back there is room enough for a range or two of hills, which probably exist.' Your readers will probably think so too in a country of 1500 miles by 1000. Few will deny that there is room for a tribe or two of blacks in that space. Trying to spell through twaddle makes me tired. I have no patience to follow the brave explorer any further, and in leaving him to the public I merely remark that Mr. Carnegie may believe he is the hero of all those exploits, but I am certain he has never been within 300 miles of the place which I have described.

Carnegie's dull schoolmasterly style was no match for De Rougemont's acerbic humour. Readers who had fast tired of Carnegie's endless meandering in the Australian desert applauded, yet De Rougemont's efforts to disparage the Scot indicated he still considered the 'lavender water explorer' his most dangerous adversary.

19
Stage Names

On the stage he was natural, simple, affecting
Twas only that when he was off he was acting
                    Oliver Goldsmith, *Retaliation: a poem*, 1774

DE ROUGEMONT'S THEATRICAL style caught the eye of expatriate Australian George Darrell, who had observed the sensation caused by the Frenchman's British Association appearances and his spat with Carnegie with keen interest. Darrell was an actor, playwright and producer who had enjoyed success with 'stage spectaculars' in the colonies. He had arrived in England in December 1897 with the intention of collaborating on a mining melodrama with Arthur Conan Doyle. The play never saw light, but in 1898 Darrell managed to find backing for his most popular Australian work, *The Sunny South*, at the Surrey Theatre in London. It closed after only fifteen performances and he was left looking for new ventures. As his own star fell, Darrell became mesmerised by De Rougemont's astonishing rise.

Darrell went to see another Australian, George Musgrove, also a theatrical promoter, who lived near Hyde Park Corner. Musgrove was then producing a successful run of a musical comedy entitled *The Belle of New York* at the Shaftesbury Theatre. Darrell proposed to him that they present De Rougemont on the provincial circuit. Together they rapidly sketched a plan for a series of lectures to be privately financed by George's company.

Neither of them wished to risk their name on the venture, so they agreed to invite Musgrove's brother Harry, who had little reputation left to lose, to manage the show. Harry Musgrove was an ex-cricketer who had managed the Australian eleven's previous tour of England. He had also been at the helm of a disastrous tour of America by an Australian baseball team, which concluded in London in July 1897 with allegations Musgrove had done a runner with the gate receipts.

There was only one problem — none of them had ever met De Rougemont and had no idea how to contact him. On Saturday 1 October, the London editor for Melbourne's *Argus* rang Harry Musgrove to solicit tickets for that evening's Shaftesbury Theatre show. Musgrove obliged but as he hurried to get the *Argus* man off the line, the editor stopped him.

'By the way, I've got a curiosity in the office just now. He's looking up some Sydney files in the reading room. It's that chap De Rougemont.'

Musgrove grabbed his opportunity.

'Hold him till I can get over. That's the fellow I've been looking for. Give him a turtle or two to amuse him but for the love of Peter don't lose sight of him.'[24]

Musgrove flung down the phone, rushed to the *Argus* office and bailed up the editor.

'Where is he?'

The editor pointed to a wiry-looking fellow standing at a bookshelf studying an archive copy of *The Argus*. Musgrove walked over and shot out a hand in greeting.

'Might I have the pleasure of meeting the new Crusoe?'

De Rougemont glanced up at the sharply dressed promoter and shrugged.

Musgrove withdrew his hand.

'Free to talk business?'

De Rougemont returned his eyes to the newspaper. It was not the first such approach he had been subject to. Celebrity, he found, drew more parasites than a shipboard wound. He offered a slight nod of his head.

'Yes.'

'Want to make some money?'

De Rougemont shrugged again.

'Yes.'

Musgrove thought him the most monosyllabic man he had ever met but proceeded to introduce himself and outline the lecture plan. De Rougemont agreed to consider it. Fearful he might never see him again, Musgrove waited for De Rougemont to finish with the newspaper files and then suggested they walk together down through Covent Garden.

On the way, Musgrove pointed out to De Rougemont the sites of the eighteenth-century coffee houses on Russell Street — Button's, Tom's and Will's — and told him they had once been frequented by the luminaries of London's literati, including Daniel Defoe.

Near the entrance to the glass-roofed Central Market building, construction of the new Jubilee Hall was underway and, to make provision for the work, fruit and vegetable stalls now spilt far out into the surrounding streets. As they navigated their way through, De Rougemont avoided the eye of stallholders who might remember him from his scrounging days of the not-too-distant past. At the piazza end of the market abounded wooden tables laden with freshly cut English and imported blooms.

'Would you like a flower for your buttonhole?' Musgrove offered.

'No,' replied De Rougemont, 'every flower has a soul. I would not take its life.'

Musgrove searched for safer ground. Confident that a beer had no soul, he invited De Rougemont to have a drink with him at the nearby Tavistock Hotel.

'No,' said De Rougemont, adding perplexingly, 'I have never taken drink that way in my life.'

In desperation, Musgrove asked if he would like to see a matinee performance of *The Belle.* De Rougemont coyly replied he had never been to the theatre, but agreed to go nevertheless. They strolled away from Covent Garden up Endell Street to Shaftesbury Avenue. The theatre was only a short distance from De Rougemont's Frith Street boarding-room and he had often passed it en route to the British Museum in those first hungry weeks. As they walked, De Rougemont told Musgrove how his adventures had come to be written up in *Wide World Magazine.* They were all true, he told the promoter, but had been exaggerated and rewritten by a subeditor at Fitzgerald's office.

As they approached the Shaftesbury, Musgrove suddenly remembered that they were running a skit on De Rougemont's tales as part of the show and panicked. If the Frenchman thought he was mocking him it would spell doom for the lecture tour. He ushered De Rougemont to a front stall and then rushed around to the stage door to tell the director, a friend, to cut all reference to his guest. The show went on — without the skit — and De Rougemont's agreement to the tour was secured.

Musgrove organised an initial series of four lecture appearances over the following month, taking in Brighton, Manchester, Birmingham and Bradford. Meanwhile George Darrell penned a four-act melodrama entitled *The Adventures of Louis De Rougemont* in which the man himself was cast to play the lead, but before rehearsals could even commence a story emerged in Sydney with the potential to destroy the new star's fledgling career.

'Louis De Rougemont is the man of the moment in London', began *The Daily Telegraph*'s leader:

> Poor old Robinson Crusoe stands eclipsed . . . not even such heroes of the 'Dark Continent' as Stanley and Gordon can be held to triumph over the glories ascribed to the man who reached London recently in a penniless condition, after working his passage from the Antipodes.

The Sydney newspaper editor then delivered his coup de grâce. The publication of the sketch of De Rougemont's photograph, he said, had excited a great deal of interest.

> During the day several persons called at the office anxious to establish the identity of the portrait with a man of their acquaintance. All of them supplied the addresses of other people who they said could give fuller information.

The curious point about all the information, continued the editor, was that it referred to one and the same man:

> He was said to have been well known in Sydney up to within the last two years. In every instance quoted he was known by the name of Henri Louis Grien.

20

A Case of Identity

Strange Story of Identity

REMINISCENCES OF SYDNEY RESIDENTS

The Daily Telegraph, Sydney

Whether there is any real identity between Henri Louis Grien and M. Louis De Rougemont remains to be seen, but quite a number of people to whom the magazine photograph was shown emphatically declared that it was the portrait of Grien.

A lady at Newtown, with whom Grien had lodged for 18 months, was positive in her identification. Her information regarding Grien, too, tends to corroborate certain statements published concerning Rougemont. Grien claimed to be Swiss. He left Sydney in May of last year for New Zealand, 'hard up' to use the landlady's expression, with the avowed purpose of prosecuting some search for copper. He has not been heard of for the past nine months, and she thinks it would be quite like him to have worked his passage to England. Since his departure from Sydney, letters have come to hand from Grien's brother in Switzerland, and been returned to the postal authorities. Grien, it is stated, became separated from his wife while in Sydney. She is still believed to reside with her children in one of the suburbs. The landlady speaks kindly of Grien, though she regarded him as eccentric. He professed to have travelled everywhere, and was never weary of relating strange adventures, especially about diving and pearl fishing. He is also said to have been a believer in Spiritualism.

Another informant describes Grien as a little man, usually dressed in a black frock coat, with a low hard felt hat, and always carrying an umbrella. Two city businessmen speak of him as a man of undoubted education and any amount of assurance. They would not be at all surprised to learn that he is identical with the man De Rougemont. Grien was 'a bit of an artist and looked it', they told our representative yesterday. He had also a wonderful gift of spinning yarns. He claimed to have visited the Solomon Islands and been adrift there three times. He imparted the information that there was a mountain of copper on one of the islands 'beautiful to behold when the sun shone'. On this testimony a syndicate was formed to work the mountain. Grien was to lead the expedition, and if successful receive £25,000. He left Sydney for the promised land but has not since been heard of.

The focus in London had been on what Louis De Rougemont had *said*. In the colonies it now rested solely upon who De Rougemont was. At the *Telegraph* offices in Sydney, more readers came forward to claim his acquaintance, but their recollections of the man in the sketch seemed to describe several different people. Some remembered Grien to be the inventor of a patent deep-sea diving dress involved in a trial on the harbour in which a diver had died. Another claimed he had had an interest in a 'patent garbage exterminator'. Still others knew him as a photographic salesman. A city assayer said Grien was a mining syndicate operator and provided evidence of having inspected gold samples for him ten years before. This Grien, he said, told of 'hair-breadth encounters with the Blacks up north' and discovering a 'mountain of gold' in the interior. His syndicates, however, had fallen through before any gold was unearthed. In one case, said the assayer, a man sent to look for Grien in northern Queensland had himself disappeared. As the mystery deepened, dozens of people visited the paper's offices in King Street claiming to have known the man intimately in Sydney. The circumstances of their encounters differed markedly, but each identified the man by the name of Grien.

Could there be some mistake? With other men, the possibility of the existence of a double, a look-alike, within the same city or somewhere across the seas, could be readily entertained, but it defied reason to imagine another man resembling Louis De Rougemont. To find another face so distinctively engraved with that spiral of whorls would be as rare as discovering an identical pair of thumbprints. On the other hand, it seemed this man Grien had gone out of his way to become well known in Sydney. It was an unusual ploy for a would-be impostor.

In Sydney, unlike London, investigations were not limited to a circulation-hungry press and its curious readership. When the name Henri Grien emerged in the *Telegraph*, it also attracted the attention of the Sydney police. The Grien who had left behind his wife and children and fled to New Zealand was wanted under warrant for deserting his family. Under police direction a court had ordered the absent Grien to contribute twenty shillings per week toward the support of his wife. Nothing had been paid. Two plain-clothes detectives from Redfern, Senior Constable Wilson and Constable Bannan, had initially been assigned to the case, but until now it had remained unexplored, set aside with the other deserters, runaways, pickpockets and suicides. The display of De Rougemont's photograph on the cover of *Wide World Magazine* in every Sydney bookshop and newsagency changed all that.

Armed with the information unearthed by the *Telegraph*, the detectives commenced their enquiries. After two fruitless days of chasing readers' leads they pronounced themselves 'temporarily baffled'. Then a positive identification was made. A man was discovered lying ill in a Sydney private hospital whom the two police were certain was Grien. A man whose countenance was so weathered and worry-beaten that if he wasn't Grien, they said, 'there were two men in the world as like as two peas'.

Yet it couldn't be De Rougemont. The *Telegraph* reporter, frustrated at the speed with which the law was proceeding, continued with his own enquiries and located Grien's wife in the inner-western suburb of Stanmore. Taking a copy of *Wide World* with him, the reporter visited the address only to be told by a neighbour the woman had taken a journey to the city and would not return for some hours. Promising to return, the *Telegraph* reporter set out to take the train back to his office. As he approached Stanmore railway station he saw a young lady walking in the opposite direction accompanied by a little girl. As they passed, the woman looked up. Catching sight of the magazine in his hand, she suddenly seized the girl's hand and hurried along the street. Realising what had alarmed the woman, the reporter began to follow her. She traced the same path he had just taken, finally turning in at the residence he had visited in Stanmore Road. He reached her gate just as she was opening her door.

'I'm from the *Telegraph*. Are you Mrs Grien?'

The young lady told her daughter to go inside the house and turned to reply. The reporter thought her too young to be married to the man in the sketch.

'Yes, I am. What is it you want?'

The reporter walked up the path to her and exhibited the *Wide World* portrait.

'Is this your husband?'

Mrs Grien looked at the photograph quickly and nodded her head in affirmation. The reporter held the picture closer to her.

'Are you sure? Could it not simply be someone else who looks like him? A brother, or a twin, perhaps?'

Mrs Grien offered a tired smile.

'There is no-one else who looks like Henri. It is him, without a doubt. But he does not live here. He left more than a year ago.'

It was not the first time the photograph had been brought to her notice. Her eldest daughter Blanche had seen the cover of *Wide World Magazine* in the front window of the local newsagency a few days before. The picture of De Rougemont on the wrapper had impelled her to enter the store and ask if she could see the magazine. The proprietor, James Ruble, who had himself known the Grien family for over ten years, asked her if she was interested in the story of the 'famous traveller'. After studying the reproduction for some minutes Blanche Grien had turned to Ruble and said, 'I know who that is. It is not Mr Rougemont. It is my father.'

The *Telegraph* man reported that it had taken only one glance at *Wide World* to convince Mrs Grien that this was the man she had married. Moreover, he wrote:

> ... she had news that he was at the other side of the world. His brother, a clergyman, had written telling her he had been informed of the separation from her husband, who had just been on a visit to him, at a place called Yverdon in Switzerland, and inquired as to the welfare of the children. Nothing, however, was mentioned of Grien having been in London, or of his intending to go there. The letter also contained a remittance order for a small amount to assist Mrs Grien.

The reporter observed that Grien's wife was not surprised to learn her husband might have achieved notoriety.

She was not able to say of her own knowledge that her husband had actually experienced all that he claimed to have done in his story, but she knew that he had travelled a great deal. When she first met him in Sydney, he was engaged in the pearl-fishing industry, and owned a small vessel. He was fond of telling the children his adventures, and she particularly remembers his stories about riding the turtles, and experiences among the blacks. On his body were marks which he had told her were inflicted by the spears of the blacks in the far north of Australia. Beyond his own statements, however, she has no direct knowledge of her husband's history previous to their marriage.

After filing his story, the reporter contacted Redfern police station and suggested to detectives Bannan and Wilson they speak with the deserter's wife. They made haste to Stanmore and, to their surprise, confirmed the *Telegraph*'s story. A reporter from Sydney's *Evening News* followed. He asked Mrs Grien when she had last seen her husband, and was given an exact date: 22 May 1897. She remembered, she said, because it was a Saturday two days before the Queen's Birthday. By then they were already living apart and had met in the street. Mrs Grien had their daughter Blanche with her and her husband had asked if she could accompany him to a party. She declined and had not seen him since.

The reporter recalled their subsequent conversation:

— Did you know anything of your husband's life previous to your marriage, other than what he had related himself?

— He told me that he had been many years in the South Seas, and had been cast away among savages, with whom he had been called upon to do battle for his life. My husband had a tooth missing from his right jaw and he said that it had been smashed in a fight with cannibal islanders.

— Have you read Monsieur De Rougemont's adventures?

— No, but my husband was ever relating stirring adventures that he had passed through. He was very fond of our boy, De Courcey, who died. He was rather delicate. His father often entertained him with sensational stories of what he had passed through in savage lands, and I remember him telling the boy of how he used to capture and ride turtles . . . my husband was always drawing pictures of savages and of strange looking sea monsters.

— Then your husband was something of an artist?

— Oh yes: he could draw very well, and he was always happy with a piece of charcoal or a slate and pencil.

— Had you ever heard the name De Rougemont before seeing *The Wide World Magazine*?

— Oh yes, my eldest son's name is Cecil De Rougemont Grien. It was my husband's wish that he should bear that name. He said that he had a cousin named De Rougemont of whom he was very fond.

— Did this cousin bear any resemblance to your husband?

— I cannot say. I have not seen my husband's cousin and do not know which part of the world he was born in. I do not know if he is dead or alive.

— Where was your husband born?

— In France, but he lived in Switzerland for many years. I married him in Sydney. We first met when I was in a shop in George Street North. He was then pearl fishing he told me. He went away and came back in about two years, when he asked me to be his wife. We were married on 15 April 1883, by the Rev. Mr Collier, a Presbyterian minister, at his private house in Enmore. Of course, I am much younger than my husband. He would be about sixty-two now. He was forty-seven when we were married.

— Did you ever hear your husband talk of going to London or of writing of his experiences?

— No, but I would not be surprised to learn that he has done one, or both.

Bannan and Wilson, embarrassed by their blunder in identifying the wrong man, stepped up the pace of their investigation. They confirmed Mrs Grien's absent husband to be the same person recognised by callers to the *Daily Telegraph* office — Henri Louis Grien.

Their enquiries revealed Grien had arrived in Sydney about the latter end of 1881 after engaging in pearl fishing off the north Australian coast. At that time, Mrs Grien, then Elizabeth Ravenscroft, a girl of fifteen, kept a fancy-goods shop with her parents. One day Henri Grien had entered the George Street shop to make some purchases, became entranced by the young saleswoman and lingered to converse with her. He called frequently afterward and courtship ensued. He told her thrilling tales of his past life and of losing several vessels in the pearling trade. Soon afterward he disappeared, but on his return eighteen months later he proposed marriage.

According to the police, Grien told his fiancée that the pearl fishing had not gone well and consented to give up the sea to settle in Sydney. He had then found work making photographic enlargements. The couple lived first in Petersham and then in the Enmore district. For some years all was well. Elizabeth Grien bore seven children in eleven years, although only four had survived to the present day – Blanche, Cecil, Charlie and Gladys. When business turned bad, the family had moved from their house in Marian Street, Enmore, to furnished lodgings in nearby Station Street. Domestic differences arose and worsened over time; eventually Elizabeth took the children and moved out. Henri Grien remained in the Station Street boarding house. The police showed the landlady there the *Wide World Magazine* photograph, which she identified as her lodger Grien. He had altered little, she said, since last seen eighteen months previously. Soon after the estrangement of Grien from his family, police had launched court proceedings. The court documents described Grien as 'an artist'.

Bannan and Wilson also reported that Grien, through his business, had become known to many people in Sydney. All of those with whom they had spoken had described Grien as an educated man and an excellent raconteur who had travelled extensively. Those who knew him intimately had no doubt he had journeyed to the South Seas and northern Australia. Even while court action was pending, Grien had disappeared to Queensland, apparently pursuing an interest in a goldmine he had discovered in Cloncurry. Several times during his married life Grien had visited Queensland; once, around ten years earlier, for a period of twelve months. During this time his son, De Courcey, of whom Grien was passionately fond, had taken ill and died. Grien received the news by wire but arrived back in Sydney after the funeral. He told his wife that, owing to his hurried departure, his Cloncurry gold claim had been jumped.

The police had spoken to several people familiar with Grien in the Enmore district. One, a Mr Duff, had lived in the same street as Grien and become friendly with him about three years previously, after Grien had solicited an order from him for a photographic enlargement. Until fifteen months ago the two had met frequently. Duff corroborated the story regarding Grien's Queensland mining interests, recalling that Grien had accosted him one day in Pitt Street, Sydney, and invited his investment in the venture, telling him it was 'a good thing'. Duff had declined. The last time Duff had encountered Grien, the good thing had gone bad and he looked 'very much down on his luck'. Duff told the police he had forgotten about Grien until a few days before, when he saw the photo published in a newspaper. *The Evening News* recorded Duff's statement:

> One glance was enough to tell me that it was Grien and no-one else. There could be no mistaking the man. I saw Grien often, and conversed with him, and I am positive that he is De Rougemont.

Duff was to reveal another surprise. A few months earlier, he said, the mail had brought him an envelope bearing a foreign postmark and unknown handwriting.

La Pelouse
Yverdon, Switzerland
5/7/98

Dear Sir,

Your name has been given me as the name of a gentleman to whom I can apply in a case of the utmost importance for my family. In the parish, lives the wife of my brother with her four children. As husband and wife had to part, and the children are left to the care of the mother, I am extremely anxious about the care of my nephews and nieces. I hope I am not trespassing too much on your kindness if I appeal to you for visiting now and then, and giving a little advice to Mrs Grien, and seeing that the children go regularly to school and receive a proper education. I wish you would kindly communicate these lines to your

clergyman; from whom I would like to get the same kindness. I suppose the best way for you to see Mrs Grien would be to write to her, Post Office Newtown, and make sure that you can see her, I don't know her address in town. I might just as well state, that, after having fully examined the case, man and wife are equally responsible for the distressing collapse of their family life. Mr W. Bowen of Regent Street and Mrs C—— of Station Street, could if you kindly call upon them, acquaint you with the details of the case. If, after having seen Mrs Grien and the children, you will grant me the favour of a few lines, I shall feel very thankful. Trusting you will excuse the liberty I am taking in my troubling you so much, and with many thanks for your kindness.
I remain, dear sir, yours sincerely,

Rev. F. Grien
Pasteur, La Pelouse
Quai de la Thiele
Yverdon, Switzerland

Duff did as Grien's brother requested, locating the Grien family residence in Stanmore Road. Elizabeth Grien subsequently received letters from the Swiss pastor containing remittances totalling thirty shillings. Only the first, however, contained any news of her husband and none made any reference to Louis De Rougemont.

The *Telegraph* already considered the case closed. Dubbing De Rougemont a second Robinson Crusoe and 'a man of many parts', the paper declared:

> If a wife's identification of her husband by means of a photograph can be accepted as indisputable evidence, there seems no longer any room for doubt that M. De Rougemont, whose sensational experiences in Australia have caused so much excitement in England, is a Sydney man; that his wife and family actually reside in a Sydney suburb; and that he has simply adopted 'De Rougemont' as his family name.

The *Telegraph* reported interest in the De Rougemont story to have swept the continent:

Telegrams received from all the colonies bear testimony on that point. In Sydney, copies of the magazine have been eagerly bought up since particulars were given in the 'Daily Telegraph'.

Across the seas, *Wide World* sales had been trebled by a genuine fascination for De Rougemont's adventures. In Australia they were being driven to new heights by a seemingly universal desire to unmask the author. In Melbourne, a businessman by the name of Lee came forward to tell *The Argus* he had frequently met with De Rougemont in that city, although under a different name, which he had unfortunately now forgotten. Lee said he had recognised the portrait instantly. 'In fact,' said Lee, 'he was the most curiously wrinkled man I ever met.'

Lee had previously had an interest in the Mount Dockrell goldmine in the Kimberley, about sixty miles from Halls Creek. He had journeyed there in 1893. Due to the wildness of the region and reported conflicts with Aboriginals, Governor Forrest had provided Lee with a police escort from Wyndham at the head of the Cambridge Gulf for the entire 400-mile journey to the mine. The trip took some thirty days, during which time Lee had encountered many Aboriginals of the region. What had struck him most, he said, was 'their superiority in all respects to the Victorian blacks' and the 'barbarous severity' with which they were treated by the West Australian police. Their resulting hatred for the white man had resulted in the spearing and death of the Mount Dockrell mine manager prior to Lee's visit. After Lee had left, one of his escorting troopers was also killed in a raid.

In late July, Lee had returned to Melbourne with a collection of native weapons, clothing and ornaments. It was then he had met De Rougemont, who had displayed a keen interest in his experiences in the Kimberley. In subsequent meetings, Lee said, De Rougemont never failed to bring up the subject of West Australia, the blacks and the gold discoveries. He had been particularly curious about the native weapons and frequently inspected the collection. According to Lee, the man was French but had a perfect command of English. De Rougemont had shown Lee a notebook, telling him that he made a record of all his own strange experiences, 'though not with any idea of publication'. To the businessman's surprise, De Rougemont also told him he had been recording the details of their conversations. He explained that he had a good memory and never took notes at the time, but that it sometimes took half the night to write down what Lee had told him. Lee read over some of the notes and found them to be an accurate representation of what he had said. The businessman commented that De Rougemont:

> ... never at any time professed to know anything of the West Australian blacks, though he had evidently travelled a good deal on the northern coast of Australia, was a man of fair culture and an interesting talker. One of his mannerisms was the taking of snuff when deeply interested in any particular topic. He was a man with all sorts of schemes in his head and talked often of inventions.

At the time, De Rougemont appeared to Lee to be 'doing nothing in particular'. He was living somewhere in St Kilda and was often seen on The Esplanade. Upon departing Melbourne, De Rougemont had told Lee that he was returning to Sydney, then travelling to Queensland where he had an interest in a mine near Cloncurry. Lee said that he had nearly forgotten the man until he saw the *Wide World* picture, but then 'could have picked him out amongst ten thousand'.

If Lee had met with De Rougemont in Melbourne, it seemed the French consul based there had not. De Rougemont had claimed that when he finally escaped the wilderness he had sought the consul's aid; however, when he tried to communicate his experiences to him, he had discovered he had almost forgotten his native language, and doubts were cast on his story. The consul, Monsieur Dejardin, who had been in the position for ten years, told newspapers that he had no recollection of any such man calling on him. Nor did consular records contain the name De Rougemont. It appeared the consul was one of few people in the colonies not to have encountered his compatriot.

Another was William Tietkens. Following his cabled denial to London, Giles's first officer issued a full statement to the Australian newspapers defending his expedition party from the charge of firing upon Aboriginals:

> The statement that the Giles party fired upon him and inoffensive blacks is absolutely untrue. I look upon it as impossible for a man to reach the western interior of Australia on foot and alone, even

now, after so many positions have been fixed by different travellers. It was still more impossible twenty-five years ago when the map was a blank . . .

However, Tietkens admitted that members of the expedition had frequently found it necessary to fire their rifles over the heads of Aboriginals who had swarmed around them when they took control of local waterholes to replenish their waterbags. The noise of the firearms, he said, always kept the tribespeople at bay, and at a distance that prevented them using their spears against the intruders. Tietkens added that he thought De Rougemont had studied Giles's journal and then fabricated elements of his adventures:

> De Rougemont's stories about the pots and pans of virgin gold etc. are absolutely puerile. The man is evidently a visionary. He has studied the journals of the explorers, and knows that opinions have been expressed concerning the probability of precious minerals being found in Central Australia . . .

Any syndicate, Tietkens said, which put together an expedition with De Rougemont as leader would 'surely meet with disaster, if not death'.

Such dismissive derision from one of the colonies' most respected pioneers inevitably spelt disaster for Murphy's syndicate, but Louis De Rougemont still had backers. Word of the impossibly alike Henri Grien and his abandoned family in suburban Sydney had not yet reached London.

2 I

The Piccadilly Explorer

Fame, like the river, is narrowest where it is bred,
and broadest afar off.

Sir William Davenant, English poet laureate, 1606–68

THE ST JAMES HALL in Piccadilly, once London's chief concert hall, had in its forty-year life played host to magicians, illusionists, marionettes, comedians and minstrels. Here Charles Dickens had performed his famous readings to mesmerised audiences and Stanley had returned from Zanzibar to a royal reception by Prince Albert — but none who had come to stand upon its broad stage had been more keenly anticipated than Louis De Rougemont. Two months had elapsed since William Fitzgerald had first introduced this astonishing man to the world. Three weeks of sensation had followed the British Association Congress, and now, for the first time, the London public was to be granted the opportunity to witness De Rougemont in person.

From mid-afternoon on Monday 3 October, a queue grew down Regent Street. Despite the *Chronicle*'s best efforts, the majority still seemed decidedly in favour of the Frenchman. The fact that De Rougemont had voluntarily presented himself for public scrutiny seemed sufficient to convince many of his sincerity. By the advertised commencement time of eight pm, an audience of 3000 had filled the hall. Seated on a platform looking out onto the massive auditorium were De Rougemont's patrons — George Newnes; William Fitzgerald; and John Henneker Heaton and his wife. The presence of Newnes and Heaton was an unexpected show of strength. It was the first time Heaton had publicly associated himself with De Rougemont. Also on stage were the chairman for the evening, Mr J. G. Chapman; and the respected barrister and Liberal parliamentarian, Mr Llewelyn Atherley-Jones, a Newnes ally. Next to the monocled Atherley-Jones sat a slickly dressed man none in the hall could identify. James Murphy had wangled a seat on stage by offering Fitzgerald a stake in his fast-sinking syndicate. It was the Irishman's last-ditch effort to present the venture in a respectable light. None spoke until, at precisely eight o'clock, Chapman stood to address the audience. After formally welcoming the dignitaries seated on stage, he told the audience De Rougemont had not intended to lecture at present, did not consider himself qualified to appear before a large audience, and did not have the time to undergo the necessary training:

> It was represented to De Rougemont, however, that the public who had patronised his work so extensively felt he ought to show himself and speak personally. It is only in deference to you that he will appear this evening.

There was light applause and the chairman continued:

> I myself have interviewed De Rougemont, and what is more I believe in him. I should think his remarkable book will be a godsend to all the young folk of England. Despite the treatment he has received, Louis De Rougemont will this evening answer the questions posed by his critics.
>
> I would therefore ask you to pay Monsieur De Rougemont the respect he so fully deserves. It is my responsibility as this evening's chairman to warn that no direct interrogation or heckling will be tolerated.

When the chairman had concluded, Louis De Rougemont, formally attired in black frockcoat and white tie, ascended the stage stairs to polite applause. He carried no notes. When he reached the podium he bowed, gripped the lectern with both hands and started at once to speak. His voice wavered slightly as he told the audience he was exceedingly pleased to address so large a gathering, which made him feel his work was appreciated, and inspired him with the courage to speak of his adventures:

> You will readily understand that a man who has been away from civilisation for so many years cannot be expected to use a language such as you have been used to. I have been chaffed by some critics because I used language which was not called discreet or courteous in my

replies to them. I shall be very glad to tell them that it is not out of discourtesy. It was simply a want of knowledge. I am not used to courtesy because we savages are not so. We say things very rudely sometimes although we do not mean to.

There was laughter. De Rougemont wiped his brow and went on:

I want specially to thank my critics, for they have been very kind to me, for they have brought this gathering together, and they have also sent many readers to my publishing firm, and that is the most important part to me.

More laughter arose. De Rougemont then set about relating the various episodes of his adventures, as he had to the British Association. He told of his meeting with Jensen in Singapore, their pearling expedition on the *Veielland* off Batavia and the encounter with the giant octopus. As some in his audience began to mutter their disbelief, De Rougemont raised a hand to silence them. He may, he said, have been mistaken about the size of the octopus because 'in my boyish sight I might have seen things very large'.

We are apt when we are young to see things very large, especially when we are frightened by them. I do not know if any of you have happened to be in a wood and seen a cat, and called it a wolf. I have done the same thing in my narrative, and I hope you will not throw stones at me because I have done similar things.

Sensing support, De Rougemont relaxed. He strolled the breadth of the stage as he told the story of his life as a castaway and his rescue and acceptance by the Cambridge Gulf Aboriginals. He observed that life in the desert had been in some ways easier than in London.

'If you left anything anywhere,' joked De Rougemont, 'you could always be sure to find it ... you can't always be sure of that in a civilised country.' After describing his life with the tribe, he told the crowd he proposed to answer some questions:

I have been asked a good many questions to which I have not replied and I will tell you why. If you were to ask me questions which I would consider personal, I would tell you, as I told a gentleman whom you all have read of, that I considered those questions impertinent, and I should not reply. I have been asked as to my birth register. Well, that

is a very strange question to ask me, because although no doubt I was
there when I was born I do not remember the spot. I have no idea, and
I never said positively I was born in any one spot. I did say I thought I
was. If I cannot prove it to you today, I shall of a certainty prove it to
you before I have finished in the *Wide World*. It will be there.

The second question is with regard to my assertion that I was
living in the Boulevard Haussmann. They have said I was born there
and I never said anything of the kind. When I went there I was a good
size lad, and therefore could remember it, and if it was not exactly the
place of my birth it was certainly a place where I did go and see my
parents when they lived there.

Another question is with regard to the mystery of the two girls . . .
It is a painful subject to me and I do not like it mentioned. I have
written about it certainly and will write about it again before I have
finished my story. I shall say the truth, the whole truth and nothing
but the truth about those two girls. You will not have to wait long,
because, I am told, by the Christmas number you will know all about
it. You wait till Christmas!

Fitzgerald rose and handed De Rougemont a book. The Frenchman
informed the audience it was Ernest Giles's journal. Turning to a
marked page, De Rougemont read an excerpt in which Giles admitted
to firing on Aboriginals after being attacked near a waterhole in the
Musgrave Ranges. Might not Giles have also fired upon De Rougemont's party? But De Rougemont was conciliatory, telling the
gathering that, as he had been indistinguishable from his black
companions, he did not blame Giles for his actions.

De Rougemont returned the journal to Fitzgerald and moved on to
a new topic:

Now, as to my knowledge of English. It is rather a strange question to
put to a foreigner, but I will try and answer it. First let me tell you
that before, when I lived in Switzerland, I spoke very well indeed.
The best time I ever spent was among English boys. Among them I
received the best training a man can possibly get. They thrashed me
over and over again. This is the best education a lad can possibly
have, and if any of them happen to be here, I shall be pleased for
them to come up. And I shall shake hands most heartily with them. I
took this thrashing from the boys in the same way that I did from my

critics. As long as my critics can earn a sixpence by thrashing me I shall be the first to say, 'Well done, my boy, go on and earn another sixpence.'

Loud applause showed the audience to be almost unanimously onside. De Rougemont proceeded to describe his life after escaping the desert.

When I came to civilisation, I was debarred from earning my living . . . but I took to what I could get, and it was this. I became a canvasser, and in canvassing I had to convince people I called upon that my principal was anxious about their welfare, and that he had sent me to induce them to buy something they did not want. Well, if there is anything that will sharpen a man's wits, it is making — I will not say women, because they generally buy what they do not want — but men buy something they do not want.

The laughter resumed and De Rougemont looked to Murphy.

There is a gentleman on this platform I had to sell land for. I had to represent it as beautiful land where wildflowers grew, and this gentleman can tell you it was a lot of rocks and nothing else. Still, I sold the land. Then I travelled for pictures, and I sold a great many. I had to make people believe I could get pictures of their fathers whether they had fathers or not. It required a very sharp man to convince these people and make them buy what they did not want. Therefore if my English is somewhat out of the run of that of foreigners, do not blame me but your so-called civilisation. They made me do it, they sharpened my wits. If I have replied somewhat acrimoniously, do not blame me but my want of knowing. I know I have put a great deal of pepper and salt into my replies. That was because I wanted not only my critics to enjoy the joke, but you to enjoy the joke, and I hope you will agree that some of my replies were quite worthy of my critics.

St James Hall filled with cheering. De Rougemont, adventurer-entertainer, marked the moment with several shallow bows to each section of the audience, waving a triumphant hand to supporters in the boxes above.

The chairman rose and invited three cheers. They were willingly given, but as De Rougemont made to depart the stage a voice from the back of the hall arrested his step.

'Will M. De Rougemont show us his arm?'

De Rougemont paused and the chairman peered out into the stalls. Chapman spotted the heckler and addressed him directly.

'This question is a delicate one. I am hesitant to ask M. De Rougemont to comply with it.'

The audience began to hiss and jeer and Chapman looked to De Rougemont. The Frenchman nodded.

'Nevertheless,' said Chapman, 'I personally would like to see the arm, as no doubt would a great many present. I will ask M. De Rougemont if he would be so kind as to show us.'

The Frenchman returned to the lectern.

'If this question had been asked anywhere outside this hall I should certainly have said it was an impertinent question, but as you are all here to see it, I shall show it to you.'

The audience roared its approval. De Rougemont removed his frockcoat and vest and handed them to Chapman. He then rolled the shirtsleeves on both arms up to the shoulder. The skin below was the same tan shade as his face, though decidedly less worn and wrinkled. Several long scars ran across the sinewy flesh but there were no visible tattoos or brands. Chapman invited the heckler to join them on stage and inspect De Rougemont's arms. He did so and after a moment declared the bare limbs to be 'to his satisfaction'. De Rougemont kissed the man thrice, then replaced his vest and frockcoat and again faced the audience.

'If I had been a convict,' said De Rougemont, 'I might have done what I have done, but I could never have accepted the invitation from the British Association.'

De Rougemont bowed again and left the platform to clapping and cheering. His first public performance had only served to galvanise support. Newnes and Fitzgerald were now confident that whatever spears the critics might hurl, the sympathies of their readership remained with De Rougemont. They left the hall to celebrate their victory with their star.

The next morning's reviews were unusually generous. The *Daily News* was impressed with De Rougemont's deportment and elocution, noting that:

[He] was by no means unsuited for lecturing, bearing himself quite straight, walking gently to and fro ... De Rougemont made use throughout of quite appropriate diction, and was never at a loss for a plain and suitable word.

De Rougemont's performance had convinced Sydney's *Daily Telegraph*'s correspondent that he was familiar with the Australian wilds, possibly even experienced in entertaining audiences:

Whoever De Rougemont is, there can be no doubt he knows the back blocks intimately, and has an extensive and peculiar acquaintance with bush slang. Also, I should suspect him of some time or other having run a show.

Inevitably, the *Chronicle* was less impressed:

He was rather nervous at first. There was an indication of this in the way he drew his hand across his forehead now and then. Later, he got more at ease and, indeed, moved about the stage with a certain personal grace. Of that at least his life with the Australian savages had not robbed him.

The *Chronicle* said that 'as far as anybody expected a consecutive narrative, with dates and precise localities, it was not given'. De Rougemont had 'gossiped broadly of his experiences' and was 'invariably rambling and disconnected'. The baring of his brown arms, said the *Chronicle*, was 'a splendid drop curtain'.

Few readers that morning, however, had got so far as to read the notices of De Rougemont's Piccadilly premiere. Emblazoned across *Chronicle* placards throughout the city were the words 'De Rougemont Exposed'. Those fast enough to secure a copy at railway stalls and newsagencies turned straight to the leader pages to see a name with which they were not yet familiar.

22

De Rougemont Undone

Grien Alias De Rougemont

AN EARLIER APPEARANCE AND ANOTHER TALE

The Daily Chronicle, Tuesday 4 October 1898

We asked the other day what was de Rougemont's name in Australia? We asked first because this gentleman had made an answer to a question of our own which was on the face of it incredible – namely, that he changed his name with every firm employing him; secondly because it was impossible for us to discover that there was any Louis de Rougemont ever born in Paris, ever baptised at the Madeleine, or ever possessing a father called by the names suggested to us; and, thirdly, because a gentleman has communicated with us stating that in the month of May last . . . he had repeated interviews with a man calling himself Grien or Green, whom he subsequently identified with 'de Rougemont' . . . The writer we may say is Mr. F. W. Solomon, who is a representative of a company occupying large premises in Finsbury-square. The manager director of the firm is a Swiss by nationality, and he has a son also prominently engaged in the business.

In his letter, Solomon recalled meeting with a Swiss man by the name of Mr Green at his company offices in May. A conversation had ensued with regard to 'a wonderful diving apparatus' this man had invented, but which unfortunately had been lost in a shipwreck while Green was en route to England. He was awaiting the delivery of a duplicate set of designs from Australia and was compelled to remain in London until they arrived. Green had shown Solomon several letters of recommendation, one from a bishop in Australia, and also mentioned gentlemen of high social standing in London who were willing to assist him. Solomon took Green to see another executive in the firm, but his request for assistance with the diving costume was rejected. Green had then claimed to be an artist, offering to make drawings of Solomon or his family. Solomon gave Green a pencil and paper and asked him to make a sketch of his likeness, but 'he cleverly dodged this by various excuses'. Green left soon after.

Solomon had not seen Green again until a fortnight ago at the Earl's Court Exhibition. After shaking hands and exchanging compliments, Green, to Solomon's disgust, had simply walked away. Seeing the picture of De Rougemont in the *Strand* had brought these incidents vividly to mind and Solomon had not the slightest hesitation in declaring Mr Green and M. De Rougemont to be one and the same person.

> I do not doubt that all his adventures may be true, but I should like to know why, after invitation, he did not make a sketch, why he did not mention this marvellous diving apparatus to the British Association and why did he leave me so abruptly at the exhibition after so many interesting conversations?

A *Chronicle* reporter had called on Solomon's firm to obtain the full detail of Green's visits. At no stage had Green mentioned his thirty years among the Aboriginals to Solomon and his colleagues. All three members of the firm who had met with Green identified him from the magazine photograph as De Rougemont. In his report, the journalist revealed details of a final test that had been applied at St James Hall the previous evening:

> At our suggestion, the younger member of the firm and Mr. Solomon were kind enough to go to the de Rougemont lecture. They at once identified the lecturer by appearance, and by voice, as the man Grien or Green. We may add that the doubt as to the spelling arises from the fact that the visitor did not write his name, though on its being represented that Green was not a Swiss name, he stated that the spelling was Grien.

Solomon's testimony inspired Massingham to send his Paris correspondent foraging deeper into the Alps. The editor told readers that the *Chronicle* was also in possession of further information relating to

Grien's identity and published a transcript of a cable which he had just received from Sydney:

> The Sydney Daily Telegraph is publishing a series of articles dealing with M. Louis de Rougemont's life in Sydney. The writer affirms that M. de Rougemont resided in the city for many years under the name of Henri Grien, but left the colony eighteen months ago, his wife and family remaining here.

William Fitzgerald, having barely recovered from celebrating De Rougemont's triumph at St James Hall, despatched a letter to the *Chronicle* office assuring Massingham that his attitude was 'deplored by a great number of people'.

> This morning you have in huge type on your placards 'De Rougemont Exposed'. Now, Sir, every sensible person must agree that the only sensible conclusion one can come to on seeing this on the placards is that you possess proof positive that M. de Rougemont is an out and out impostor, who has never been through the adventures he alleges he has been through, and who has fabricated the whole story from beginning to end.

On turning to the article in the paper, said Fitzgerald, all one found was that De Rougemont, in a destitute state, had called on a firm under the name of Green and tried to sell them a diving apparatus.

> Let me tell you, Sir, that M. de Rougemont sought my advice on this very subject when he first came into this office, and I advised him to call upon Mr. W. A. Gorman, of the well-known firm of submarine engineers . . .

Fitzgerald said Massingham had also misrepresented the matter of the sketches. De Rougemont was simply acting as canvasser on behalf of an artist for whom he was soliciting orders. Said Fitzgerald:

> Now, I appeal again, to the great body of the public, and I ask them whether the fact that De Rougemont had called upon a gentleman in the City, giving his name as Green (a name which it is perfectly

well-known he gave to officers of the SS Waikato, in which he came over to England) justifies even in the smallest degree, the surprising Daily Chronicle placard, 'De Rougemont Exposed'.

If Fitzgerald was aware of the enquiries in Australia he would not yet admit it, but in his letter he had inadvertently provided Massingham with a further clue. It was not, as he claimed, generally known that De Rougemont had travelled to England under the name of Green. Upon receiving his letter, Massingham immediately despatched a cadet to interview the *Waikato*'s captain and then set about writing his response to Fitzgerald. Both letters were published in the *Chronicle* the following day.

The adventurer, Massingham said, had every chance to prove his integrity and the *Chronicle* had been impartial in its treatment throughout. If De Rougemont was telling the truth his story was 'the most marvellous in history'. But why had he concealed it from all in Australia? And why had he used false names in both the colonies and England? Why were all claims as to his identity unverifiable? In a bid to flush out further facts, Massingham invoked the good name of Fitzgerald's employer:

> Sir George Newnes is a thoroughly honourable man, who, if he were himself convinced [that De Rougemont was a fraud], would not lend himself to any kind of plan for deceiving the public. We have confidence in his good faith; if he finds that he has been deceived, he will readily admit the fact. We suggest, therefore, that instead of sending an expedition to 'find Jensen' he should send a reliable investigator to find Grien. He will then be dealing with facts that are verifiable . . .

Meanwhile Massingham's cadet had tracked down Captain Croucher of the *Waikato*. The captain told him he had taken the man in question on in Wellington, immediately prior to the *Waikato*'s departure.

The man came aboard under the name of Green and was paid no wages, but provided with passage and food. Green was formally engaged as a 'gentleman's servant', but had been employed in stoking. To Croucher's knowledge, Green had not mentioned his wonderful adventures during the voyage.

The *Chronicle* also located Green's certificate of discharge from the *Waikato* in London. The document stated that H. L. Green was discharged from the *Waikato* in March 1898. His age was given as fifty and his birthplace, London.

However, upon reading the *Chronicle*'s version of his interview, the captain of the SS *Waikato* contacted Massingham to tell him the inexperienced cadet had the story wrong. Croucher had in fact heard during the voyage that Green was writing the story of his life, and was also told of various 'wonderful accounts, to which, as being commander, he had little time to pay attention'. There were also reports among the crew of hearing Green's stories.

Suddenly Massingham was seeing connections that had eluded him for weeks on end. Then, just two days after De Rougemont's lecture at St James Hall, a broad-chested man walked into the *Chronicle* office and asked to see the editor. He told Massingham that he had read the account of Green's interview with Solomon regarding diving apparatus. Being a diver himself, and the holder of the world record for the deepest dive — thirty-one fathoms — it was a subject he knew a little about. He introduced himself as William May and told Massingham that the name of Green had a familiar ring. The editor showed May the portrait of De Rougemont in *Wide World*. May nodded.

— That is Green.

— And what do you know of him?

— Well, I knew him well for three or four years in Sydney.

— In what capacity?

— As a member of a firm called, I think, McQuillan and Green. Mr Green endeavoured to get customers for a diving apparatus, to secure trials of it, and to induce people to put money in the concern, I believe with considerable success.

— What was the material?

— It was a copper arrangement, with an ordinary diver's headdress screwed on to it — the diver passing his arms through the holes in the armpits, and having the rest of the apparatus fitted to him. But it had one defect. It gave the diver about four and a half pounds of air to live upon when he wanted about thirty. One day about two years ago, I was asked to inspect the invention. I did so and I said to the firm that in my opinion they had discovered a highly successful murdering machine. However, my advice was not taken. No doubt Mr Green and his partner were honestly confident of the value of their invention, for it was tried in Sydney Harbour. A man, who was, I believe, a Dane, went down in it and died of the experiment. There was an inquest, but apparently the firm were not held to be blameable.

— You said, Mr May, that you have known Mr Green, alias De Rougemont, for three or four years. Then you knew him in 1895?

— Yes, and I would be glad to make his acquaintance again in London.

— When you knew him, did he look like he had just returned from the savages?

— Not at all. He was as settled and civilised as most people you meet in Sydney.

Massingham laughed. May looked back to the portrait in the copy of *Wide World* in his hands and began to thumb through the pages, pausing at an illustration of De Rougemont astride a turtle. A question occurred to Massingham.

— By the way, Mr May, have you ever ridden a turtle?

— Yes I have.

— On the surface of the water?

— Never.

— How did your ride take place?

— In diving I struck a turtle at the bottom of the water and I got astride his back. The moment he felt my touch he raised his head and swam straight up. I signalled to the boat to be pulled in; but I could not communicate and so slid off the turtle to avoid an accident.

— But a ride on the surface of the water, is that possible?

May shook his head and Massingham concluded the interview. After he had shown the diver out, he sent a telegram by cable to the editor of the Sydney *Daily Telegraph*:

> Kindly wire how long Grien lived Sydney, and age eldest child.

Massingham hounded the cable office operator for a response. On the morning of Thursday 6 October, the details surfaced via the submarine wire:

> Seventeen years. Frequently away. Eldest child fourteen.

News was also to hand from the *Chronicle*'s correspondent in Switzerland. On Friday 7 October, Massingham delivered his verdict, declaring the bubble to have burst. The man was not De Rougemont, not even Grien, but Grin.

> Who is de Rougemont? Well, his name is not Louis de Rougemont. It is Henri Louis Grin. He was not born in Paris. His father had not a warehouse or a shop in the Boulevard Haussmann. He has no right to bear the name of de Rougemont and never had. After inquiries in France, Switzerland and elsewhere, we are convinced that he is Swiss by nationality and that he was born near Yverdon, a town in the Canton Vaud, on the borders of Lake Neuchâtel. The year of his birth was not 1842, but 1847.

Massingham then recounted the interview with the diver, William May:

> Mr. May tells us that when he first met Green in 1895 he was to all appearances a settled inhabitant of Sydney. What are Mr. Green's statements to us and to the British Association? 'I only reached civilisation', he said, 'in 1895, after an exile of upwards of thirty years.' As he further stated in this office that before going to Sydney he was at Mount Margaret, Fremantle and Melbourne, it must have been some time before he reached Sydney. As a matter of fact, he was at Sydney some years before. Another point. De Rougemont stated to us that he used the name of the firm that he was travelling for. If Mr. May is correct that again is an obvious untruth. For three years at least, he was known by the name of Green; he comes by that name

to England; he gives it to the firm he wishes to interest in his diving apparatus. It is an English variant of his own name – Grin – he even retained the initials H. L. and he generally used it. In a word, the names he has given in the 'Wide World' magazine do not fit, the dates do not fit, the story does not fit.

Now we go a step further. We quoted some days ago a cablegram from Sydney stating that the 'Daily Telegraph', a well known and responsible paper, had been publishing a series of articles stating that de Rougemont was not de Rougemont at all but a certain Henri Grien; that he lived in that city many years; and that he had left a wife and family there . . . seventeen years in Sydney, with intervals for disappearances. This of course takes fourteen years out of the thirty years spent among savages. In a word it renders the whole story impossible. We shall in a future issue lift the veil from this historic imposture some way further . . .

The following day, under the heading, 'De Rougemont Fraud', Mass-ingham continued his exposé. De Rougemont's stories were 'an ingenious tissue of lies palmed upon the public'. It was proof, the editor said, that 'nothing is more true than that truth is stranger than fiction'.

We leave our readers to draw the moral for themselves. For our part, while we regret the passing of a pleasant fancy, and even accord a certain admiration to the clever audacity which created it, we are bound in the public interest to remark that the de Rouge-mont fiction bears a curious likeness to the Tichborne case.

It is true that M. Grin had not laid claim to an ancient estate. On the other hand he has not merely claimed, but to all appearances succeeded in obtaining, a very large sum of money. If the evidence produced to us is true, or anything like the truth, he has obtained that money by false pretences.

Having raised the spectre of criminal consequences for De Rouge-mont, Massingham turned to the 'veiled figure' of Murphy.

Of this gentleman we have heard one or two things. He was in business in Australia and knew M. de Rougemont there. In London, he was alleged to be the leading spirit in a great syndicate which was arranging to exploit the goldfield opened up by M. de Rougemont's residence amongst the undiscovered blacks ... For the present we cast no aspersions on Mr. Murphy. He may be the most genuine of persons. He may indeed be deceived by a wily adventurer. Our reporter called twice at his address in Bloomsbury but failed to find him. We invite him, therefore, in his own interest, to clear himself of the suspicion which would attach to him if it should appear that he was acquainted with the fact that de Rougemont's story was not in substance true, and assisted him to deceive the persons to whom he sold it and the public at large ...

Murphy, of course, was no longer resident in the streets of Bloomsbury. The *Chronicle*'s reports had already persuaded him that the best avenue was flight. Meanwhile, a reporter had identified De Rougemont's original lodgings in Soho. The Frith Street landlady was happy to furnish a description of Mr Green, the name under which the destitute De Rougemont had rented her room. He had arrived, she said, with 'no more luggage than would fit in a matchbox' and kept to himself. He had seemed in 'needy circumstances' and on more than one occasion had been unable to meet his rent. He had no visitors and occasionally in conversation had referred to foreign parts. The landlady understood him to have recently arrived from Sydney. Later, Green's circumstances seemed to improve suddenly and, before leaving, he had paid the landlady his rent in full.

According to schedule but with perfect bad timing, Harry Musgrove's touring show starring Louis De Rougemont now commenced in Brighton. With cracks in the modern Crusoe's story widening by the hour, Musgrove took the precaution of planting allies in the audience to ward off difficult customers. They included a sharp West Australian journalist by the name of Edwin 'Dryblower' Murphy and sometime explorer and prospector William Carr-Boyd. The latter was himself renowned for stretching the truth, having once told lecture audiences he had been captured by Aboriginals and had his nasal septum perforated as part of an initiation rite. In fact, Carr-Boyd's 'initiation' was known to have taken place during a drinking bout in a Kimberley miners' camp. Notwithstanding the doubtful credibility of his ring-ins, Musgrove's ploy succeeded. When

De Rougemont took the stage in Brighton a man rose almost at once to enquire about turtle riding and was quickly talked down.

De Rougemont's success at St James Hall could not be repeated in the face of the *Chronicle*'s revelations. The lectures struggled to draw crowds. The exposure of De Rougemont's identity and doubt over his motivations conspired to lose Musgrove money, if not face. Ever the promoter, Musgrove concocted a stunt to excite attendance. He suggested to De Rougemont he sue the *Chronicle* for calling him a liar. De Rougemont initially agreed but reneged half an hour later. The crook's tour was finished. A disappointed Musgrove later blamed its failure on a British public who disapproved of 'anyone else's vices but their own and those only if committed with decent secrecy'. The venture folded, and George Darrell's play never opened on the stages of Covent Garden.

The *Chronicle*'s man in Europe had been following fresh trails through the mountains of Switzerland. He had wasted three weeks pursuing the elusive family De Rougemont from Paris to Lausanne. Now within only days of commencing his enquiries regarding Henri Grin in Switzerland he had extracted practically his entire history in that country. There were more Grins in Canton Vaud than a cartload of Cheshire cats. As he tramped thirty miles through the sleepy communes of Gressy and Belmont, Grin's family and friends came out to greet him. Did they know Henri? Why, of course; he had grown up with them. In any case, they had seen him only months before. The same response was given across the countryside. It seemed that on his recent holiday, Henri had made a point of visiting all the villages and people he remembered from boyhood, even re-acquainting himself with his place of birth in Gressy. There, in a creeper-covered stone cottage, Henri had introduced himself to the current residents, Monsieur Burtaud and his family. Now when they were shown the portrait of Louis De Rougemont in *Wide World*, Madame Burtaud jumped up with astonishment. 'It is he himself — a speaking likeness of him!' Even the children gathered around, saying '*C'est le monsieur qui est venu ici.*' All the villagers, the correspondent said, felt there was something very mysterious about the sudden reappearance of their long-lost neighbour. One told him, '*Il y avait quelque chose de louche*', meaning 'there was something shady about him'. But none could identify exactly what.

Across the hills in Belmont, Grin's innkeeper cousin exclaimed 'He is the living image of his father, and of his brother François.' At the Café de Commerce, another cousin, Madame Emmanuelle Grin, ridiculed the notion of thirty years among the savages, declaring that his immediate relatives had received frequent communications from him over the previous twenty years. When the correspondent mentioned Paris and the supposed shop on the Boulevard Haussmann he was howled down with laughter.

He made his way to Suchy, where he had been told Grin's brother was a Protestant pastor. François Grin was absent, but his wife instantly recognised the picture of her brother-in-law. She recalled his visit around the start of August, but had left home almost immediately after his arrival. The pastor's wife seemed distressed by discussion of Grin, but revealed that her husband visited England often and was aware of the controversy in the English press. In town, at the Café Jura and the Café National, regulars recognised the man in the photograph as '*le frère du pasteur*'. The correspondent also claimed to have unearthed in Yverdon the roots of Grin's pseudonym, discovering evidence of a boyhood friend by name of De Rougemont.

The *Chronicle*'s persistent investigations had finally reaped reward. On 11 October, Massingham called upon Sir George Newnes to 'stop this egregious imposture and leave this strange creature, who has gulled even the British Association, to the derision of the public'. No doubt, noted the editor, 'De Rougemont' was 'at this moment arranging to give seeming proof of certain notable incidents, which to the unwary might seem to be a brilliant vindication of his veracity'.

Newnes was yet unbowed. No denial or explanation was offered to the *Chronicle*. Instead, Fitzgerald placed an item in the *Westminster Gazette* informing the public that, regardless of the *Chronicle*'s allegations, publication of the Christmas number of *Wide World* would proceed as planned. Indeed, the magazine had already been prepared for export to its many markets in distant parts. Massingham responded with astonishment that Newnes would not 'honourably retire from an impossible position'. The *Chronicle* editor had previously resisted implicating the proprietor in the fraud. Politically, the liberal Newnes was a valued ally, a freethinker who, like Massingham, strongly believed in social reform. Now the editor suggested that De Rougemont had not acted alone:

We confess to thinking that he is sinned against as well as sinning. There is someone behind him who has, apparently, egged him on, and the prospects which opened before him have carried him much further than he himself had at first intended. In order to clear up therefore, one point which the editor of the 'Wide World' magazine will doubtless himself desire to set right with the public, we suggest to him that the original shorthand notes taken from de Rougemont's lips should be submitted to some impartial expert for comparison with the printed tale.

Massingham was now poised to inflict damage not only on the reputation of the imitation adventurer but the Newnes publishing empire. It demanded response. Newnes summoned Fitzgerald to the Reform Club. Later that day De Rougemont was witnessed entering the Southampton Street offices and during the evening a letter arrived at the *Chronicle* office addressed to Massingham. In this letter, Fitzgerald refused to back down. He stated that he was not interested in what De Rougemont had done while he was in 'civilization'. He reiterated his belief that, no matter how many years the man had spent among the Aborigines, the substance of what he said was true. The publication of the fourth instalment would go ahead, said Fitzgerald, as it had long been printed, but he would include a slip saying the story was currently being verified.

Massingham smelt blood. Newnes, he told his readers, had invested substantial money in the story and seemed to prefer to continue to circulate a falsehood than face pecuniary loss. The company was simply buying time in order to avoid loss on numbers already in preparation and 'afford this adventurer the opportunity of concocting some further childish lie'. He dismissed Fitzgerald's letter as 'so monstrous as that is difficult to discuss it as a piece of sane reasoning'.

No reference had been made, continued Massingham, to the shorthand notes requested by the *Chronicle*. And despite Newnes's claims to have no evidence beyond what the man had himself witnessed, Fitzgerald had once offered to provide a vocabulary of the tribe over which the 'cannibal king' had reigned. The offer had been withdrawn on grounds that it would damage the interests of Murphy's newly formed mining syndicate. That in itself, said Massingham, was a further fraud.

Unless 'de Rougemont' has found them in the British Museum or in the library of the Royal Geographical Society, he cannot produce on demand a score of genuine words. We further say that the syndicate is a myth, and we challenge Mr. Murphy to produce anyone who has been fool enough to put actual cash into the enterprise which Mr. Fitzgerald so triumphantly announced.

Massingham asserted his newspaper to have proved De Rougemont an impostor and stated that if Fitzgerald was 'an honourable man', he was bound to hand over the £500 reward offered. This, said the editor, would be invested for the benefit of Mrs Grien and her sons and daughters, whom the charlatan had abandoned.

Fitzgerald was not in London to read Massingham's response. He was already on his way to Switzerland, travelling at Newnes's command to verify the details of De Rougemont's background. If he sought to stem the flow of information now flooding across the border from the *Chronicle* correspondent, he was too late. The day of Fitzgerald's departure the *Chronicle* published an interview with Henri Louis Grin's one-time fiancée, Adèle. Now married to the local postmaster in Yverdon, the woman reported that Grin had paid her a surprise visit at the end of July. She had scarcely recognised him until they began talking about the past. She told him she was happy that things had turned out as they had and that she was married to a good husband. Grin had told her he was also a married man and had a wife and four children, the eldest daughter being fourteen years old. He also said he was 'fairly prosperous, and had several inventions on hand, one a diving machine'. Grin had stayed for half an hour but, Adèle told the correspondent, was all the time 'vague, mysterious and unsatisfactory'.

> He did not please me at all. It was all so indefinite. He did not know whether he was going back to England, America or Australia. When he went away I congratulated myself on not having become his wife. I am very glad now that my aunt was always opposed to the engagement at that period . . . To give you an instance of the vanity of the man, he talked with my aunt after leaving me and he said 'Adèle never moved a muscle of her face when she received me. She must have quite forgotten me.'

'Why, of course,' said my aunt, 'she is a happy married woman now.' What, did he think I was going to swoon into his arms on seeing him again?'

After Grin had left, Adèle had asked her aunt what she thought of him. 'He is a *blageur*,' she replied. A teasing joker, explained Adèle. She told the correspondent she had never received a letter during those twenty-five years, though his family had often received them, and she was told that in them he had asked after her.

The correspondent had also called at La Pelouse, the nearby home of Grin's mother and sister. The sister, Mme Rouille, confirmed that Henri wrote home often, particularly to his brother. There had been a lull in correspondence at one early point, she said, but 'nothing like twenty years'.

The *Chronicle* had also discovered that before departing London for his family reunion, 'De Rougemont' had ordered a local Swiss map from a Lausanne bookseller to guide him on his tour.

If we are not mistaken in the dates, all this happened after 'M. de Rougemont' had arranged with Mr. Fitzgerald, and the latter part of his stay in Switzerland was actually subsequent to the appearance of the first number of the fraudulent story. Did he tell any of those in the Canton Vaud, or at Zermatt, who know him as a long-absent member of the Grin family, that he had borrowed a false name, and that he was selling to a veracious journal a biography *pour rire*?

According to the *Chronicle*'s exhaustive enquiries, he had not. Now Fitzgerald himself tramped the hills and hamlets of Vaud in Massingham's reporter's footsteps. Several residents told him they had already spoken with a man from *The Wide World Magazine* only days before. It appeared the *Chronicle* correspondent had extracted his information by deceit. Dishearteningly, the locals also confirmed the inescapable fact that Henri Louis Grin was the very same man Fitzgerald had sent on holiday in July. While its extent remained uncertain, the evidence of De Rougemont's fraud was undeniable and conclusive. On Thursday 13 October, however, an undated handwritten letter without return address was received at the *Chronicle* office.

Dear Sirs,

I have seen the number of yesterday of The Daily Chronicle, and my master has shown to me my portrait in the Wide World magazine. I beg to ascertain you:

1. That I never called myself De Rougemont and never been amongst any savage people
2. That — as I am a quite private person — you ran a risque in publishing the disobligeant details relating to my life and the life of my father

Yours Truly,
H. L. Grin

Was this the 'childish lie' that Massingham had warned readers to expect upon De Rougemont's exposure? The garbled patois seemed to suggest a man of low station and education — perhaps one who had remained a servant rather than experienced a life of high adventure. Massingham rejected all such possibilities. Publishing a facsimile of the letter, he derided it as a 'silly trick' intended to frighten the *Chronicle* into caution. It was hardly believable, he said, that it could simply be an outsider's practical joke.

> The idea seems to be that H. L. Grin is ... a footman, and has always been so; and that the writer of this letter, and not the illustrious traveller, is the son of the unhappy *charretier* of Yverdon.

The letter, said Massingham, was a concoction worthy of the author of the De Rougemont tales. As the newspaper had already identified Grin as De Rougemont by 'dozens and scores of methods of identification' and traced his life nearly year by year, 'all rational doubt is ridiculous'.

Ridicule now abounded. Parodies and satires at De Rougemont's expense proliferated in the press. *Punch* magazine delighted in the publication of derogatory verse, shooting down the Frenchman's mock turtles and flying wombats before concluding:

> Though possibly your name is 'Green'
> Yet you yourself are not so.

Massingham also taunted Fitzgerald for journeying to Switzerland in the *Chronicle*'s wake. Why now, after the story had already exploded? Why hadn't the *Wide World* instead taken steps to verify De Rougemont's identity prior to publishing his autobiography, a procedure Massingham claimed would only have occupied forty-eight hours? Fitzgerald knew well that his author had been going to Switzerland in summer. Were they in communication during his time there? The final question remaining, Massingham said, was as to whether 'another hand' was responsible for working up the story.

As for De Rougemont — or Grin — himself, he had been observed by a Massingham informant on the morning of Friday 14 October leaving James Murphy's Bloomsbury address. The informant followed him to the Victoria railway station. Carrying a rug but no luggage, he had bought a ticket for Lausanne and departed on the 8.50 am train. With the protagonist out of the picture, Massingham finished by requesting that the man who wrote the letter in H. L. Grin's name visit the *Chronicle* office. 'We shall publish,' said the editor, 'anything he has to say.'

No such man came forward. A telegram was received, also lacking a return address, conveying the message 'letter follows'. The letter never arrived.

As famous murder cases attracted false confessions, so the impostor's fame was now inspiring imitations. Apparitions of the vanished Grin were miraculously materialising all over England. One man made the error of supposing that simply because his name was also Louis Grin, there could be no other — but he himself bore no resemblance to the Swiss itinerant. Some merely wished to claim acquaintance with Grin, perhaps hopeful their own rank might somehow be elevated by association. One man, signing himself Thomas Singleton, writing from the Union Bar in Birmingham, informed Massingham that he knew Grin well and that he was not the man identified with Louis De Rougemont. Several Thomas Singletons then wrote to deny they had written the letter. Meanwhile, there had been no word of the actual adventurer since his departure for Lausanne.

There was, however, a letter from his brother in Suchy, sent to the *Chronicle*'s correspondent. Complaining of the intrusion in his affairs, François Grin berated the reporter for having shown the picture of his brother to every one in the town without explanation or 'care for the consequences'.

No-one except myself can say anything about him. Ever since he left for Australia he wrote to no-one except myself . . . he was only some six or seven days here and saw no-one, spoke to no-one and yet you go about asking questions.

The pastor demanded that the correspondent never return. Undeterred, the *Chronicle*'s man set off on the final leg of his Alpine quest, making his way to Zermatt where the brothers Grin had enjoyed a brief holiday. By the time he reached his destination, it was season's end and every hotel would close the following day. The correspondent trudged his way to each, displaying the now tattered *Wide World* photograph to staff and checking registers. Finally, at the Hotel Zermatt, he found a souvenir of the adventurer's vacation by the Matterhorn. There in the arrivals book, dated 15 July 1898, was printed his name. It was not Henri Louis Grin. On the page alongside the pastor's signature was the name Louis De Rougemont. It was final proof of the inseparable identity of Grin and his alter ego. The hotel manager also recognised his photograph. It seemed the adventurer had left an indelible impression wherever he went.

Massingham pondered the possibility that Grin suffered from mental infirmity — 'a sort of megalomania with which the poor man is afflicted'. He noted that Grin had chosen names of noble French origin for two of his sons: De Rougemont for one and De Courcey for another. (Ironically, the aristocratic De Courcey family motto was *vincit omnia veritas*, or 'truth conquers all things'.) One correspondent had already suggested a phrenological study of De Rougemont's skull might prove advantageous.

Was Grin's reign as king of an Aboriginal tribe purely delusion? Could thirty, or even three, years spent among the Aboriginals of remote Australia be explained away simply as the wild imaginings of an afflicted mind? Massingham was unsure. Between arriving in Australia in 1875, undertaking pearling operations in the Torres Strait and courting his fiancée in Sydney there seemed to be limited opportunity for Grin to have made his home in the desert. While he had lived as a married man in Enmore there appeared to have been frequent occasions when Grin was away, but on the available evidence these periods were relatively brief. Massingham concluded that the 'possible intervals available for any sort of residence, even of the more commonplace character, among the aborigines are narrowed down to a question of a few months'. The editor pondered if Grin ever knew any more of Aboriginal society than 'that smattering of common knowledge which hundreds of Australians have picked up on the fringe of civilisation at the pearling stations and elsewhere along the coast'.

Now that the adventurer's true identity had been revealed, others were rapidly filling in the gaps between his departure from the Wellington dock and his arrival at Newnes's offices. A New Zealand crewman revealed that the man he knew not as Grin but 'Green' had staged a seance prior to the sailing of the SS *Mataura* and warned Captain Milward of 'forebodings of disaster gathered around his vessel'. The sailor also gave an account of a seance attempted by this fellow while aboard ship. In the absence of a table, a ouija board had been placed on the legs of one of the parties present. Green then rubbed the board vigorously with both hands. When anyone spoke, he would admonish them, saying, 'You must keep silent or you will bring the evil spirits.' On this occasion, however, no spirits of any type materialised, which he had ascribed to the presence of a 'heretic'. According to the New Zealander, a number of the crew would tease the man by whispering his name repeatedly when he was asleep, causing him to wake and seek in vain for the speaker. Another shipmate claimed he would sometimes enter a trance and speak in an incoherent tongue to a 'Professor Denton', whom he said had been dead for fifteen years.

Other stories of Grin's belief in the spirit world were also emerging. A *Chronicle* informant revealed that shortly after disembarking in London Grin had consulted a medium on the safety of trialling his deadly diving suit in the English Channel. The medium told him, 'If you do, the spirits will be with you.' Grin had then applied for a provisional patent for the apparatus, furnishing the name of Henri Louis Grin and Murphy's Bloomsbury address, but the trial had not gone ahead.

Another man told a *Chronicle* reporter that the superstitious traveller had called on him and enquired where spiritualist meetings might be held. He told him he had just arrived from New Zealand and had lost all his belongings, including some sort of diving apparatus, aboard another ship. He also spoke with him of his adventures in Australia with the Aboriginals. The traveller became a regular visitor and their conversation included pearling and diving, but not once did he offer the man his name. On one occasion, the man had lent his visitor a copy of a diving story by Arthur Conan Doyle that had appeared in the *Strand*, which he had never returned. On another, the traveller had asked how he might arrange to have his own story published.

> My answer was, why not try Newnes or Harmsworth or Pearson? I suggested those three large publishing houses. I advised him there was no use going around with a verbal story merely, that he should have some manuscript written out to show. He declared that he would set to work on those lines, and wouldn't I be good enough to help him in getting an introduction to one of those publishing houses in question. To this my reply was, 'Oh, I'll go down with you one afternoon when I'm not very busy, if you'll bring your manuscript along. The next time he called he said he had met an old Sydney friend, a Mr. Murphy, and I gathered that he was helping him. Then later I noticed the first instalment of the de Rougemont narrative in the 'Wide World' magazine. On his visit following that I observed to him, 'You've begun to tell your story: you're de Rougemont then?' He smiled. He was evidently well pleased with himself.

De Rougemont had also told the man of his visit to Switzerland and of being at the *Wide World* office almost daily, correcting proofs and approving illustrations. Even as the pressure of exposure in the *Chronicle* began to mount, De Rougemont had continued to visit, sometimes in the company of James Murphy. The Irishman would then dominate conversation. De Rougemont made light of the *Chronicle* attacks, but did observe that the *Wide World* illustrations 'rather exaggerated' his text. De Rougemont had carried on calling even after he was exposed by the *Chronicle* as Henri Grin. The last time the man had seen him was less than a week prior, when he and Murphy had visited together. Murphy had asked the man what he thought of the state of affairs.

> 'Well,' I answered, 'it's getting pretty hot isn't it?' 'Oh,' said Mr. Murphy, 'we have a complete answer, a complete answer to all these allegations'. 'Yes,' echoed de Rougemont, 'A complete answer – a complete answer.' My comment was emphatic: 'You had better get it out, for this thing is a long distance past an advertisement for

you.' As they were leaving de Rougemont turned back and cried to me, 'You understand, all engagements are cancelled!'

De Rougemont's cryptic farewell seemed a final concession of defeat. If there was a complete answer only he knew it. Yet even as the evidence mounted, *Wide World* refused to concede defeat. Fitzgerald returned from his futile hike through Switzerland to be confronted by the *Chronicle*'s victory dance and allegations of his personal complicity in duping the English public, as well as Massingham's claim on his £500. His indignant response was published in the *Chronicle* the day after his return. It was a revelation, Fitzgerald said, to see a great London newspaper freely devoting vast amounts of money and space in order to show the world what manner of man a *Wide World* contributor was. After chiding the *Chronicle* correspondent for falsely posing as one of his own magazine's reporters in Switzerland, Fitzgerald turned to the matter of the cash.

> Did any sane person suppose I staked my humble hundreds on the man with the same fervour I displayed in backing the STORY? I know and knew that men who have lived among the blacks are by no means uncommon in Australia, and, as Mr. Henneker Heaton will tell you, no one *who knows* could talk with de Rougemont for ten minutes without being satisfied that he had done so . . . No, I am afraid I must return an amused negative to your demand for my cheque until you disprove de Rougemont's residence among the blacks . . .

His money safe in his pocket, Fitzgerald signed off with a last dig at the *Chronicle*'s motives.

> One other undignified little hint that you give – that the story has been of great value to the 'Wide World' magazine. I don't deny it; but I ask: *Are we alone in this?*

Across the ocean, *The New York Times* suggested the *Chronicle* might also have had another object in debunking De Rougemont:

> We do not remember any case on this side of the water in which half as much trouble has been taken, half as much expense incurred, or

half as much space used in the accomplishment of this pious task as the London *Chronicle* has taken, incurred and used for the purpose of demonstrating that M. Louis De Rougemont is a humbug. If Sir George Newnes were not a dangerously successful invader of London's journalistic field, it is altogether probable De Rougemont's narrative would have been classed as 'interesting, if true'.

A further letter from Fitzgerald to the *Chronicle* the following day contained the belated testimony of Newnes's shorthand writer, R. J. Bremner Smith. Smith said De Rougemont's story was 'unquestionably his own', and that it had been pieced together from a series of interviews. The fullest details were obtained by 'persistent interrogation'. From the shorthand notes a preliminary transcript had been written, which De Rougemont had read. He had later supplied some further details. Throughout the whole proceeding, added Fitzgerald, no fact or incident was suggested to De Rougemont. The only alterations, he said, were those that 'every journalist knows must take place under such circumstances'.

Having saddled responsibility for the story firmly upon the author, *Wide World* now hastened the retreat. Foreign newspapers that had purchased the rights to the De Rougemont serial cancelled publication. The man himself had been found by the *Chronicle* correspondent, now lodging with his brother in Suchy. According to the reporter, Grin had only left the house once during his stay to visit the town cafes. There, in his local newspaper, the *Journal d'Yverdon*, under the heading '*Le Faux Robinson*', were the details of his dethronement as 'king of the cannibals'. There was no indication if or when the deposed monarch would return to England.

Other stories 'stranger than fiction' published in *Wide World* were now also falling under closer scrutiny. Newnes's *Tit-Bits* had several years earlier published a special issue on newspaper hoaxes, exposing as fraud a story on an Indian guru called Ram Pershad. Now it was revealed that the same story had also appeared as 'an absolutely true account' in *Wide World*. Another tale was detected to have been lifted verbatim from a popular teenage adventure novel published over four decades earlier. To Newnes's chagrin, 'spot the difference' was becoming a popular pastime in the clubs of Pall Mall.

The embarrassment had become intolerable. *The London Morning* gave the situation bluntly, calling on Newnes to 'shake himself free from the coils of a deception' before his reputation was irrevocably tarnished. On Friday 21 October, the newspaper tycoon released a public statement declaring he could no longer 'vouch for the truth of Louis De Rougemont's story currently appearing in a serialised form in *The Wide World Magazine*'. At Newnes's direction, a prominent advertisement also appeared in London newspapers, stating that the company could no longer publish 'The Adventures of Louis De Rougemont' as a true narrative. However, if Grin was not speaking the truth, said Newnes, he was 'the greatest master of fiction since Daniel Defoe'. The magazine would continue to publish the work as fiction and 'leave it to the public to believe as much or as little as they please'.

For Massingham's part that would be very little. In the eyes of the *Chronicle*, the man Heaton had only four months earlier declared the 'most interesting man in the world, or the biggest liar in the universe' was irrevocably confirmed as the latter.

23

Henri Louis Grin

The one duty we owe to history is to re-write it.
                    Oscar Wilde, *The Critic as Artist*, 1891

'On the borders of the lake of Neuchâtel, about the year 1847, there
lived a farmer of the name of Antoine Samuel Emanuel Grin and his
wife Jeanne.'

So began the true story of Henri Louis Grin. The *Chronicle* correspondent had discovered Antoine had not been a prosperous man of
business and never a shoe merchant. He had in fact been a notorious
drunk, who survived to buy his next schnapps by working occasionally
as a *charretier*, carting in the district. On 12 November 1847, in the
Gressy cottage, Jeanne Grin had borne a boy, her second. The young
Henri did not have his keen grasp of English punched into him by
English boarding-school boys but attended a basic *école primaire* in his
native canton. By the time Henri was ten years old, the family had
been forced by declining circumstances to move into the town of
Yverdon. Henri spent his days going to school and assisting his father in
his work as a town carter. He fell to quarrelling with his parents and
when he was sixteen left home. Henri's mother did not provide him
with a single centime, let alone 7000 francs, and nor did escapades
ensue in Cairo and Singapore. Moreover, according to those who knew
him, Henri did not know a single word of English prior to his departure.
After his son left, Antoine Grin disintegrated into alcoholic vagrancy,
sleeping behind bars in police cells before finally hanging himself in
1885 in the village of Vallorbe. For a year, nothing was heard of Henri.
His family had given him up for dead when word came in early 1863
that he had fallen in with the travelling company of a famous English
actress, Fanny Kemble.

It seemed scarcely believable. Young Henri, with no experience
of the wide world beyond the lakes, hills and hamlets of Canton

Vaud, was now set upon a course which would carry him to the opposite end of the earth.

His new employer was descended from two generations of theatre actors. Frances Anne Kemble had first appeared on stage at Covent Garden as a teenager, playing Juliet. Her father and uncle were among the most renowned Shakespearean actors of their time. Marriage to a slave-keeping American cotton heir fired Fanny Kemble's social conscience and when Henri Grin entered her service, she was a socially committed, well-connected theatrical star, travelling the world lecturing and presenting Shakespearean readings. Her second book, *Journal of a Residence on a Georgian Plantation*, calling for the abolition of slavery, had just been published in London. Fanny also had a passion for the picturesque heights of the Swiss Alps and, in the summer of 1863, undertook a climbing tour with her American daughter. While in Switzerland, her path would cross with that of the young Henri Grin, and she hired the extroverted youth to act as her 'courier', managing her various travel arrangements. In her service Grin first visited Italy, before briefly returning to Yverdon. Over the next six years their itinerary took in the United States, France and England. Henri was sometimes granted the privilege of watching Kemble perform from the stage wings. It was the boy adventurer's first brush with fame. According to those who knew her, Kemble found the young Grin amusing, teasing him and taking a personal interest, but in 1869 there was a falling out which, Henri later informed his friends, was due to the actress 'having a temper'.

The *Chronicle*'s research had revealed that at the age of twenty-two, cast again to the fates, Henri Grin had chanced upon a servant's position in London with a well-to-do Swiss family who owned a summer house in Yverdon. The master was a banker by the name of Mieville, and in his service Henri became commonly known as 'Louis'. The pale-faced young man with the high forehead was clever and astute but unpopular with the other staff. Mieville's housekeeper at Yverdon, Mme Henrieux, remembered Louis had a 'sneering, independent manner' and 'seemed to think he was a very important personage'. He also had a devouring passion for reading, 'filling his mind with books of travel, and nursing a secret taste for adventures'. While in the service of the family, the *Chronicle* reported, Grin had suffered a severe accident by falling from a window, injuring his skull.

He was long ill, and it appears to be the opinion of some of those who knew him before and after that mishap that the accident to some extent affected his brain.

Grin accompanied the banker on his many trips abroad. Mieville found him to be 'exceedingly useful' but did not like the young man's overbearing nature, complaining that it was 'Louis who [was] the master and I the servant'. He found Grin's demeanour toward other underlings such as hotel servants and customs staff particularly offensive. Once when crossing the French border at Pontarlier, Grin's insolence to the border officers resulted in their searching his baggage to the bottom, where they discovered several new gold Swiss watches. Grin's audacity cost him 700 francs and Mieville's trust. Another incident brought him under suspicion of theft again, and in 1873, Mieville released Grin from his service. He returned to the family home in Yverdon and considered his options. With time on his hands, the romance with the young local girl Adèle developed. They soon became engaged but the girl's aunt, wary of Grin's wandering ways, stepped in to prevent the marriage.

Grin was not destined to make happy home in the green hills of Vaud. The *Chronicle* observed that despite his misdemeanours in the Mievilles' service and his brain-affecting fall, Louis had managed to continue his career in domestic service, somehow maintaining 'so creditable a record that he kept in the higher branches of the profession'. The paper discovered that a friend in London had soon heard Henri was seeking a new position and introduced him to the family of Sir William Robinson.

Robinson, whose brother Hercules was the incumbent Governor of New South Wales, was soon to depart England to take up the position of Governor of the Colony of West Australia. He had previously served the Empire in its remotest parts. At twenty-eight he had been appointed president of the tiny West Indian isle of Monserrat and four years later received a posting to the Falkland Islands, a collection of frozen rocks off Patagonia described by Robinson himself as 'the fag end of the world'. Now he was being despatched to the most isolated colony in the Antipodes. Henri Grin made his way to London and was appointed butler to Lady Robinson. He would not return to Switzerland for twenty-four years.

In December 1874, the twenty-eight-year-old Grin travelled in the retinue of the new governor on the SS *Pera* via Ceylon to Albany, Western Australia. The hundred-metre-long steamer, once the pride of the Peninsular & Oriental Line fleet, was the largest and most luxurious ship the sea-seasoned Grin had ever been aboard. The passage was completed by leisurely mail boat to Fremantle. Nothing he had experienced in his travels had prepared him for the height of Perth summer. The dry air tore at his throat and sweat rendered his butler's garb leaden as he tended to Lady Robinson on an endless round of civic receptions. The tiny Swan River settlement numbered only 5000, less than Grin's native Yverdon, but it seemed all had turned out to celebrate the new governor's arrival and have their glass filled by his wife's servant. Eventually arrangements were made to relocate Robinson and his company to the breeze-tempered comfort of the Governor's summer residence on Rottnest Island.

Here Grin had his first encounter with Australia's native peoples. For thirty-five years the island had served as a prison for Aboriginals. Their forced labour had built the very means of their incarceration. They had erected the cells; constructed the walls that held back the imprisoning sea and the lighthouse that guided their jailers' boats; heaved and dragged the quarried stone and jarrah wood to build the fine colonial residence that now sheltered Grin. His own term of exile was a far lighter burden. Heeding Lady Robinson's call left ample time to study his surrounds and the local inhabitants. The Governor read lessons to the unfortunate prisoners at the little stone church on Sundays and much of the rest of the week was devoted to recreations — shooting Rottnest snipe, fishing, and hunting wallaby driven out by setting the scrub alight. A bathing box provided modesty to swimmers at the summerhouse jetty. But Grin was dissatisfied; he had not travelled 12,000 miles to idle on a prison isle amid defeated natives. He only escaped when, after summer's worst had passed, the Governor's company returned to the mainland.

The neo-gothic facade of Government House in Perth's main street, replete with high-capped turrets, was reminiscent of another prison — the Tower of London. Here Grin resentfully discharged his duties and shunned his domestic colleagues. According to the *Chronicle*, Lady Robinson thought her butler 'very conceited and somewhat troublesome'. Life at Government House offered Grin the opportunity of observing the colony's men of influence first hand. Robinson was a skilled public speaker and musician who liked to exercise his social talents. To the banquet hall at St Georges Terrace came a stream of guests, including the explorer John Forrest. Robinson's predecessor Governor Weld had been an enthusiastic patron of exploration in the colony, and Forrest his favoured expedition leader. Only a few months prior to Robinson's arrival, Forrest had successfully completed a courageous Central Australian crossing. On his return to Perth he was met with a hero's welcome. Now he was a regular at Robinson's table and Henri Grin hungrily devoured the explorer's tales of survival and discovery.

Forrest's first foray into the interior had been a wild-goose chase inspired by long-circulating rumours that a party of white men travelling from the east had been killed by Aboriginal people on the shores of a salt lake. After a local Aboriginal man claimed to have found human bones, speculation arose they may have been the last vestige of Leichhardt and his party. The twenty-two-year-old surveyor Forrest embarked on a 2000-mile murder investigation only to discover they were the remains of horses from an earlier expedition.

Next followed a successful trek in the footsteps of Eyre around the Great Australian Bight to Adelaide, his hardships on horseback eased by a following schooner, the *Adur*, laden with supplies. Forrest's ego was dented when he returned to discover that some of his fellows considered taking a boat along for the ride to be cheating. He proposed a new expedition, plotting a virgin course from the west coast near Geraldton across the bare interior.

In March 1874, aided only by horses, Forrest's party set out. Their route would take them across the tracks of Ernest Giles's ill-fated meanderings of the previous year. After their own deathly struggle with thirst and a diet consisting near solely of damper, the party finally met with the Overland Telegraph at Peake Station. Forrest's name was made. In December 1874, he made his triumphant return to Perth borne in a horsedrawn carriage along a route jammed with well-wishers. A banquet and ball were thrown in the expedition party's honour at the Town Hall and the legislature voted Forrest an honorarium of £500.

Still, the explorer's reports of desolate, waterless landscapes yielded little hope for settlement of the colony's interior regions. Without further reason to expend funds, it was clear the era of exploration on the continent's last frontier would soon come to a close. Yet even now, while Forrest's exploits fired Henri Grin's imagination at Government House, Ernest Giles was on the edge of the Nullarbor, preparing a final assault on the territory that had nearly killed him and swallowed up Gibson. At Fowlers Bay in South Australia, Giles mustered camels and horses to cross the desert country from east to west.

By the time Giles set out in May, Henri Grin's five-month tenure at Government House was coming to an end. Grin had spent his spare hours in Fremantle, making acquaintance with pearling crews preparing to voyage to the northern coast. The notion appealed to Henri, who had never had it in mind to remain a butler longer than necessary. Acting the part of the lowly servant had transported him to the new world – now was time to realise the new man. Inland from Perth, pastoral land fast dissolved into desert, but the open sea offered adventure and, if the pearlers' wealth of stories were to be believed, the chance of fortune.

Pearls, the gold of the deep, had been known to the Aboriginals of the north-west coast for millennia, and were discovered by the *Beagle* in 1839. In Grin's day, a single white shining sphere sold in London for £260, the equivalent of a 64 oz gold nugget. In 1873 a pearl valued at £2500 had been brought up at Nickel Bay. Their pursuit was fraught with danger: frequent cyclones harried the Dampier Archipelago and destroyed fleets, scurvy abounded, shark attacks were common. The unmarked graves of pearlers and divers dotted the coast, but the perils were fast forgotten when a new strike was made and an oyster-rich reef offered up its rewards. In seven years the number of pearl luggers and boats working the north-west coast had multiplied more than ten times.

Foregoing his disdain for underlings, Grin struck up a liaison with an attractive young housemaid at Government House. The girl was already engaged to a fifty-year-old English eccentric, James Coulson, who had also travelled out to the colony on the SS *Pera* in the Governor's service. Grin befriended Coulson and, after the betrothed couple had married, resigned his position and followed in their wake. So well did he ingratiate himself with the newlyweds that the decision was made for the three to lodge together at a smart boarding house run by a Mrs Seubert in Fremantle. The landlady's husband had been a pearler in the north-west and the house was now a popular resort for holidaying pearlers and visiting ships' captains.

Perth's *Daily News* later published a letter received from a fellow boarder who recalled Grien, Coulson and his wife well:

> The lady was a brilliant conversationalist, and could talk on almost any subject, and although the old gentleman himself [Coulson] did not perceive it, all the other boarders were not slow to discern relations between her and Grin were far too lover-like to be merely platonic. She . . . gave herself out as Grin's cousin, though she was as unmistakably English as he was unmistakably foreign.[25]

Grin's relationship with other residents was stormy, and a fight with a pearler by the name of John Finnerty ended up in court. A Captain Embleton, who had been present at the scene but was too intoxicated to recall what had happened, nevertheless swore in court that Finnerty had committed an unprovoked assault on Grin. Finnerty was fined five shillings. (He would later give Coolgardie its name, become the town's warden and employ the retired Ernest Giles as his clerk.) A renowned raconteur, Finnerty would one day boast that during his stay in the boarding house, Grin had filched some of his best tales of the far north for use in creating Louis De Rougemont.

Having stolen Coulson's wife's heart, Grin now set about relieving him of his money. He convinced Coulson there were riches to be made in fitting out a vessel for pearling and bêche-de-mer fishing and running it north. Coulson agreed to put up the money for the boat, and Grin purchased an eleven-ton cutter from Henry Dixon of Fremantle. It was christened *Ada* but was derisively known on the waterfront as *The Sudden Jerk*. Designed for government work in the cleaning of buoys, the unlikely vessel was high at each end and low in the middle. The dupe Coulson funded the fitting out of the boat as a pearler and Grin charmed locals into providing stores on credit. In order to register the boat, Grin became naturalised as a British citizen, adapting his surname to 'Grien' in the process. So successful was he in conning Coulson that, in June 1875, Henri Grien was duly listed as the ship's master. Joining he and Coulson for the *Ada*'s maiden voyage to Broome were eight Aboriginals recently liberated from Rottnest Island and a young man named Stewart. The use of Aboriginal convicts' labour for the purposes of pearling had previously triggered the moral indignation of *The West Australian Times*. 'By what law,' the *Times* editor had written, 'can the government justify the shipping of native prisoners for private employment which is in effect treating them as slaves?' It fell on deaf ears — few other settlers cared for the fate of these men.

Upon arrival of the *Ada* in the north-west, Stewart died of unknown causes. Coulson soon returned alone, having had his fill of Grien and his pearling scheme. He collected his wife from Seubert's seaside lair and together they sailed for England. Henri Grien was now an adventurer of independent means and the *Ada* could take him wherever he chose — but without Coulson's cash, life was hard. Grien's Aboriginal crew jumped ship at the first opportunity. For twelve months he ran the boat profitlessly up and down the north-west coast, inexperience and poverty strangling his every effort. Yet 1875 and 1876 were souvenir years for pearlers: theirs was the single most lucrative industry in the colony. From Broome up north through the Timor Sea and Torres Strait, Australian and Dutch pearlers crewed by a seemingly inexhaustible supply of Malay and Aboriginal divers were plundering riches from the ocean floor. In a boom market, Grien was bust. All around him the men he had met at Seubert's and on the docks at Fremantle were doing a roaring trade. In the remote seas, rogue pearlers flourished. 'Blackbirding', the kidnapping and enslaving of Aboriginals as divers, had become rife along the Dampier Peninsula. The practice had been outlawed by the colonial legislature, but the closest police were 350 nautical miles south of Broome at Roebourne — and they didn't have a boat.

Many of the captive divers were literally worked to death. 'No dark man's life is valued,' said one observer, 'but the utmost amount of diving must be sucked out of a man, kill or not. For who knows who will be his owner next season . . . these poor creatures are forced to dive from morn to eve irrespective of the depth of the water caused by the rise and fall of the tide.'[26] Even those Aboriginals who joined the oyster hunt voluntarily were paid less than a pittance — their reward being a few ragged items of clothing, tea and tobacco in place of cash. The desperate Grien saw an opening. In June that year, he recruited two white men from Broome, Henry Hickey and John Riley, and entered business. *The Sunday Times* in Perth later recalled the complete story of their violent venture. Four Aboriginal men — Yaningbiddy, Perala (alias Jacky-Jacky), Womengar (alias Tommy) and one other — were taken by force before 'they were in turn forced to assist in the kidnapping of natives from Beagle Bay and King's Sound'.[27] Once they were imprisoned by sea aboard the *Ada*, they were set to work by Grien and his partners as pearl divers and shellers.

Two months later Henry Hickey arrived alone at Roebourne. The *Ada* was nowhere in sight. He had sailed from King's Sound aboard another vessel, the *Baningarra*. Hickey visited the Roebourne police station and volunteered a statement, which was subsequently produced in the Perth Criminal Court:

> I have just returned from a trip to King's Sound. About the middle of August last I was on board the *Ada* cutter, on board of which there were Louis Grien, John Riley and myself. There were also on board four natives who had come to us willingly at King's Sound. Being short of meat we started for the Lacepede Islands, to procure turtle. When about three miles off shore and 30 miles this side of King's Sound the natives, who remained in the hold from the time we started, showed a hostile appearance and attacked any of us who had occasion to go into the hold with spears, firewood or anything they could get hold of. We were forced to go into the hold for flour and water. I opened a sliding door from the cabin into the hold for that purpose, and was in the act of passing through the door when one of the natives struck me across the chest with a *dowak* [throwing stick], and the other natives began to throw wood at me. A gun was lying on a hose close to the door. I picked it up and fired it into the hold with the intention of scaring the natives.

Half an hour later, he said, he had found one of the Aboriginals lying dead from a shot in the neck. Together with Grien and Riley he had brought the body up on deck, attached weights to it and thrown it overboard. All this had occurred, said Hickey, around seven or eight o'clock in the morning. He told the police that one of the remaining Aboriginal men had then gone ashore at the Lacepede Islands, another was left in Beagle Bay and the third had made the journey with Hickey aboard the *Baningarra* and was now in Roebourne's port, Port Walcott.

The Sunday Times said that when the police fetched this man from the *Baningarra* for questioning, a different scenario emerged. Police in Broome were despatched to locate the other Aboriginal men present aboard the *Ada* and they were brought to give evidence in the Roebourne courthouse. The testimony of one, Yaningbiddy, further implicated Henri Grien.

Yaningbiddy told the court he had been on board the *Ada* at King's Sound when six local Aboriginals, including one old man, had been lured aboard with the promise of food. After the white men had given them something to eat, Hickey had come to him and another Aboriginal man known as Jacky-Jacky and said, 'You must help us to put these natives down the hold.' They had then taken one man each and forced them into the hold. The white men secured the hatches.

A second cutter, the *Anne*, was with them, crewed by two other white men, Bill and Alick. The two boats went west to another place where they saw more local Aboriginals on the shore. Grien, Riley, Alick and Jacky-Jacky had then gone ashore and brought a lot of these men to the *Anne*. Three came on board the *Ada* and were forced into the hold. All the others became frightened and leapt from the *Anne* to swim ashore. Both boats continued west. Yanningbiddy's version of how the shooting had taken place was transcribed by the court:

> When sailing along early one morning, Grien was near the hatches aft, Riley and Hickey were in the cabin, myself and the boy Tommy were by the mast. Hickey put his head up the companion way and said to Grien who was on deck: 'You open the hatches Grien. You makem light, me see him well. It is too dark below, I can't see.' Hickey then went below.
>
> Grien opened the hatches and I heard the gun fired. I saw smoke coming out of the cabin and also out of the hatchway. Hickey came on deck, when Grien said to him: 'You have hit him hard. You have killed him dead.' Hickey said nothing. I went to the hatches and saw the legs and part of the body of a native. I saw blood on the legs and breast, but I could not see the upper part of the body. Immediately after, Hickey came on deck after firing the gun in the cabin. Grien put the hatches on again immediately. The natives in the hold cried a good deal.

Yaningbiddy told how some of the men were then exchanged between the *Anne* and the *Ada* and the old man put ashore. Both boats then went to the Lacepede Islands, and while they were there the *Baningarra* arrived with more Aboriginals on board. Hickey went on board the *Baningarra* and took four Aboriginals with him. The boat then sailed for Port Walcott. Later, *The Sunday Times* said, Grien had taken the *Ada* in the same direction but en route met another boat called the *Aurora* just north of Roebourne at the mouth of the Yule River. The *Aurora*'s captain, a man with the unlikely name of Sam Sustenance, gave Henri Grien a letter notifying that Hickey had been arrested and charged with wilful murder. Grien became very frightened, took some provisions from the *Aurora* and put the *Ada* about, sailing away in the opposite direction.

After hearing Yaningbiddy's evidence the police immediately issued an arrest warrant for Henri Grien and John Riley, charging them with aiding and abetting Hickey's murder of the Aboriginal. The hunt for Grien and Riley was half-hearted and short-lived. The land-bound police could do little to prevent their quarry's escape in the *Ada*. Meanwhile Hickey was committed to trial in Perth, found guilty of manslaughter and sentenced to five years' hard labour.

Grien and his remaining crew made for the Timor Sea, hoping to elude capture and resurrect their pearling fortunes. They made shore at Lacrosse Island at the mouth of Cambridge Gulf, apparently encountering members of an Aboriginal tribe there before continuing east to the Arafura Sea.

The *Ada* was officially listed as missing in Roebourne in February 1877, but only two months later, three men arrived on foot at Cooktown on the opposite side of the continent. They told slack-jawed locals they had landed a small craft on the other side of the Cape York Peninsula at the mouth of the Mitchell River and simply walked the 150 miles through crocodile-infested mangroves, river and rainforest. A resident, Thomas Williams, later told a Melbourne *Argus* reporter that one glance at their shiny new boots had sufficed to discredit the tale. Three days later the Cooktown pilot boat went to the assistance of a cutter drifting with a single sailor aboard fifteen miles away at Cape Bedford. It was the *Ada*, and the man was Henri Grien. He was brought to Cooktown, where he gave police a false name and reported that the rest of his crew had been landed at the Kennedy River in Princess Charlotte Bay, 160 miles north of Cooktown. They had gone to seek water but when they had not returned he had supposed them killed by blacks. He had been windbound in those waters for six weeks, during which time he only narrowly averted an attack by local tribespeople, who came aboard and danced on deck while he hid in the locked hold. Finally winds had blown up and he had fled alone down the coast. Grien offered no explanation of where the *Ada* had been before entering Princess Charlotte Bay. The police were sceptical. It seemed obvious that the three men in mudless boots who had walked into town were the *Ada*'s crew and that, for a reason they did not wish to disclose, they had gone ashore a few miles out of Cooktown and come in with a false report. Grien denied the men were his crew, but despite their suspicions, the police could find no grounds for arrest and let him go.

Grien knew it was only a matter of time before his craft was identified and its sordid history known. He kept the *Ada* moored at Cooktown only as long as it took to obtain new crew. Three locals were induced to join him and provisions acquired. They sailed for the Kennedy River, purportedly to search for the men Grien had told the police had gone ashore there. Neither Grien's vessel nor his crew were heard of again in Cooktown, and were thought to have been lost at sea.

In his flight from the West Australian authorities, Grien was fast learning the art of elusion. Sydney's *Daily Telegraph* later reported he had made his way to Port Douglas and dispensed with *The Sudden Jerk*, the ungainly buoy-cleaner *Ada* that had survived the thousands of nautical miles from Fremantle. He had no need to do so. Unbeknown to Grien, the police had now abandoned their search for the suspected killers after fruitlessly combing the north-west coast on horseback.

In Cooktown, Grien had observed the human traffic flowing back and forth to the goldfields on the Normanby and Palmer rivers. The rush on the alluvial fields of the Palmer, the richest ever found in Queensland, was past its peak, yet still diggers flooded in from the south. Cooktown and Port Douglas were awash with the tents of men whose fortunes would never be made. Grien had not liked what he had seen of the state of miners returning from the Palmer, and few seemed actually to possess gold. On the fields and in the towns, sickness and crime were endemic. One Danish miner reported 'all the loafers, pickpockets and card-sharpers seemed to have trooped in from Brisbane, Sydney and Melbourne'. Dysentery was an equal scourge. In Cooktown, he observed 'men lying helpless, writhing with pain on the ground, some of them bellowing out for pity or mercy'.[28] Doctors were scarce and their mercy only came 'cash down'. This shortage of medical facilities inspired Grien to explore a new career as a miner's doctor on the Palmer fields. The fact that he had no training beyond tending to his own fishing wounds aboard the *Ada* seemed no deterrent. Grien saw Australia as a land where anything might be possible, one which seemed to invite and even reward self-invention. But the resurrection of men halfway through death's door proved to be beyond even his powers.

According to local miners, Grien had then returned to Port Douglas, obtained a rusting camera and set up as a photographer, taking shots of diggers with their strikes, but the dwindling supply of gold made work difficult to find. Without further prospects on land, Grien scoured the port for a ticket out, secured a position as cook on a pearl lugger and took to sea once more. It was the very job Louis De Rougemont had assumed aboard the *Veielland* under the captaincy of Peter Jensen, before disaster and shipwreck led to his terrible isolation in the Sea of Timor.

24

Perpetual Motion

A prophet has no honour in his own country.

John 4:44

WHEN HENRI GRIEN surfaced again a year later it was not on the shores of a skerrick of semi-submerged sand, and the fearless terrier Bruno was nowhere to be seen. Instead, Grien washed up penniless in Australia's most populous city. His clockwise circumnavigation of the continent had wound up in Sydney, with Swiss precision, in time for the biggest event ever staged in the colonies: the International Exhibition of 1879, showcase for the industrialised world's achievements. On the streets of Sydney the excitement was palpable.

In the Botanical Gardens, builders working through the night by the light of imported electric lamps had erected the Garden Palace, a stupendous edifice of towers, turrets and arches culminating in a huge glass dome over 300 feet in diameter. Inside, exhibits from around the globe spread out over eight and a half acres. A steam tram service was installed to carry the flood of visitors from Circular Quay. Over the next eight months, one million people from the colonies and beyond — four times Sydney's population — would come to ogle everything from the American elevator to German cuckoo clocks; ice-making machines to opossum rugs. Over 9000 exhibits were on display from twenty-one countries. They radiated out from a fountain surmounted by a huge bronze statue of Queen Victoria even more grandiose than the giant portrait De Rougemont would claim to have drawn to impress his Aboriginal hosts in the Cambridge Gulf. Fellow Exhibition workers would later report that Grien had wangled a job at the Swiss stand, plying his smooth tongue and rich accent to advantage as he touted the wonders of the Swiss watch. It was a business he knew well; one that owed him 700 francs.

Nearly twenty years later, Grien's further adventures in Sydney became the focus of an ongoing police investigation. Sydney's *Evening News* reported that Constables Wilson and Bannan were removed from the case and a notorious detective called Jules Rochaix was assigned to trace Grien's movements from his arrival in 1879.[29] The French-born Rochaix was one of only fourteen elite detectives in the New South Wales force. He had developed a reputation for infiltrating immigrant circles and bringing in suspected anarchists, radicals, labour agitators and other anti-establishment types. Roundly despised by his fellow Europeans, Rochaix nevertheless successfully worked his contacts to flush out Grien's past. Setting the detective on the Swiss itinerant's scent was using a sledgehammer to crack a walnut. Rochaix set to the task with zeal. One man who proved particularly useful to the detective was Adolphe Guymuller, a Swiss national who ran a cafe called Adolphe's in Hunter Street.

Rochaix's questioning established that, in his free time, Grien had gravitated to the Giuliani Brothers wine shop opposite the Theatre Royal in King Street, a cosmopolitan haunt frequented by Swiss, Italians, French and Germans. There Grien had befriended Guymuller, then a chef at the nearby Weber's Post Office Hotel, who displayed a taste for Grien's stock of tales. Grien told him that immediately prior to coming to Sydney he had been aboard a pearl sheller in the Torres Strait and had there contracted fever and ague. Before that time, he said, his own vessel had been lost, consigning him to the depths of poverty. When the closure of the International Exhibition threatened to return him to that state, Grien visited Guymuller at his hotel and begged employment in his kitchen. The chef swallowed Grien's sob story and installed him as kitchen hand.

The fearless adventurer was now a common drudge. It could not last. After two weeks, Grien complained that while he could suffer the tropics, the heat of the kitchen was too much for him. He quit the hotel, only to return several weeks later with a proposition for Guymuller. Grien told him he had obtained an undertaking from a Sydney firm to fit out a pearling expedition to the Torres Strait, provided he could find five men willing to join him as crew. Each of the members of the party, with the exception of Grien, was to contribute £50 to the venture. Guymuller was tempted to join Grien, but his loyal friends at the wine shop dissuaded him and knocked

back the offer themselves. Grien told them they would regret their
decision as an 'expedition under his leadership was sure to make a
fortune'. Only one, a Swiss man called Ruchty who had worked at
the Exhibition in an oyster saloon, agreed to take part. On the waterfront Grien found four Englishmen willing to make up the balance.
Prior to their departure, Guymuller was invited by Grien to inspect
the vessel that would carry them north. He accompanied him to
Woolloomooloo where Grien pointed out a cut-down barque.
Guymuller was impressed and commented that the boat looked very
strong. 'Not at all,' replied Grien with a smile, 'she will break her
back on the first reef we strike.' The chef was uncertain whether he
was joking or not.

The vessel sailed shortly after. Several months later, a regretful
Ruchty slunk into Giuliani's wine bar, decidedly the worse for wear.
Asked about the expedition, he related how the barque had been
wrecked on a reef in the Gulf of Carpentaria, and the entire party had
lost everything. Grien and crew had floated about in lifeboats for two
days without food and water before being picked up. Grien's prophecy
had proven correct. Ruchty said the boat had 'the choicest assortment
of ruffians on board that he had ever met or heard of'. After clearing
Sydney Harbour heads, the men had taken to quarrelling among
themselves. They were all armed and revolvers had been drawn on the
slightest provocation, pot shots being taken at other crew members for
recreation. Terrified, he and Grien had slept in an aft cabin, too afraid
to venture on deck. The cabin door was kept locked and they 'always
had a revolver handy and slept with one eye open'. At night the other
men 'blazed away at each other', but their marksmanship was as 'wide
as their moral code'.

A few days after Ruchty's return, Grien reappeared at Giuliani's,
boatless, battered and broke, but not broken. He obtained new work
soliciting orders for photographic enlargements and within weeks was
enthusing to his fellow Europeans over a revolutionary new photographic enamelling process he had discovered. There was money in it,
he assured them; all that was required was a little extra capital to take
him to France to perfect his invention. Grien's audience, now inured
to his get-poor-quick schemes, knew it was unlikely that investors
would ever see him — or their money — again.

Adolphe Guymuller told Detective Rochaix that after this Grien had seemed to 'steady down', though Guymuller had then lost contact with him for a period of some ten years.

Between 1880 and 1888 there had been sporadic sightings from a variety of tropical locales. Some said Grien had been set adrift in the Solomon Islands. Others claimed that he had been in Queensland. Nat Gould, a popular novelist, would later claim his wife remembered Grien 'blackbirding' on schooners off Brisbane, capturing local people to work on sugar plantations.[30] Yet another report said Grien had turned up in New Caledonia in April 1881 after being marooned on a South Sea island, and had taken up work for a short time for a German called Knoblaugh who ran a store on the Rue de l'Alma in Noumea. Might there have been a connection between the stories? It was like trying to construct a jigsaw which had not too few, but too many, pieces. How many of the reports might simply have been concocted by the storyteller himself before being transformed by time into 'fact'? Or had Grien truly been shipwrecked, perhaps on one of the schooners used for blackbirding around the Pacific?

Whether he had been pearling, marooned or simply wandering the country's backblocks, Grien returned to Sydney in time to walk down the aisle with fancy-goods salesgirl Elizabeth Ravenscroft in Newtown in 1883. For a time he appeared to live the life of the happily married man in inner-suburban Sydney, supporting his ever-growing family by working as a photographic canvasser, enameller and colourist. When earnings from Henri's photographic endeavours became insufficient to support the brood, he turned to waiting tables at cafes in Newtown, an area cluttered with cheap boarding houses and bare brick residences 'utterly unrelieved by tree and grass'.[31] The Grien family changed address within the same district five times in seven years. Grien found escape from the dream-destroying suburban desert by undertaking frequent stints at syndicate share selling, surveying exhausted Queensland mines, working defunct claims and combing the New South Wales countryside for photographic work, but between 1883 and 1890 there still remained unexplained absences, mysterious lacunae of weeks and months when it was feasible Grien may have been further afield. Stationhands at Newry Station south of the Cambridge Gulf recognised Grien's photograph in Sydney's *Daily Telegraph* and reported that he had worked there for a time as a cook. They remembered Grien to have spent much of his spare time reading and re-reading two books. The first was *The Adventures of Telemachus*, a famous seventeenth-century text by François Fenelon based on the imaginary adventures of Odysseus's son Telemachus while searching for his father. The second was *La Fontaine's Fables*, a childhood classic, comprising a series of witty and deceptively simple moral parables involving animals. Both were published in their original French.

Grien was home often enough to father, if not foster, more children. By the time he was forty-six years old, Henri had four children below the age of ten and no stable job. A picture-frame maker who employed him on occasion after 1890 told *The Daily Telegraph* he was 'weird, eccentric and marvellous'. Grien had often related his plans to visit unexplored portions of Australia and to get up syndicates to work old goldmines, in which he was convinced there were still fortunes to be found. The framer said Grien spoke fluent English and could also converse in French, German and 'Swiss', but claimed to be Swedish. 'The man was all life,' he said, 'and full of vigour.'

The *Telegraph* would later report that Grien had also been identified as the proprietor of a cafe in the Blue Mountains, west of Sydney. Locals in the town of Lawson recognised Grien from the published photos of De Rougemont. They claimed he had run the Lawson Coffee Palace for a time in 1892, gaining a large circle of acquaintances and driving a thriving business. Eventually, they said, Grien had 'quietly disappeared'.

A woman who had encountered Grien at the Gresham Hotel in Brisbane in 1895 described him as a busybody who 'was continually boring us with his spiritualistic experiences, and who never returned the photo I gave him to enlarge'. *The Argus* reported that the woman had recently run into Grien in the *Wide World* offices and recognised him immediately. He had also borrowed from her, and never returned, a book on travel in the South Sea Islands.

By the early nineties, Henri had established a reputation in Sydney for his explorations of the world beyond. A city fortune teller recalled Grien had been recommended to her by one of her clients when she was first starting out in the trade. He had recognised her as a fellow medium and it was on his advice she had successfully set up consulting offices. She described Grien as a man of fifty years of age, with dark hair and whiskers beginning to show the silver, six foot in height and of spare build. The fortune teller told *The Daily Telegraph* that when

Grien spoke he was usually 'under the influence' — in a state of self-hypnosis. He would fall into a trance and talk for hours on end. He was a plain man as far as looks went, she said, but there was something 'magnetic and fascinating' about his voice. The *Telegraph* reported:

> He used to get himself into an hypnotic condition, and do all manner of strange things ... He attended her seance meetings regularly, and when under this mysterious influence would tell her strange things about himself, his adventures with Australian blacks, and of many other curious things. He told her of the treasures of unlimited gold that he knew where to find, and was particularly anxious for the fortune-teller to get up a syndicate to send him in search of it ... He told her that people would not believe him when he told them of these things, but he knew from the way her seances were attended that many people had faith in her, and therefore considered she would be the most likely person to bring the scheme to a successful head.

While in his 'extraordinary state', Grien also showed an uncanny ability to play piano, though he declared that he did not normally know one note from another. The most amusing thing, said the fortune teller, was Grien's mimicry of Australian fauna. One evening in her private house, he suddenly 'got under the influence' and 'getting down on his hands and knees, jumped like a kangaroo over a little table that stood in the room'. The next moment, said the fortune teller, the influence left him and he did not know what he had done. He had once repaired a clock in the same state and could also perform acrobatic feats. She described Grien as 'invariably hard-up', though 'an excellent painter of portraits'. He told her he worked as a water-colour artist, and did all of his work in a trance. She said he would often walk to her house in the suburbs and upon arrival 'fall to on the victuals like a famished mortal'.

The medium expressed a strong opinion that Grien had been lost in the bush and spent time among Aboriginal tribespeople, but said the assertion that he had spent thirty years there was absurd. He had led her to believe he had spent three years in their company and claimed to have been their king. During that period, she said, he had disappeared from Sydney 'as completely as if the earth had swallowed him' and when next she saw him he was sunburnt and 'looked like a tramp'. When he returned to her house he would sometimes forget himself at meal times and lift his food to his mouth with his hands, before catching himself and looking ashamed, but the strongest proof of his residence among Aboriginals was 'the fact he disliked walking about in boots', and would go about the house with feet 'untrammelled with boots or socks'. His feet, she said, were covered in corns, indicating he had been accustomed to going barefoot.

Grien had also told her he was a Swede, that he had a wife and 'two or three' children and that his home life was unhappy. It was impossible, she thought, for Grien to have spent a very extended time among distant tribes, as he professed to know quite a number of Sydney people, and used to rattle off biographical sketches about them that demonstrated his many years' experience in the city.

Ultimately, though, all that experience had come to nothing. While his family starved, Grien fed off delusions of riches and the fortune teller's table. It was at this time that Murphy's land scheme at Como was launched, providing some temporary relief from poverty, but disaster was never distant.

In late 1896, Henri became involved in the design of a revolutionary new diving suit with two brothers called M'Quellan. The invention would allow divers to reach greater depths than previously possible and Grien convinced several insurance brokers of its potential in salvaging operations. The design was duly patented and the brass suit manufactured, but at its first trial in front of press and insurance company representatives in Sydney Harbour the Swedish diver demonstrating its use was brought up dead. Initial reports maintained that the costume was too heavy, causing the diver to fall over when he hit bottom, and as a result, the suit had leaked. *The Daily Telegraph* reported that Grien and the M'Quellan brothers had designed 'a very fine death trap'. The coroner disagreed, finding that the Swede's death was coincidental and had in fact resulted from a combination of pressure and a spinal disease contracted some time before. Henri Grien, the illusionist, the great escape artist, eluded blame once more, but his hopes of escape from destitution had perished with the diver. When, in desperation, Elizabeth Grien finally went to court to obtain a maintenance order against Henri to feed her young family, the thwarted adventurer saw no option but to seek his destiny elsewhere.

Despite Grien's most inventive efforts over more than two decades, Australia, land of possibility, had refused to surrender a single speck of its great store of treasure. Under the influence of avarice, Grien had pursued phantoms that beckoned him further and further into the unknown before simply vanishing without trace. However, his experiences, and those of men he had met, had yielded an abundance of material that might yet be transmuted into gold by one who knew the alchemy. Working in a rundown cafe in suburban Newtown, Henri Grien encountered a man who knew the hidden country's most profound secrets even better than he.

25

Ship of Fortune

Whatever way you wend, Consider well the end.

> Jean de La Fontaine,
> 'The Fox and the Goat', *Fables*, 1678

OF THE WHITE PIONEERS of Australia's remote regions, Harry Stockdale was one of the least acclaimed. Even David Carnegie, for all his disillusionment, attracted greater notice than Stockdale. His exploits were poorly advertised in the cities and, unlike Giles and his ilk, he rarely enjoyed the patronage of government or society. Nor would he have thought to promote himself as an explorer. Like many who had lived beyond the fringes of white settlement, he saw himself more simply as a bushman. In any case, 'explorer' was a designation too narrow to aptly describe his talents. To those few who knew anything of the territory he had roamed his exploits were already legend. He had once raced and beaten on horseback the fearless rider and poet Adam Lindsay Gordon. He was himself a poet and lyricist who kept detailed journals and recorded the characters he encountered in verse. Stockdale was also a proficient sketch artist who had filled several notebooks with portraits of the Aboriginals he had encountered. He had learnt much of his bushcraft from these people.

He was only six years older than Grien but had spent much of the 1860s and 1870s in the north and far north-west and knew the landscape and its inhabitants intimately. In his travels he had assembled an unparalleled collection of 640 Aboriginal weapons and implements. Stockdale's intense fascination for the ancient culture of Australia's peoples did not, however, ingratiate him with his contemporaries in the major cities. It was only under the guise of seeking out new pastoral land that Stockdale had been able to find finance for his first major expedition at the age of forty-three.

In the company of seven men and twenty-four horses, Stockdale had proceeded aboard the steamship *Whampoa* from Sydney to an area near the Cambridge Gulf. The point where he made shore on the western side of the gulf on 13 September 1884 was later named Stockdale Landing in his honour. His inland route would take him through the very domain Louis De Rougemont would claim to have surveyed as king after his salvation from the Timor Sea. To anyone's knowledge, none had landed in those parts for nearly forty years — not since the *Beagle* had returned to Australia after ferrying Darwin's secrets safely back up the Thames to London. Stockdale knew the region to be well populated by Aboriginals. While his investigations between the gulf and the Ord River had revealed some habitable land, the most exciting discovery was an immense gallery of rock art on the Kimberley cliffs. Stockdale had spent days reproducing the images in his notebooks before resuming his official purpose. When he finally returned to camp he found two of his men had exhausted his horses in kangaroo hunting and consumed rations beyond their share. Stockdale was forced to abbreviate his expedition and set out immediately for the Overland Telegraph Line, but the two men had complained they were unfit to continue. After some argument, Stockdale agreed to leave them behind on the banks of a creek with three weeks' rations, guns and fishing tackle. Stockdale and the remainder of his party finally reached the Overland Line but search parties would never locate the two men left behind.

By the time Grien waited upon him in a Newtown cafe in early 1897, Stockdale was an authority on Aboriginal life and customs in the north-west. The bushman had by now completed further expeditions through the Kimberley, Port Essington and Alligator River regions. He had also published several pamphlets, including *The Origin and Antiquity of the Boomerang* and *Love, Courtship and Marriage among the Aborigines* and had lectured to the Royal Geographical Society in Sydney.

The open-minded Stockdale was also fascinated by unexplained mysteries and in 1889 had published a work entitled *The Legend of the Petrified or Marble Man*, which explored the riddle of a petrified human body discovered in a marble quarry near Orange in New South Wales. Debate over whether it was fossil or fraud had raged in the papers and Parliament for a month and the figure had been put on public exhibition in a shopfront in Victoria Arcade, Sydney. Stockdale himself had weighed in with a tale of a petrified Aboriginal he had seen first hand near Mount Gambier. Allegations were made that the body was actually the perfectly rendered cast of a real corpse but expert sculptors rejected the possibility of the rock being shaped by human hand. After inconclusive examinations by the city coroner and independent doctors, public interest receded and the 'Marble Man' eventually disappeared. According to one observer, the episode was illustrative of the 'inborn tendency of men to deceive and the willingness of the world to be deceived'.[32]

With such common interests, Stockdale and Grien found that conversation between them flowed freely. Grien was enthralled by Stockdale's far-ranging knowledge and the meticulous detail in which he had recorded his journeys. Stockdale's notebooks, with their fine pencil sketches of the various Aboriginal peoples he had met, their adornments, weapons, ceremonies and implements, were an anthropological treasure. The neglected pioneer had failed to find a publisher for his journals and few had had the opportunity to read them, but Grien was transfixed. Stockdale was equally captivated by the endless feast of tales his Swiss waiter brought to the table. They met several times more before, at Grien's request, the bushman agreed to lend him a number of his cotton-clothed notebooks to study and transcribe. He would not see his waiter again.

The Swiss chef Guymuller was among the last of Grien's acquaintances to have seen him in Sydney. He told Detective Rochaix that in March 1897, he had bumped into Grien outside the Empire Hotel in Pitt Street. Grien had told Guymuller that he was 'off to Europe, where he had something to do that would bring money'. No further details were on offer and, relieved his investment had not been invited, Guymuller passed it off as another of Grien's vain flights.

In August 1897, Henri Grien migrated across the Tasman to New Zealand, leaving family and failure behind and taking Stockdale's journals with him. Despite his past, Grien did not seek the shelter of anonymity. At the port of Nelson, locals rapidly became acquainted with the traveller's full range of talents. Displaying what the *Nelson Evening Mail* described as 'a splendid crayon portrait' in the town's main street, Grien successfully solicited orders for more, but the results were reported as 'strongly resembling cheap photographic enlargements'.

Next, he advertised knowledge of a 'sure cure for rheumatism' and a 'talisman for consumption'. Several customers were induced to trial the former Cooktown quack's treatments for free, but still the business did not catch on. Soon, the local paper reported that Grien had lured two 'Australian capitalists' to investigate a potential copper property in Aniseed Valley, west of Nelson, but after that no more was heard of the men or the venture. At last Grien declared himself a spiritualist and a medium, capable of tracing hidden gold claims by merely studying an article of a prospector's clothing. All things considered, the *Nelson Evening Mail* declared the town's visitor to be 'a very interesting personage, half-visionary and half something else . . .'

New Zealanders were no strangers to outrageous travellers' tales. William Jackson Barry, a transported Irish convict, had arrived in Otago from Australia in 1861, having worked there as a part-time bushranger, coach driver, drover, cattle trader, whaler, prospector and butcher. After a time as an offal seller on the goldfields of Tuapeka, Jackson set up shop as a butcher in the town of Cromwell near Queenstown. He broke the existing butcher's monopoly, lowered the price of lamb and within two years had been elected the town's first mayor. After several years of ingratiating himself to great profit with all and sundry, Barry grew restless. He got up a lecture scheme and began touring the South Island presenting a mostly fictitious speech called 'Forty Years of Colonial Experience', dabbling in carcass butchery and auctioneering when funds ran low. After several years his lectures evolved into a manuscript, which after revision by a local journalist was published in London under the title *Up and Down*. Barry travelled to England in 1879, mysteriously acquiring the naval rank of captain along the way. 'Captain' Barry's tales of cruising on whales and discovering hidden valleys of gold caught the imagination of the English public, just as De Rougemont's would.

When he returned to New Zealand in 1880, Barry embarked on a lecture tour with less satisfactory results. Eggs were thrown at the Captain in Timaru, but Barry rose to the task, modifying his stories to suit the audience, and appearing with a variety of increasingly spectacular props that included the skeleton of a whale and three Maori chiefs. A lecture entitled 'Kings and Chiefs I Have Met and Cannibals I have Seen' drew charges the content was lifted from a book by Archibald Forbes, British war correspondent for *The Daily News*. But like De Rougemont, Barry was nothing if not resilient. He continued to ply his mythmaking trade across both New Zealand and Australia for the next fifteen years, before writing a final book at the age of seventy-nine. Henri Grien had much to live up to if he was to supplant William Jackson Barry in the imagination of New Zealand.

After only a month, having fast exhausted the possibilities and patience of small town Nelson, Grien sailed to Wellington. Word had reached him across Cook Strait of the wreck of the fully laden steamer SS *Tasmania*. In the treacherous, inaccessible waters off Table Cape, eighteen lives had been lost and only the ship's anchor recovered. Of particular interest to Grien was the rumour that among possessions lost was a fortune in jewellery belonging to one of the ship's passengers, Isadore Rothschild. A salvage company had been hired and Grien attempted to persuade the firm to invest in the diving suit he had invented, but was rebuffed. Undaunted, he explored other options.

Along with Stockdale's notes, Grien had brought to New Zealand a selection of quartz specimens from previous mining expeditions in Queensland. He unsuccessfully tried to use these as a basis 'for floating a company to work a certain mining ground he knew of in Australia'. The expert Grien engaged to examine the specimens, a Professor de Blumenthal, assessed them as worthless. The professor was interviewed by a local newspaper man, who reported:

> Thereupon M. De Rougemont seemed to have at once abandoned his scheme and left the stones with Mr de Blumenthal. He describes De Rougemont as a man most fascinating in conversation, and full of stories of adventures (which he seems to fully believe), but as being apparently subject to hallucinations of the most extreme kind. Spiritualism is one of his hobbies – in fact he claims to be not only a medium but a healing medium and tells of wonderful deeds he has done in that capacity. Altogether he is a cultured and well-informed man but utterly impracticable.

Henri Grien was now scraping bottom. Starving and without prospects, he fell in with a group of clairvoyants, some of whom had found sustenance in this world and staved off the next by attaching themselves to Fitzgerald's Travelling Circus. Tom Mills, a young journalist working for *The Evening Post*, met Grien and his spiritualist company at a supper party following a performance one evening.

A weird looking woman was at the head of the show; she claimed to be occult; but she was a stick of plain, very plain Spanish liquorice from Sydney. The others said they belonged to a new order of seekers after truth; but they impressed me as seekers after the food this good-natured woman provided as often as four times a day.

Grien's friends introduced him to Mills and he filled the journalist's ears with tales of the strange and wonderful. Later he sought out Mills with a business proposition: he would spin his yarns and Mills would write them up. Mills was not interested:

He had an idea of going direct into book form. I was not impressed. Candidly but very gently I told him that I was a bit of a liar myself, as became a journalist of repute with every man's hand against him, and that I could not see a market for that sort of thing.

He advised Grien to 'make fiction of it, and then you will be a best seller'. Grien would not hear of it. He wrote instead to his brother François in Yverdon. The pastor had spent time studying and teaching in England, and Henri, correctly estimating that his stories would benefit by distance, sought his advice on having a book published there. François wrote back, counselling Henri against taking such a course, warning there was little money to be made in writing, but at Henri's request he enclosed his British Museum Reader's Card.

Grien's course was set. He lacked only the means by which to reach London. One late October evening in 1897 he borrowed a dinner suit and made his way to the Army Drill Hall in Wellington where a mayoral soiree was being staged to welcome home the New Zealand Shooting Team. The team had recently returned from competing in London aboard a newly built refrigerated steamship, the SS *Mataura.* The vessel was now docked in Wellington harbour, being laden with 25,000 frozen sheep for the return voyage. Grien had seen the ship at Queen's Wharf and now saw an opportunity to waylay the *Mataura*'s captain and wangle a passage to England. He convinced his journalist friend Mills to allow him to accompany him to the reception; on arrival they were shown to seats in the press section. On the opposite side of the horseshoe table were the attending dignitaries, including the Premier of New Zealand and the head of the Navy, but to Grien's disappointment the seat reserved for the *Mataura*'s captain, Charles Milward, was empty. Suffering an upset stomach and embarrassed by his failure to realise the soiree was a full dress affair, the captain had chosen to hide in his plain black coat at the back of the hall.

As the speeches began, the shooting team began to call loudly for Milward to come forward. On the voyage out, the Captain had made his name by stringing a line of bottles on the *Mataura*'s foreyard arm and outshooting them all. He bowed to their wishes and approached the head table, but by now his place had been taken and he was obliged to sit with the press. Milward took a seat opposite the Premier, Mr Richard Seddon, who opened proceedings with a warmly appreciated joke about the lack of heating in the hall. The various toasts were then proposed. The Army representative's response was so long-winded that a man at the bottom of the hall cried out 'Give him a drink of whisky to whet his whistle!'

After he finally retreated, Milward rose to applause.

'Mr Seddon, gentlemen, I am very pleased to have been the means, under Providence, of bringing these brave New Zealand warriors to their hearths and homes, and I thank you heartily for the kind way in which you have drunk "The Reserve Forces".'

With that Milward sat down. The audience were underwhelmed, but a wrinkle-faced man immediately to the Captain's left turned to congratulate him.

'Sir, you have given the best speech of the evening.'

Milward laughed. 'If brevity be the soul of wit, as it is said to be, I certainly have, for I have made the shortest.'

'A virtue others might emulate. Tell me, Sir, might I ask if you are the captain of the big ship lying at anchor in Queen's Wharf?'

Milward confirmed that he was.

'Then I should like leave to speak with you regarding a business proposition.'

Unaware of the numerous businesses his neighbour had already proposed to the locals, the captain agreed. 'You may come and see me tomorrow morning, if you like, at ten o'clock.'

The following morning Grien went down to Wellington Dock, boarded the *Mataura* and made his way to the captain's cabin. Milward recalled their meeting in his journal:

He came at the appointed hour and told me that his name was Henri Grin, that he had been living on Thursday Island and that he had invented a diving dress by which any diver could go down to very great depths, at least 60 fathoms, with perfect safety.

He said that it was on the principle of the copper flexible hose and that he particularly wanted to get to England to offer his invention to the British Admiralty. He needed a passage to England and was willing to give one-half of anything that he might receive from all sources for his patent to the person who would give him such passage.

I wanted to learn more about his invention and he told me there had been a little accident in Sydney where the suit was first tried, that he had hired a man to go down and that when this man was pulled up, he was dead.

'But why did you not go down in the suit yourself?' I enquired.

He got very angry at this and called me a fool, and when I asked him 'Why,' he said, 'if I go down in the suit and it goes wrong and I die, who is going to say what is the matter with the suit? As it is, I know exactly what is wrong and I alter it at once.'

Finally, I agreed to give him a passage home, not so much for the sake of the half of anything that the Admiralty might give but because he had rather an interesting personality and I liked him.

Two weeks later, on the morning of 14 November, as Milward prepared to depart, Grien delivered his prophetic warning of trouble to the east and the *Mataura* sailed to meet its fate off Patagonia without him. He would make his passage to London on the *Waikato* instead. No matter his powers of clairvoyance, it seemed Henri had a powerful, and disastrous, effect on ships. The year after he had made his journey to London in the *Waikato*'s hold, she set out to return to New Zealand only to snap a propeller shaft and drift aimlessly in currents off the Cape of Good Hope for a record four months. Eventually she was found and towed to Fremantle, where a youthful Henri Grin had commenced his antipodean adventures twenty-five years earlier.

Grien and Milward would soon meet again on the steps of the New Zealand Shipping Company in London, but this would not be their last encounter. The incorrigible Grien initiated a correspondence with the captain over the following months, writing to him and asking for introductions to various people. In September 1898, as

Louis De Rougemont's fame burst into full bloom, they had an unlikely reunion at the *Wide World* offices.

Milward had received a letter from William Fitzgerald the previous month inviting him to come to London to give an account of his discovery of De Rougemont. The editor told Milward his expenses would be reimbursed and that he would receive a fee for his time.

The clean-shaven ex-captain travelled to Southampton Street, navigated his way to the editor's office and knocked two or three times at his door. Receiving no answer, he gently opened the door and walked in unannounced to find himself face to face, yet again, with the Delphic tramp, who was pacing the floor while a younger man at a desk – presumably Fitzgerald – dictated notes to a secretary. Milward approached his tramp.

'How do you do, Henri?'

Grien looked blankly at the beardless captain.

'I do not know you!' he declared.

Milward was about to explain when Fitzgerald jumped up from his chair.

'What the devil do you mean, sir, by coming in to my room without knocking and then addressing this man as Henri, when his name is Louis De Rougemont?'

Milward was unapologetic.

'Keep your hair on, young man,' he replied heatedly, 'I looked for someone to bring my card in and finding no-one to do so, I knocked twice. Receiving no answer, I came in and addressed Henri Grien by his name. As you yourself asked me to come, I certainly did expect a different reception but as you have so little manners, I will wish you good morning.'

Milward was about to leave when Grien suddenly threw his arms around his neck.

'Oh, it is my little captain! Forgive me, sir, I did not recognise you.'

The captain released himself from Grien's grip and continued to walk out the door.

'Wait, Captain, I wish to come with you!' shouted Grien and followed him out.

Fitzgerald called out to remind him of the speech they needed to prepare for the British Association that Friday, but Grien did not look back.

'I don't care for any speech. I am going with my little captain.'

Grien and Milward walked down into the Strand and strolled into a teashop, but De Rougemont's fame had already grown too great for his presence to pass unnoticed. Word quickly spread and a circle of people gathered around their table, saying to each other in awed whispers: 'That's him.'

When they eventually returned to the *Wide World* offices, Fitzgerald asked Milward to write a short account of how he had first encountered Louis De Rougemont. According to Milward:

> This I did and he sent me my first-class train fare and one guinea for an article which, however, was never used, as before it could be used, the exposé of De Rougemont took place and so it was not required.

Milward recalled that Grien had told him how he had prepared his 'adventures' for the world.

> He spent many hours a day, for a long time, studying in the British Museum and reading all manner of interesting adventures there. I once asked him how he dare to annex an albatross story and make it into a pelican story, to which he replied: 'Well, you see, zer vas no albatross zer and zer vas pelican.' 'But it is not true,' I said. 'No,' was his only excuse, 'but it does come in so very well just zer.'

In fact, Milward had closer ties with the albatross story than Grien. The shipwrecked French sailors who had attached their desperate message to the bird's neck in the Crozet Islands in the hope of rescue were very nearly saved by Milward himself. At the time of the albatross's miraculous discovery in Perth in 1887, Milward had been serving as second officer aboard a ship which was in port in Cape Town. When word of the Crozets incident reached the French consul there, he boarded Milward's vessel to ask its captain if he would call in at the islands en route to New Zealand. The captain agreed to do so if the weather was fine, but asked the consul if he or his government would pay for any delay to the mails if the weather turned out to be bad.

The consul hesitated and replied that there was a French man-of-war called the *Dougay-Trouin*, due in a fortnight, that could look for the men if necessary. Milward's ship sailed shortly after, but found the weather around the Crozets unfavourable and proceeded on its journey without stopping.

Milward told of the affair's tragic end:

The Dougay-Trouin reached the islands on 11 October and found a notice in the British Depot at Possession Island saying that the men had left for Hog Island on 6 October as they had finished the provisions in the depot and had determined to try and make their way to the next one.

The man-of-war sent to look for them found no trace of them on Hog Island; as they have never been heard of since, it is considered possible that they foundered on the way across. Thus seventeen lives were lost because the French Consul could not guarantee the paltry sum of £5 per hour, the amount the ship would have to pay for being late with the mails. This is the original of Louis De Rougemont's story of the pelican and of the relief sent by the man finding the bird.

26

The Theatre of War

Not since the time of Defoe has there been a man like
De Rougemont and there will never be another.

Lord Rosebery,
British Association Dinner, Bristol, September 1898

MASSINGHAM MAY HAVE declared victory over De Rougemont but
throughout October 1898, letters on the subject continued to choke the
Chronicle mailroom. Although his identity was exploded and the thirty
years marooned had been pruned to mere months, readers still picked
over the finer points of his narrative. Many remained in De Rougemont's camp, defending their right to believe what they chose. Apart
from those such as Becke who had suffered professional embarrassment at the fabulist's pen, many forgave his deceptions as simply the
stock-in-trade of the modern littérateur. Surely he had done no worse
than Kipling or Defoe. After all, they reasoned, who had Grien really
hurt by posing as a latter-day Crusoe? No serious money had been
stumped up for Murphy's ludicrous syndicate. In fact, De Rougemont
had done society a favour by exposing a few well-known braggarts and
windbags who had attempted to manipulate the scandal for their own
ends. Grien's exaggerations seemed mere peccadilloes compared to the
commonplace deceptions practiced by travellers to Pall Mall. Overall it
was a small price to pay for the entertainment served up.

Wide World's circulation remained at record levels and Newnes's
publication of 'The Adventures of Louis De Rougemont' in book form
proceeded as planned. Fifty thousand copies were sold in two editions.
American and foreign language versions followed in rapid succession.
The Daily Chronicle also continued to profit: in November 1898, a
thirty-three page publication by the title of *Grien on Rougemont; Or the
Story of a Modern Robinson Crusoe* appeared on railway newsstands. It

gave a potted version of the *Chronicle*'s triumphant campaign, replete with cartoons, and included a pantomime script based on the scandal for good measure.

In Australia, newspapers revelled in deriding the gullibility of the British public. The consensus was that Grien could never have worked his racket in the colonies. His stories were so well worn that upon the slightest inspection they had simply disintegrated. Grien was no different to any other pearler or prospector with his handy swag of tales ready to roll out at the first chance of a free drink.

One who defended Grien's right to profit from his yarns at the expense of the English was Henry Lawson. The colonies' larrikin laureate lauded De Rougemont's adventures as 'the most romantic, interesting and perhaps the most reliable of any writing, in connection with Australia, published by an English magazine up to date'. The only vexing thing, he said, was that he hadn't done it first.

> I must admit that I felt just as wild as any of De Rougemont's critics at the first go off, but that was mainly because he got there with his scenery and savages before I did with mine . . . and he made a bigger splash in three months than any other Australian writer has begun to make in a hundred years.[33]

Why, asked Lawson, was De Rougemont damned for merely telling a story which harmed no-one, when other writers hid venomous facts beneath a veil of fiction and nothing would be said?

> When we read a book of adventure we want to believe it's true, and if it is well written we do believe it's true — whether we know it or not. We couldn't be reading it and believing all the time that it's a pack of lies . . . And if the writer *tells* us it's all true — what do we want to slang him for? Why go to such pains to prove he's an unprincipled liar? If De Rougemont had told the British public in the first place that his work was pure (and impure) fiction from beginning to end, the chances are they would have thought he was a liar sooner than we did. Ain't it marvellous?

De Rougemont's only failing, said Lawson, was in not trusting in his own invention. The public, he said, wanted to be tricked. In order to be let alone, Lawson decided, De Rougemont needed to make himself 'ten times bigger' than Kipling. Because he did not know the tricks of the trade, 'he was only about two or maybe three times bigger, and that's what was the matter with him'.

> I've read De Rougemont's yarn, every line of it and I think the story is delightful in its force and simplicity (and frankness); as realistic and convincing as a murderer's confession taken down by a man who is intelligent enough to put down what the murderer meant to say in plain English . . .

If Grien could simply revise a few references to local fauna, Lawson was convinced his account would become:

> . . . one of the gospels of childhood of the second or third generation from here; the Australian Robinson Crusoe which grave parents will enjoy secretly or under the pretence of reading aloud to their children (expurgated edition) and even after said nippers are able to read for themselves; I want to have a bound copy of the first edition in the family.

Lest others took a less generous view, Henri Grien cooled his heels in Switzerland, lodging in Yverdon with brother François. As the remaining instalments were published he continued to receive payments from *Wide World*. By 1899 he was also receiving royalties on his book from England, America and Europe. François had been wrong. There was money to be made in writing. It was simply a matter of what one wrote — and how far one went.

The modern Crusoe's travels were by no means at an end. In September 1899, a resurrected Louis de Rougemont surfaced in South Africa. *The New York Times* reported he had arrived in Cape Town by boat, undertaking the journey on doctor's orders after contracting a throat infection, attributed by the American paper to 'too much talking'. Curious passengers had recognised De Rougemont on board the vessel but he had denied his identity until the captain called him to his quarters and confronted him with a copy of his own book. De Rougemont admitted his pretence and signed the flyleaf of the captain's book. The captain agreed to assure his passengers that De Rougemont was another man altogether.

For the first nine days in Cape Town, De Rougemont managed to maintain anonymity. When he ran short of funds, however, a visit to the city's principal bank to cash a cheque led to his detection. *The New York Times* reported:

> . . . following the usual practice, the teller enquired 'Are you Louis de Rougemont?' and immediately thirty or so heads popped up from behind the various partitions, and a murmur ran along the counter among the crowds of customers there.

From that point the paper kept a close tail on De Rougemont. It traced his residence to a seaside suburb and told readers he had been observed at 5.30 am, dressed in greatcoat and pyjamas, walking across the common to take a swim in the sea. This feat was repeated daily, marvelled the newspaper's correspondent, despite it being the wintry season. It seemed odd treatment for a sore throat; nevertheless, the reporter thought rumours De Rougemont might lecture in Cape Town were doubtful on account of this affliction. De Rougemont told *The New York Times* he expected to return to England in two weeks, but intended eventually to settle down in Sydney. He had a good bank account and a scheme in mind to dramatise his book.

But De Rougemont did not depart Cape Town for England. The following month, while the Anglo–Boer war raged in the provinces, he took advantage of the vast British military presence to revive his theatrical career with a series of lecture appearances in Durban and Maritzburg. Hoardings trumpeted the arrival of 'The Greatest Liar on Earth', echoing Browne's description of Mandeville. It was a savvy move. The front was crawling with newspaper correspondents, among them a young Winston Churchill and Arthur Conan Doyle. The hoaxer's startling reappearance was swiftly reported back in Britain.

De Rougemont also wrote letters to a woman friend in England, which he had arranged to have profitably published in *The Outlook*, the magazine that had first serialised Wells's *The Time Machine*. The old stager did not spare the dramatics as he toured the trenches, visiting the wounded and entertaining the troops.

> I leave tonight for the seat of war . . . I had a chat with the Irish wounded yesterday at their hospital before being removed to Cape Colony. They bore the marks of heavy fighting; they were in

splendid spirit, which will assist in prompt recovery, and may be heard of again in future engagements.

The rainy season, De Rougemont reported, made things hard on the troops. Even worse, it dampened the enthusiasm of his theatrical audiences. He wrote 'the rain spoiled my lecture last night, and yet at Durban it was rainy and I had a record house and a great reception'. De Rougemont had also made the most of an opportunity to 'astonish the natives'.

I have been among the Kaffirs, and had a good reception from them. I was able to join in their songs, dances and amusements; even the witch-doctors gave me a demonstration of their powers. I asked the Minister for Natives to inquire me of those who have occult powers, he promptly told me 'impossible', owing to the law against them, and, being afraid of all strangers, they would not divulge anything. Still, I'm getting it, and hope to find their system or mode of mental telegraphy . . . Maritzburg is a nice town, but I would rather be at Richmond or Bloomsbury again. How different things are in dear old England . . .

It was clear the naturalised De Rougemont now considered himself a true-born Britisher. He signed off promising to write again by next mail to tell 'of things not in general, simply of our troops and the Boers'. The thrill of battle was upon him. The following day at the besieged town of Ladysmith he wrote himself into the action.

I received my baptism of fire this morning when Ladysmith was being shelled . . . My eagerness to go to the front was the cause of my making the acquaintance of the commanding officer. Colonel Knox's batteries and the marine batteries were commanding the hill-tops, and were drawing nearer the enemy; and as I had the start of them, I entrenched myself behind the hastily formed stone shelters, and remained perfectly quiet and listened to the shells passing over me. The Boers' Big Ben 40lb shells made only noise and smoke; but our batteries were of a different handling, and every shell that fell on the Boers' station plainly seen by me from my eminence.

De Rougemont could also be seen by the British command. Upon detecting him, Colonel Knox ordered the intruder from the battlefield. According to De Rougemont this was done 'with very great courtesy and regret when I told him who I was. He would have liked me to remain, but orders are orders.' Like a man who had accidentally forgotten his theatre ticket, De Rougemont returned to town to get a permit for the front line, only to find to his great surprise that the General-in-Chief had ordered all non-residents to leave town 'without exception'. De Rougemont would not be deterred. He had come to see war and war he would see, no matter the consequence. Besides, the following day's program promised even more excitement.

> They can only arrest me, and I must put up with the result, for tomorrow's battle must see the Lyddite guns in use, and after that I think the British will be able to charge with mounted infantry and cavalry . . .

De Rougemont breathlessly signed off his letter, 'The guns are booming. I am going out. Goodbye once more.' By the next morning he had managed to persuade an officer to escort him to the front, but to his great disappointment a temporary armistice was called and the fighting came to a halt to allow for the burial of the dead on both sides.

> So today we shall be at peace, and tomorrow I shall post this just before hostilities resume . . . am so surprised they allowed the Boers to mount guns of such a calibre without any molestation from us, but I'm not a soldier.

If the tactics puzzled him, the armistice at least allowed an opportunity to socialise. According to De Rougemont, even the British military's highest ranked men were keen to make the acquaintance of the famous Louis De Rougemont, if not to discuss campaign strategy. 'I spoke to Prior and Colonel Rhodes and many others; they all recognised me.'

De Rougemont was nevertheless neither war correspondent nor soldier. His offer to serve as a volunteer was refused and eventually he was forced to leave Ladysmith. He portrayed his reluctance to depart from the front as gallantry, twice giving up his seat on the train to 'some frightened people'. It was only just in the nick of time, as the Boers were about to assume control of the railway, that he finally left — 'the last to come away on the last train'. Despite his rejection as a fighting man, his enthusiasm for war was undiminished.

> When I left things looked grand. The sound of our shells hissing and the explosion made things very lively, and I quite enjoyed it. My dear, I should have been a soldier, for old as I am, I could have stood the camping as well as any young man.

His last despatch came from Graham's Town in Cape Colony:

> I am here for a day and then go to the front. This time I shall have a permit, and I shall watch things keenly . . . The mail is leaving, and I think you shall get this as soon as my letter from Natal. Goodbye, I shall be with you in January.

If the greatest liar on earth made further theatre appearances in South Africa, he did not make mention of them. War, it seemed, was an even more potent stimulant than public acclaim. He returned to England in early 1900, but his homecoming would go unreported and for a time it seemed De Rougemont had lost his capacity to command the attention of the press. Within fourteen months, however, he would return to the stage, and the headlines — this time in Australia.

It was March 1901. Over thirty years had elapsed since De Rougemont's supposed arrival by Aboriginal catamaran at Cambridge Gulf. Now, in the guise of a vaudeville artist, he would debut on two of the country's biggest stages, at Melbourne's Bijou Theatre and the Tivoli in Sydney, promoted by theatrical entrepreneur Harry Rickards. De Rougemont had initially approached his London promoter Harry Musgrove to organise a tour. After gauging the mood of both press and public, Musgrove had declined, but happily recommended him to his competitor Rickards. At each performance his colourful tales were to be illuminated by an accompanying lantern-slide show. As in South Africa, bill posters advertised the forthcoming appearance of 'The Greatest Liar on Earth'. The Bijou program billed the act 'the engagement extraordinary of the great Louis de Rougemont', and extraordinary it was — if brief.

On opening night, the dinner-suited adventurer appeared on stage without introduction, greeted by loud cries of 'Ananias'. De Rougemont's plan was to relate twenty-five episodes from his experiences, but before he commenced the first the Saturday-night crowd began to taunt him. Disconcerted, but confident of winning over his audience, De Rougemont began to tell of his pearling adventures. The heckling abated momentarily before rising up again to completely drown out his narrative. One spectator expressed his regret that the seventy-five-foot giant octopus that had nearly seized the hero and dragged him to a watery grave had not been 'five foot longer'. Louis De Rougemont's stage career was sinking fast. *The Argus* described his rowdy reception:

> As the adventurer stood upon his few frail planks, the storm grew and howled all around him. From above a pitiless hail of rude interjections smote and stung him, while the thunder of stamping feet pealed ominously. M. de Rougemont saw that he could make no headway against the storm, so he luffed up, and ran for safety to the shelter of the wings . . .

De Rougemont was dead in the water. Melburnians, it seemed, were long of memory and short of patience. Edmund Fisher, *The Bulletin*'s Melbourne critic, timed the performance at four minutes — the shortest run in the Bijou's history. He described De Rougemont as 'a mild, worried looking person with a grizzly beard'.

> He came forward on Saturday in a swallow-tailed coat and began to relate his extraordinary experiences as though this was the awfullest situation he had ever faced. A bold de Rougey with a voice of thunder might have commanded the awe of the Indians in the gallery until he had fairly got going, but this unhappy stranger couldn't roar worth a cent. His pose was apologetic and his yarn almost inaudible.

The Melbourne *Age* characterised the event as 'not a success'. De Rougemont's audience knew him, said the reviewer, but unfortunately he did not know his audience.

The following Saturday in Sydney, an anxious Rickards took the stage in advance of De Rougemont, begging the audience to grant him 'British fair play'. At the matinee, warm applause greeted the lecturer before a copycat cry of 'Ananias' rang out once more. But this time De Rougemont continued regardless. He commenced by explaining what had occurred in Melbourne.

> I have a cold, and my voice could not reach all parts of the house. Some of my adventures are said to be pretty tall, but you know, when anyone writes a book, it is impossible for him to adhere to the truth. If he does not embellish it, it's not worth anything. And yet, Kipling says it's the book of the century.

He assured his audience that he would show the stories were 'almost true, barring the embellishments'. The promise of a near-truth experience was enough to keep the bemused Tivoli crowd in their seats and the lecturer on stage. As De Rougemont spoke, he also directed the lantern-slide show, commanding an unseen operator to move rapidly from one incident to the next in order to avoid excessive scrutiny. Alfred Pearse's colour pictures depicted De Rougemont holding on to his dog Bruno's tail with his teeth, being pursued by an alligator, charged by a buffalo and attacked by whales. When the slide operator's pace slackened, the lecturer shouted 'Next please!' and 'Hurry up and send them on as fast as you can!' Soon the audience entered into the spirit, calling out 'Next please!' whenever a particular tale became too much to swallow, but when the turtle appeared on screen with De Rougemont aboard, laughter took hold. The lecturer defended his exploits.

> This is a thing I've been kicked about more than anything else, you can believe that. I'll prove it, for I intend to get a turtle and do the same with it in Port Jackson.

The turtle riding never eventuated. On Monday morning, critics rated the performance as 'certainly amusing' and noted that, although invited, the lecturer did not return for an encore. *The Evening News* observed that while the Tivoli was 'not by any means crowded', De Rougemont was 'received with good-natured tolerance'. Many present, the report said, thought the lecturer deserved a fair show for coming before the public at all.

Looking to recoup his Melbourne losses, Rickards immediately responded with press advertisements hailing De Rougemont's 'Instantaneous and Emphatic Success'. He was engaged for a further ten matinee and evening performances over the ensuing week. At their conclusion Louis De Rougemont departed both stage and country forever. He was lucky to escape. Somewhere in the files of the West Australian Police an arrest warrant in the name of Louis Grien still lay mouldering, and there was no lack of evidence to show he and De Rougemont were one and the same person. *The Sunday Times* in Perth later reported it was only the fear of embarrassment that had kept the law at bay:

> Not wishing to make themselves ridiculous in the eyes of the world, before putting the warrant into execution they prosecuted further enquiries, when they found that all the witnesses who had given evidence at the trial of Hickey in Perth in 1877 were either dead or could not be traced, and they decided that an arrest would be abortive.[34]

De Rougemont returned to London with his liberty intact, but five years would elapse before he returned to the public gaze.

Meanwhile, a surprise appearance by his former editor revealed details of the affair hitherto unknown. William Fitzgerald returned to the spotlight in 1902 after being dismissed by George Newnes as *Wide World* editor. He promptly took the proprietor to court, seeking damages.

The Washington Post reported that Fitzgerald had alleged the idea for the magazine was originally his and revealed Newnes had agreed to pay him a royalty on top of his salary of three crowns for every 1000 copies sold. Fitzgerald testified that at the end of the first year of *Wide World*'s publication the accumulated royalty totalled approximately £1700. That figure was more than double his actual salary and put *Wide World*'s annual circulation at an astonishing 2.25 million copies. What was more, Fitzgerald claimed that his contract entitled him to a proprietary stake in the magazine. The court disagreed and Fitzgerald's suit was thrown out, but the revelation of the lucrative commission earned by the ex-editor on *Wide World* sales cast new doubt on his motives for defending the De Rougemont tales from the outset.

27

Death of a Mythomane

For there is good news yet to hear and fine things to be seen,
Before we go to Paradise by way of Kensal Green.
G. K. Chesterton, 'The English Rolling Road', 1914

AUDIENCES AT THE LONDON Hippodrome were accustomed to strange spectacles. Behind the four-storey red sandstone facade at Leicester Square was secreted one of the world's most spectacular theatres. Atop a domed tower facing Charing Cross Road perched a bronze racing chariot led by leaping horses, a mnemonic of the colossal Hippodrome of old, host to ancient Rome's Circus Maximus. The London model circa 1906 was a showpiece of luxuriant modernity. Mahogany doors opening onto a white marble vestibule admitted ticket holders to a plush velvet-trimmed foyer. Here they would mingle in anticipation under an ornamental ceiling culminating in a huge electric-lit dome, clutching programs promising entertainments beyond belief.

When they were permitted into the cantilevered auditorium and took seats looking out on to the gigantic, wire-caged arena, anything became possible. The first notes of a dramatic overture sounded from an orchestra situated high in the Minstrels' Gallery. From below their very seats could be heard the rumbling growls of wild beasts as they prowled underground runs. Overhead a circular glass roof slid open to reveal the skies above. Then a dazzling storm of lights heralded the sudden appearance of performers, human and otherwise, from entrances around, below and above. At any moment, the entire floor of the circus arena could fall away to reveal a tank filled with 100,000 gallons of water, the whole transformation being achieved in one minute flat. Glass screens rose at its perimeter to protect spectators as fountains played twenty-foot-high jets into the pool's centre and divers plunged from the galleries.

Since its opening at the turn of the century, the Hippodrome had hosted every imaginable type of circus act: lions, polar bears and sea lions, as well as a cavalcade of acrobats, bareback riders and trapeze artists. The program also offered less predictable fare. A one-legged cyclist by the name of Eddie Gifford dove seventy feet from the roof of the building while seated on a bicycle. Trained Chinese cormorants swooped from the sky to pluck fish from the water and deliver them to Oriental fisherman afloat in skiffs. Blind pianists, armless violin players, boomerang throwers, anacondas and acrobatic elephants all shared the bill. Only weeks earlier Houdini had been borne off in triumph by the crowd after performing a series of miraculous escapes.

Still, nothing had prepared the Hippodrome audience for the sight that would greet them in the summer of 1906. On the edge of the water-filled arena appeared a white-bearded, balding and elderly man in a bathing costume with a rug hugged around his shoulders. Next to him on a platform was a very large and even more aged turtle. After surveying the audience, the man spoke in a quiet, controlled voice:

> Ladies and gentlemen, I am an old man. More than three score years have passed over my head. Throughout my long life I have met with many misfortunes, but the greatest of all my misfortunes was when I ventured to write down the experiences and adventures that befell me. They were strange — so much stranger than fiction — that those who could not judge said they were untrue. I said that when I was living on an island I amused myself by riding turtles in water. They jeered and said it could not be done. I am old, my strength is not what it was, my limbs have lost the suppleness of youth, but still I am prepared to show you that I can do it.

The turtle, he said, had been recently captured on the coast of Nicaragua. It was unfortunately a female — the male being better equipped to bear a man of his size and weight. After waving his hands across the reptile's shell to mesmerise her, the old man pushed the turtle into the water and climbed on her back. The creature baulked but did not dive. After only a moment's uncertainty she began to swim toward the centre of the pool, her pilot upright upon her back and holding onto her shell above her neck with one hand. With the other he beat the water, all the while shouting 'Yatali, yatali!'

Upon successfully reaching the middle, the rider dismounted. Though the pool was deep enough to swim in, six-foot-tall De Rougemont stood comfortably, with his head and torso well above the water. With a flourish he lifted the turtle bodily and wrestled her onto her back before righting her again and climbing back aboard. The audience applauded. The old man guided the turtle back to the arena's edge and the steel platform below his feet rose to elevate him triumphantly out of the water. In dripping costume, Louis De Rougemont delivered a modest bow to the stalls.

The Times was amused:

> There are some animals designed by nature to be beasts of burden as well as articles of food, but the turtle is not one of these. It is a degradation of the noble estate of that animal that he should serve the purpose of an aquatic beast of burden and at the same time afford entertainment to an audience as he now does at the Hippodrome ... Not the least amusing part of the performance is the recital by Mr. De Rougemont of the way in which he first came to ride turtles, and one cannot but admire the plucky way in which a man of seventy years of age thus dares to do what few would dare to attempt owing to the sharpness of the animal's fins. After seeing the struggles between the turtle and his would-be rider in the shallow waters of the Hippodrome one is more convinced than ever that the animal is intended primarily for soup ...

After a subsequent performance, a spectator, John Kirwan, one-time editor-in-chief of the *Kalgoorlie Miner*, described a fearful splashing and commented that 'whether De Rougemont was riding the turtle or the turtle De Rougemont was not clear'. An American journalist for *The Washington Post* timed the entire routine and found it was even shorter than De Rougemont's record-setting four-minute run at Melbourne's Bijou Theatre:

> The whole turn lasted two and one-half minutes, 30 seconds of which De Rougemont spent in speechmaking, 20 seconds in cajoling the turtle, 20 seconds in finding the turtle after it disappeared under water, 58 seconds in clinging to the turtle, 10 seconds underneath it – and two seconds on the turtle's back.

For once, though, Louis De Rougemont had carried the day. Even if his island and its turtles did not exist, he had at least proved the possibility of the feat he had described taking place. Seen through the looking glass of the self-proclaimed cannibal king, if a thing were remotely possible then it might just as well be true. For a week he shared top billing with a plunging bull, a diving horse and 'three small heads — fragments of a lost race', but his success at the Hippodrome would not satisfy him long; it only gave rise to greater aspirations. The following month a letter was received at the *Daily Mail*:

> Dear Sir,
>
> I am in treaty to buy a turtle weighing half a ton (the largest ever caught) which is now exhibited in Italy. I intend to cross from Dover to Calais on its back. Should you care to be present the matter could be arranged. I will call on you tomorrow to give you further information,
>
> yours, etc,
> Louis De Rougemont

De Rougemont secured his turtle but the Channel crossing never happened. Instead, a less ambitious public demonstration was organised off the pier at Southport. Three weeks later the *Daily Mail* published a further missive from De Rougemont explaining the failure of the event:

> I had to go in mid-stream so that every one of the immense crowd (a record one) on the pier could see me. On arriving at the spot I lowered my mount in the sea and then jumped on its back. Unfortunately it 'turned turtle' and both of us were thrown under the boat. Owing to the lumpy sea my steed was struck by the boat, and after three attempts I was compelled to give up, for my turtle seemed quite exhausted, or practically dead. The crowd was very sympathetic and praised my daring in facing such a sea.

De Rougemont would never ride again. Once again, the modern Crusoe sank from view, but this time his disappearance would be almost total. Over the next eight years, a report would surface from time to time of a supposed sighting, like the seasonal sightings of sea serpents. His name became synonymous with any impossible tale, and 'De Rougemont Outdone' was a favourite of newspaper subeditors. Then, in July 1915, news emerged that De Rougemont, now aged sixty-seven, had wed again in London, with his old *Wide World* illustrator, Alfred Pearse, attending as a witness. The wedding certificate gave his occupation as a 'mining engineer and author'. His age was erroneously recorded as eighty-two years. The fact that his abandoned first wife, Elizabeth Grien, was still living in Sydney seemed no impediment to his remarriage in London under the adopted identity of Louis De Rougemont. It appeared bigamy could now be added to his long résumé of fraud. What was more, the press reported, he was planning to revisit the Antipodes on a prospecting honeymoon.

> Louis De Rougemont, whose story of amazing adventures once astonished the world is – with the bride he recently married – preparing for a trip to Australia, in connection with a 'highly interesting discovery', the nature of which is being kept a profound secret. For the present they are quietly residing in London, Monsieur engaging in playwriting and in the study of the occult, in which latter science he has always delved deeply.

De Rougemont's new bride, Thirza Ann Wolf (nee Ellis) was reported to be 'a strikingly handsome woman, possessed of considerable charm of manner'. She was described by *The New York Times* as a financial agent and teacher of languages who had made De Rougemont's acquaintance when doing translation work for him. It was her third marriage. The first, to a French stockbroker, had ended with his suicide; the second, to a Karl Wolf, in divorce. She said she had met Louis De Rougemont in London and found him a 'delightful child of nature', recounting for hours tales true and marvellous. It seemed the old romancer had found a new believer. She told the newspapers:

> One cannot be dull in the company of Louis. His imagination is livelier than that of other men. And then when he presented the truth interestingly, the world called him an outrageous liar ... I believe in Louis De Rougemont. He will yet startle the world with the revelation of a great truth, and those who have thrown stones at him will live to see his name vindicated before the world.

To those who could recall Louis's defiant speeches made sixteen years earlier, Thirza De Rougemont's words seemed laughably familiar. The 'great truth' that would vindicate her husband's name was to prove as elusive as his name itself. As England became immersed in the Great War and food supplies dwindled, the man who had invented himself claimed to have conceived a patent foodstuff that could replace meat, but there was no-one willing to swallow another patent fraud. De Rougemont could find no substitute for money. It was to be his last hurrah. The much-married Mme De Rougemont lost faith in her latest husband and vanished. This time his descent into obscurity was near complete.

Even in penury, though, the wanderer remained in motion. When the Armistice was signed at the end of World War I, he was known to be living on charity in a Surrey village. A friend from Australia, Bernard Freeman, later claimed in his own autobiography to have put De Rougemont up at his house in Bedford. Louis, he said, was 'a broken man in health and spirit'. Occasionally the old man would break down and weep. He told Freeman he had never been through so much trouble as he had gone through in London: 'The people there are more vicious, more unscrupulous than they are in the wilds of Australia. They robbed me of my name, they robbed me of my fortune, and then they are not satisfied. They follow me in the streets and laugh at me.'

His final public appearances came in Piccadilly, selling books of matches alongside beggars and ex-soldiers close to the scene of his fleeting triumph at St James Hall. The writer Osbert Sitwell remembered him as 'a tall, bearded figure, lank and stooping'.

> This ghost of the streets was dressed in a long, old ragged coat, over the collar of which the thin hair fell, and showed above it a calm, philosophical, curiously intelligent face. I was told repeatedly that this man was Louis De Rougemont.[35]

In January 1920, Henri Grien *né* Grin alias Louis De Rougemont went to London Homeopathic Hospital in Great Ormond Street gravely ill with an internal complaint. An operation was immediately performed. He had been referred by a London doctor and admitted under the name 'Louis Redmond'. He had provided an address in Queen's Gate, Kensington, but given his condition it seemed likely his real home was either on the street itself or in the Kensington poorhouse. A few days later a letter arrived addressed to Louis

De Rougemont. No such name was found on the hospital register but an official noted its similarity to that of the recent admission and checked with the patient, who claimed the identity. His report would later be quoted in *The West Australian*:

> De Rougemont (or Redmond) is in a ward with fifteen other patients, but does not talk to any of them. He has, however, told the sisters and nurses that he is the real and famous De Rougemont. A gaunt, much wrinkled old man, with a full white beard, he gives his age as eighty-five. He stated that most of his money was lost during the war in German banks. Friends of the patient also say that he is Louis De Rougemont, and that he used the name Redmond to save himself from annoyance.[36]

It was the first time Henri Grin had ever changed his name to escape publicity. Eighteen months later, lacking funds for further medical treatment, Grin arrived at the infirmary of the Kensington workhouse and was again admitted under the name Louis Redmond. A few days later, on 9 June 1921, he was dead. The death certificate declared he had died from an enlarged prostate and cystitis at the age of seventy-three years. His occupation was given as handyman. Eight years later, Thirza De Rougemont and Alfred Pearse would apply to change the notation on the death certificate to 'mining engineer and author'. It was a belated attempt to salvage some truth from a life of fraud.

The *Times* obituary was brief. It described Louis De Rougemont's 'strange tales' as having caused 'a widespread sensation in the late nineties'. If the late medium was checking his notices from beyond, he would at least have gained satisfaction from seeing his passing acknowledged in London's most respected newspaper. In the United States, *The New York Times* recalled the 'historic hoax' that had caught the public imagination. In Australia, however, De Rougemont's death passed largely unnoticed.

He was buried five days later at Kensal Green. There, in the same cemetery as his one-time patron, Fanny Kemble, lay the earthly remains of the second Crusoe: impostor, romancer, adventurer, black-birder, mystic and *un homme extraordinaire*. Beneath the poor soil of a pauper's grave, his final journey to the beyond was undertaken in a thin wooden vessel inscribed 'Louis Redman'.

A fabulist to the last.

28

A Final Proof

As the pearl ripens in the obscurity of the shell,
so ripens in the tomb all the fame that is truly precious.

Walter Savage Landor, 1775–1864

ONLY THREE MONTHS AFTER Louis De Rougemont's inglorious exit, his name once more graced the headlines. At the Philharmonic Hall in Great Portland Street, audiences were flocking to regular screenings of travel and exploration epics. Film had brought the last frontiers ever closer, providing a first-hand experience even the stories in the pages of *Wide World* could not hope to match. *With Scott in the Antarctic*, depicting the conquest of the pole, had held audiences spellbound. Now another film, entitled *Australia's Wild Nor' West*, was being hailed by *The Times* as 'a revelation of an unknown outpost of Empire which must attract widespread attention'.[37]

The sixteen-minute silent film chronicled the 1917 North-West Scientific and Exploration Expedition, led by E. J. Stuart. Backed by a private syndicate, Stuart and his party had a charter to prospect for minerals and make cinematographic records of items of interest. Much time was spent surveying the Kimberley hinterland and nearby islands. The film was shot by William Jackson and featured 'photographs of districts which had never before been visited by white men'. It also included unprecedented footage of local Aboriginals engaged in fishing, recreation and rituals. Stuart had now brought the film to England to attract foreign investment in the mineral-rich north-west and open up the territory to mining. But it was the Aboriginal sequences that attracted the greatest interest. The *Times* reporter was invited to a private screening in the company of expedition member M. P. Adams, and immediately recognised the film's significance.

The film is wonderfully interesting, and there is hardly a section of it which does not teach the onlooker something of Australia which he did not know before. Ceremonies are reproduced on screen which probably have not been photographed before, and one gets a vivid impression of the magnificent physique of the natives of the North-West. Some of the men from the islands of Cambridge Gulf are 7 ft high and we can quite believe Mr. Adams when he says that it was only possible to obtain brief glimpses – because they are the kind of savages who cannot be induced to pose before the camera.

In one case, said the reporter, the film was obtained by concealing a gramophone behind the rocks playing a recording of a song called 'Stop Your Tickling, Jock'. The camera captured footage of the men gathering huge stones, although the reporter was unsure whether their purpose was to 'demolish the Scottish record or the cameraman'.

The most controversial aspect, said *The Times*, was that the 'film suggests, on more than one occasion that, after all, De Rougemont may have been speaking the truth when he wrote of his remarkable adventures'.

Mr. Adams holds, and the film supports him, that many of the statements made by De Rougemont were perfectly true. There are photographs of the dugong, or giant sea-cow, which is undoubtedly the thing that De Rougemont describes as a small whale. De Rougemont referred to large flounder with a tail which secretes a spear, and the description applies exactly to the giant stingray.

It was the reporter's next statement that would have given the late adventurer the most satisfaction. 'De Rougemont claimed to have ridden turtles, and here one sees the giant natives performing the act, both on land and by water.'

Australia's Wild Nor' West proved hugely popular with audiences keen to see the famous liar vindicated. Following its successful season at the Philharmonic Hall, the film screened daily at Australia House in London for six months, yet still failed to attract the investment Stuart sought. Just as at Bristol, De Rougemont had stolen the spotlight. A year later Stuart redoubled his efforts with the publication of an account of the expedition entitled *Land of Opportunities*. Its opening words acknowledged the debt owed De Rougemont:

> It is a little more than twenty years ago since Louis De Rougemont startled the world with a story of his experience in the Wild North-West of Western Australia, and it seems regrettable that the statements published then by the intrepid old Frenchman should have remained discredited until after his death. He was disbelieved by the scientific world, and the reading public laughed derisively. De Rougemont was referred to as a second Baron Munchhausen with the imaginative powers of a Jules Verne. Many of the imaginings of the latter have, however, since become established facts, and it has rested with Mr. E. J. Stuart, and the best camera kit available, to vindicate De Rougemont. Had the latter been equipped in the same manner as the North-West Scientific and Exploration Expedition, of which Mr. Stuart was leader, he would have been in a position to produce evidence to silence his detractors, and twenty years would not have elapsed without anything being done to develop the natural resources of this wonderful land of opportunities.

The Wide World Magazine was now in its twenty-fifth year of publication. Thriving on the publicity generated by Louis De Rougemont, Newnes's compilation of cast-offs had evolved into one of England's best-loved colour magazines. By now its founder was dead and Fitzgerald had moved on, but the company still relished the opportunity to have the last word. The February 1922 edition of *Wide World* contained an article by sometime mystery writer Elliot Bailey headed 'De Rougemont Was Right'.

> Absolutely unknown twenty years ago, when the startling stories of Louis De Rougemont first brought it into prominence, this great country is still practically a virgin wilderness, trackless and unexplored, the home of wild animals and wilder savages, many of them cannibals. The explorers underwent many remarkable experiences and saw many wonderful sights, and incidentally their discoveries went to substantiate the claims – widely ridiculed at the time – of Louis De Rougemont. Did De Rougemont speak the truth after all when he told his tales of wonderful adventures among the blacks?

The written testimony of the members of this expedition proves it. More importantly still, his statements are corroborated by the all-seeing eye of the camera . . . It may be the world owes a greater apology to the memory of De Rougemont than is realized even now. It is typical of the irony of things that he should have died just as the all-conquering cinematograph began to substantiate his claims . . . Much of the strangest portion of De Rougemont's narrative is now proved to have a solid basis of fact. He must have actually seen the wonders he described, lived among the curious people whose ways and doings he pictured so accurately.

'By exporting his adventures to England, De Rougemont had escaped the more rigorous scrutiny he might have experienced in Australia.'

Postscript

Splendaciously mendacious rolled the Brass-bound Man ashore.
Rudyard Kipling, 'Poseidon's Law', 1904

WHAT HENRY MASSINGHAM, the *Daily Chronicle* editor who had worked so assiduously to prove Louis De Rougemont a fake, made of *Wide World*'s celebration of De Rougemont's supposed vindication two decades later is unrecorded. Following a celebrated editorial career he himself died in 1923, only two years after De Rougemont. William Fitzgerald's replacement at *Wide World*'s helm, Francis Jones, wrote a letter to *The New York Times* stating that he had been present on many occasions at Southampton Street when De Rougemont dictated his adventures. He said that De Rougemont had believed implicitly in every detail and never once acknowledged that the incidents in his narrative were fictitious. In fact, Jones wrote, 'De Rougemont took his exposé with arctic-like coolness, and simply expressed a disappointment and hurt surprise that his statements should be in any way doubted.' Additionally, Jones noted, De Rougemont had been required by Newnes to sign an affidavit to the truthfulness of his story prior to its publication.

The modern Crusoe would continue to resurface in unlikely locations. In his 1925 book, *The Everlasting Man*, G. K. Chesterton recalled an encounter with De Rougemont in Kent some years earlier. In the course of his research into alternative religions, Chesterton had become familiar with a group called 'Higher Thought' to which the spiritualistic De Rougemont belonged. Chesterton had been walking in the woods with him where he 'could not help but feel that his sunburnt face and fierce tufted eyebrows and pointed beard gave him something of the look of Pan'. They came upon a small village church. As they sat looking at it in contemplation, De Rougemont turned to Chesterton and said, 'Do you know why the spire of that church goes up like that?' Chesterton responded he did not and De Rougemont replied, 'The same as the obelisks; the phallic worship of antiquity.' Chesterton was shocked and for a moment saw in his companion 'not Pan but the Devil'.

Some would later claim the mantle of 'Exposer of De Rougemont'; others freely wove tales of meeting De Rougemont into their own embellished memoirs. Professor Bernard Freeman, who declared in his 1934 autobiography *Freeman of Stamboul* that he himself had staged a revolution in Honolulu, struck oil in New Zealand and lived for six weeks in a hollow tree, devoted an entire chapter to 'How I Discovered De Rougemont'. The remarkable account merged actual and imagined events with De Rougemont's own tales.

Freeman stated that he first hired De Rougemont, under that name, to assay mines in Queensland in 1895. The two men then travelled to Victoria to survey goldmining prospects. On their return journey De Rougemont predicted the onset of a bushfire two days in advance and won a fight to the death with a twenty-foot carpet python. Heading north through Queensland, he proved himself adept at various native languages and, according to the professor, appeared to be known by almost every Aboriginal they encountered. Freeman also recalled De Rougemont's incredible ability as a water diviner, boomerang thrower, gold panner, bird imitator, food finder and cook. Attacked by a band of long-haired Aboriginals not dissimilar to Landor's 'hairy Ainu', De Rougemont carried the day by donning a pair of stilts and firing over their heads with a double-barrelled shotgun. On another action-packed foray to the Gulf of Carpentaria, De Rougemont conducted a corroboree, which concluded with a cannibal feast that made Freeman 'turn away sick and disgusted'. Each night by the campfire he entertained the professor with his repertoire of extraordinary stories, which by this time Freeman was certain had a 'basis of truth'. They returned via Townsville, where De Rougemont organised a parade of boys riding on goats in honour of the visiting Queensland governor, before reaching Brisbane in time for the great flood of 1896. When the steamer *Pearl* sank in the swollen Brisbane River, De Rougemont leapt in and rescued two people from drowning. After they eventually parted, Freeman found himself in England, and on a visit to Madame Tussaud's was astonished to discover his old friend's effigy wearing the very suit he had given him in Sydney. Even more astonishingly, fate reunited the professor with his old friend in person a little time later on a London railway station.

Freeman's account was without doubt the most remarkable instance of 'De Rougemont Outdone', but it was not the last. De Rougemont's name would continue to be invoked, especially when a particularly outrageous hoax captured the imagination of press or public.

In 1929, the exposure of the forgery of documents relating to the secret of making Stradivarius violins led *The Times* to editorialise on what drove De Rougemont and his ilk to take such pleasure in deceiving the public. All of us, the paper said, could count a man like him amongst our friends, a man who delighted in converting the most trivial events of his life into sensational incidents:

> His account is always rich in circumstantiality and detail. The least sign of scepticism spurs him on to higher flights ... And yet his hearers know, and he knows that they know, that it is all splendid fiction. The extraordinary thing about it is that the confirmed long bowman is often a good fellow, with a high standard of morality in every other department of his life. He seems to spin his yarns out of sheer delight in his narrative ability. They do not bring him, and are usually in no way designed to bring him, any perceptible gain. They are often persisted in when they have become a real drawback to him. We may be sorry for him or irritated by him, but before we reprobate him utterly, it is well to reflect upon the tiny grain of the same seed that is sown in most of us ...

Nor would De Rougemont's turtle-riding exploits be readily forgotten. In 1930, further confirmation of the plausibility of his feats came with the publication of *The Book of Puka Puka*. This autobiographical work recounted the idyllic South Sea life of an American, Robert Dean Frisbie, who had cast himself away to live on Puka Puka, an atoll also known as Danger Island, to escape the annoyances of the twentieth century. Puka Puka, 715 miles north of Rarotonga in the Cook Islands group, was, and is, home to one of the most isolated communities in the Pacific. The island was not much bigger than De Rougemont's Timor Sea refuge and Frisbie discovered the inhabitants there practiced a method of turtle fishing that exactly replicated the fabulist's famous aquatic cruises, catching the turtle at sea and surfing to shore astride its shell. Frisbie was told that the females were much easier to ride than the males, which could explain De Rougemont's selection of the female turtle for his Hippodrome performances.

When, shortly after the cessation of World War II, officials fell for a Winston Churchill impostor spotted in the bleachers at a Cuban baseball game, smoking one of Havana's finest, flashing his V sign and signing autographs for the enthusiastic crowd, *The Times* again saw parallels to the De Rougemont case. The paper now suggested that De Rougemont's error had been in continuing the deception too long.

> Hoaxers can count with confidence on the amused indulgence of the public so long as there is someone in an official capacity to bear the odium, but if the deception is kept going long enough the officials will have time to combine and then the impostors can hope for little in the way of kindness. The fabulous adventures of poor Louis De Rougemont as a cannibal chief in the wilds of Australia gave innocent pleasure to thousands who read of them. Even if those thousands had dimly suspected the uneventful threadbare life of the romancer they would still, in all probability, have gone on reading him, grateful for his luxuriant fancies.

Frank Clune, author of a brief biographical account of De Rougemont published in 1945, *The Greatest Liar on Earth*, was inspired to imitate his subject when travelling on the Great Barrier Reef. After capturing a '300 pound greenback' near Lindeman Island, the maverick Clune was challenged by his companions to ride it ashore.

> I thought of my bronco-busting days in the United States Cavalry and reckoned it wouldn't be far to fall . . . if De Rougemont could do it, why not Clune? . . . I sprang on his carapace as he headed for shore; but whether Clune rode the turtle or the turtle rode Clune, it was impossible to tell in the turmoil. All I know is that we had turtle soup for dinner.

In 1950, the forgery of a series of Dutch old masters prompted *The Times* once again to raise De Rougemont from the dead, placing at least some of the blame for his and other impostors' successes on the naivety of the British public. *The Times* observed 'alien hoaxers seem to be received here with open arms. Louis De Rougemont may have been Swiss but he certainly found his mark here in Britain'.

Almost twenty years later, in 1969, the reported rescue of an over-board South Korean seaman by a giant turtle who permitted him to cling to its shell for fifteen hours again roused recollections of the Hippodrome act in London papers.

Several years later, writer Bruce Chatwin had a chance encounter with the modern Crusoe that would eventually appear in his first book, *In Patagonia*. Exploring the dusty journals of his seafaring distant cousin Charles Milward, Chatwin discovered that Louis De Rougemont was the 'mythomane' who had prophesied the loss of his cousin's ship, the *Mataura*. Milward's journal included the description of his reunion with De Rougemont in London and the encounter at the *Wide World* offices.

Some would borrow De Rougemont's name as their own pseudo-nym. When the late Prince Rainier of Monaco entered a florally decorated workbench in the *Concours International De Bouquets* in Monte Carlo in 1980, it was Louis De Rougemont who was announced as the winner of second prize. It was fitting tribute to the man who had told Harry Musgrove he believed every flower had a soul.

De Rougemont's name persisted in the theatre as it did in the press. Musgrove and his partner George Darrell's 1898 play was not the last performance work to be based on the fabulist's life. A radio production entitled *The Strange Story of Louis De Rougemont*, written by James Potter, was broadcast on the BBC nationally in the late 1930s. In 1975, writer Geoffrey Maslen, also author of a biographical work on De Rougemont, composed a radio play entitled *Louis De Rougemont: Australia's Only Cannibal Chief*.

De Rougemont's motivations have remained the subject of specula-tion. On the surface, his impulse to promote a concocted life seemed a heady mix of self-aggrandisement and avarice. There is no doubt he was a dangerous person to permit upon your ship — or to loan a book. He was also a man of irrepressible energy who could resist no opportu-nity to broaden his horizons. As in his work as a photographic enlarger, every experience became magnified in his hands. Like the best adven-turers and scientists of his age, De Rougemont expended his energies upon moving beyond accepted boundaries to explore the unknown: in the physical world, by travelling to the remotest parts, both real and imagined; in the spiritual, by seeking answers beyond the visible.

Whether by reason of vanity or a confessional instinct, De Rougemont appeared to have been unable to resist providing clues to his identity. In Australia, he seemed to have left a lasting impression on all he met, resulting finally in his inevitable and rapid exposure.

The fabulist's life was full of contradictions. De Rougemont's often sympathetic attitudes to Australia's Indigenous people, so out of kilter with those of many of his contemporaries, belied his own actions. By pointing the finger at the behaviour of white explorers in contact with Aboriginals, was De Rougemont simply seeking to transfer the guilt Henri Grien felt over his murderous blackbirding activities? Another striking example of this hypocrisy was evident in his professions of undying love for Yamba; which were in stark contrast to his near criminal neglect of his family in Sydney.

De Rougemont's fabulous tales have never been elevated to a position among the classics of Australian literature, as Henry Lawson suggested at the time they ought to be. Aside from the question of their actual literary worth, this is perhaps also due to the author's observable moral hypocrisy; to the fact that much of his material was thought to be stolen; and to his refusal to concede the deception.

Nevertheless, although it is no longer widely read, *The Adventures of Louis De Rougemont* remains a looking glass to a time when Australia was a land in which anything seemed possible and its history, described by Mark Twain as 'like the most beautiful lies', was an elastic concept.

Perhaps the last word should belong to William Fitzgerald, who, after all had been revealed, still supported the authenticity of his author's experience, if not his identity. At the conclusion of his preface to *The Adventures of Louis De Rougemont (as told by himself)*, published by George Newnes Limited in 1899, the editor proclaimed his unwavering faith: 'I believe now, and have believed from the first, that every single incident in the narrative is actual fact.'

Acknowledgements

The author owes a debt to those who have previously followed the extraordinary turnings of the fabulist Louis De Rougemont's life. Foremost among these are the late Australian journalist and writer Frank Clune, author of *The Greatest Liar on Earth*, and Geoffrey Maslen, author of *The Most Amazing Story a Man Ever Did Live to Tell*. Christopher J. Barnett gave invaluable assistance by generously providing access to the relevant pages of his grandfather Captain Charles Milward's original journal. These provide the factual basis for my retelling of Louis De Rougemont's encounters with Captain Milward and the story of the SS *Mataura*.

The author would like to thank: Tara Wynne, literary agent of Curtis Brown Australia, for her belief, expertise and guidance; Meredith Curnow, commissioning publisher at Random House Australia, for her enthusiasm and commitment; Elizabeth Cowell at Random House Australia for her editorial wisdom, insight and ability to detect a fabulism; Catherine Aldred for her constant support, undervalued assistance and utterly unfounded faith; Aileen Howard for researching the details of Henri Grin's passage to Western Australia; Sophie Short for her generous assistance in French translation; Anna Grien, Ross Grien and Peter Grien for their kind help; for their interest and assistance, Judy and David Aldred, Heidi Aldred, David Astle, Rob Howard, Tracy O'Shaughnessy and Melanie Ostell; Sarah Strong at the Royal Geographical Society; Tricia Andrews of British Library Newspapers at Colindale, England; the staff of the British Library, the National Library of Australia, the State Library of Victoria and the Stonnington Library; Gary, Danny and Ian at SMC; Max for the office space and Charlie for the early mornings.

The portrait of Louis De Rougemont on page ii and Alfred Pearse's original illustrations reproduced on pages 32, 35, 37 and 45 are taken from *The Wide World Magazine: Vol. 1, April to September 1898*, published by George Newnes Ltd in London in 1898.

The cartoon images on the inside front and back covers, and those on pages vi and 272 come from *Grien on Rougemont, or, the Story of a Modern Robinson Crusoe: as told in the pages of the 'Daily Chronicle'*, published by Edward Lloyd in London in 1898.

Bibliography

Books

Atkinson, Alan, *The Europeans in Australia: a history*, vol. 1, Oxford University Press, Melbourne, 1997

Barrett, Charles, *White Blackfellows: the strange adventures of Europeans who lived among savages*, Hallcraft Publishing, Melbourne, 1948

Battye, JS, *Western Australia: a history from its discovery to the inauguration of the Commonwealth* (facsimile edn), University of Western Australia Press, Nedlands, WA, 1978

Battye, JS, *The History of the North West of Australia, embracing Kimberley, Gascoyne and Murchison districts*, Hesperian Press, Carlisle, WA, 1985

Bird, Isabella L, *Letters to Henrietta/Isabella Bird*, ed. Kay Chubbuck, John Murray, London, 2002

Blackburn, Geoff, *Calvert's Golden West: Albert Frederick Calvert: a biography and bibliography*, Hesperian Press, Carlisle, WA, 1997

Brokken, Jan, *The Rainbird: a central African journey*, Lonely Planet Publications, Hawthorn, Victoria, 1997

Browne, Spencer, *A Journalist's Memories*, Read Press, Brisbane, 1927

Calvert, Albert F, *The Aborigines of Western Australia*, W. Milligan & Co., London, 1892

Carnegie, David, *Letters from Nigeria*, Black & Johnston, Brechin, Scotland, 1902

Carnegie, David, *Spinifex and Sand: a narrative of five years' pioneering and exploration in Western Australia*, C. Arthur Pearson, London, 1898

Caygill, Marjorie, *The British Museum Reading Room*, The Trustees of the British Museum, London, 2000

Chatwin, Bruce, *In Patagonia*, Cape, London, 1977

Chesterton, GK, *The Everlasting Man*, Hodder & Stoughton, London, 1925

Clune, Frank, *Free and Easy Land*, Angus & Robertson, Sydney, 1938

Clune, Frank, *The Greatest Liar on Earth*, The Hawthorn Press, Melbourne, 1945

Collins, Peter & Roy MacLeod (eds), *The Parliament of Science: the British Association for the Advancement of Science 1831–1981*, Science Reviews, Northwood, Middlesex, c. 1981

Day, Arthur Grove, *Louis Becke*, Hill of Content, Melbourne, 1967

De Rougemont, Louis, *The Adventures of Louis De Rougemont (as told by himself)*, Newnes, London, 1899

De Serville, Paul, *Rolf Boldrewood: a life*, Melbourne University Press, Melbourne, 2000

Dutton, Geoffrey, *Australia's Last Explorer: Ernest Giles*, Faber, London, 1970

Edwards, Hugh, *Port of Pearls: a history of Broome*, Rigby, Adelaide, 1983

Favenc, Ernest, *The Explorers of Australia and their Life-work*, Whitcombe and Tombs, Christchurch, 1908

Favenc, Ernest, *The History of Australian Exploration from 1788–1888*, Turner & Henderson, Sydney, 1888

Finkelstein, David, *The House of Blackwood: author–publisher relations in the Victorian era*, Pennsylvania State University Press, University Park, PA, 2002

Forrest, Kay, *The Challenge and the Chance: the colonisation and settlement of north west Australia 1861–1914*, Hesperian Press, Victoria Park, WA, 1996

Freeman, Prof. Bernard, *Freeman of Stamboul: being the memoirs of Professor Freeman*, Angus & Robertson, Sydney, 1934

Friederichs, H, *Life of Sir George Newnes*, Hodder & Stoughton, London/New York, 1911

Frisbie, Robert Dean, *The Book of Puka Puka*, John Murray, London, 1930

Frost, Cheryl, *The Last Explorer: the life and work of Ernest Favenc*, Foundation for Australian Literary Studies, James Cook University of North Queensland, Townsville, 1983

Giles, Ernest, *Australia Twice Traversed*, Sampson Low, Marston, Searle & Rivington, London, 1889

Gould, Nat, *The Magic of Sport*, J. Long, London, 1909

Grien on Rougemont, or, the Story of a Modern Robinson Crusoe: as told in the pages of the 'Daily Chronicle', Edward Lloyd, London, 1898

Groom, Nick, *The Forger's Shadow: how forgery changed the course of literature*, Picador, London, 2002

Havinghurst, Alfred Freeman, *Radical Journalist: H. W. Massingham (1860– 1924)*, Cambridge University Press, London/New York, 1974

Heaton, John Henneker, *Australian Dictionary of Dates and Men of the Time*, George Robertson, Sydney, 1879

Hill, JG, *The Calvert Scientific Exploring Expedition (Australia, 1896)*, George Philip & Son, London, 1905

Hodgson, Barbara, *No Place for a Lady: tales of adventurous women travellers*, Greystone Books, Canada, 2003

International Exhibition (1879: Sydney, N.S.W.), *Official record of the Sydney International Exhibition, 1879*, Thomas Richards, Government Printer, Sydney, 1881

Irvin, Eric, *Gentleman George, King of Melodrama: the theatrical life and times of George Darrell, 1841– 1921*, University of Queensland Press, St Lucia, 1980

Jackson, Kate, *George Newnes and the New Journalism in Britain 1880– 1910: culture and profit*, Ashgate, Aldershot, 2001

Keesing, Nancy, *History of the Australian Gold Rushes by Those Who Were There*, O'Neil, Hawthorn, Victoria, 1971

Keevak, Michael, *The Pretended Asian: George Psalmanazar's eighteenth century Formosan hoax*, Wayne State University Press, Detroit, Michigan, 2004

Kirwan, Sir John, *An Empty Land*, Eyre & Spottiswoode, London, 1934

Kretchmer, Max H, *Journey beyond the Seas*, M. H. Kretchmer, Mortdale, NSW, 1980

Liebowitz, Daniel & Charlie Pearson, *The Last Expedition*, Piatkus Books, London, 2005

Lumholtz, Carl, *Among Cannibals: an account of four years' travels in Australia and of camp life with the Aborigines of Queensland*, J. Murray, London, 1889

Macleod R & P Collins, *The Parliament of Science: the British Association for the Advancement of Science 1831–1981*, Science Reviews Limited, Northwood, Middlesex, c. 1981

Mallett, Ashley, *The Black Lords of Summer: the story of the 1868 Aboriginal tour of England and beyond*, University of Queensland Press, St Lucia, 2002

Maslen, Geoffrey, *The Most Amazing Story a Man Ever Did Live to Tell*, Angus & Robertson Publishers, Sydney, 1977

Merland, C, *Dix-Sept Ans Chez Les Sauvages: les aventures de Narcisse Pelletier*, E. Dentu, Paris, 1876

Mill, Hugh Robert, *Hugh Robert Mill: an autobiography*, Longmans, Green, London, 1951

Mill, Hugh Robert, *The Record of the Royal Geographical Society 1830–1930*, Royal Geographical Society, London, 1930

Milward, Charles Amherst, unpublished original journal, written circa 1898–1899, as transcribed by Monica Milward Barnett (copyright Monica Milward Barnett)

Morrell, Jack & Arnold Thackray, *Gentlemen of Science: early years of the British Association for the Advancement of Science*, Clarendon Press, New York & Oxford University Press, Oxford, 1981

Peasley, WJ, *In the Hands of Providence: the desert journeys of David Carnegie*, St George Books, Perth, WA, 1995

Petrie, Sir CA, *The Carlton Club*, Eyre & Spottiswoode, London, 1955

Porter, Mrs Adrian, *The Life and Letters of Sir John Henneker Heaton*, John Lane – The Bodley Head, London, 1911

Shakespeare, Nicholas, *Bruce Chatwin*, Vintage, London, 2000

Sitwell, Edith, *The English Eccentrics*, Faber and Faber, London, 1932

Sitwell, Osbert, *Sober Truth: a collection of nineteenth-century episodes, fantastic, grotesque and mysterious*, Macdonald, London, 1944

Souhami, Diana, *Selkirk's Island*, Weidenfeld & Nicolson, London, 2001

Spencer, Sir Baldwin, *Wanderings in Wild Australia*, Macmillan, London, 1928

Stockdale, Harry, *The Legend of the Petrified or Marble Man*,
F. Cunninghame & Co., Sydney, 1889

Stuart, EJ, *A Land of Opportunities: being an account of the author's recent expedition to explore the northern territories of Australia*, John Lane – The Bodley Head, London, 1923

Wiener, Joel H (ed.), *Papers for the Millions: the new journalism in Britain, 1850s to 1914*, Greenwood Press, New York, 1988

Articles

'The Adventures of Louis De Rougemont', *Bookman*, vol. 10, no. 4, December 1899

Bellanta, Melissa, 'Fabulating the Australian Desert: Australia's lost race romances, 1890–1908', *Philament*, issue 3, April 2004, viewed October 2005, <http://www.arts.usyd.edu.au/publications/philament/issue3_Critique_Bellanta.htm>

Blair, JB, 'Grin's Fairytales', *The Etruscan* (Bank of NSW Journal), vol. 6, 1956, p. 34

De Rougemont, Louis, 'Mr. Louis De Rougemont under Fire', *The Outlook*, 2 December 1899, p. 567

Genoni, Paul, 'The Disappearance of Ludwig Leichhardt in Young Adult Fiction', *Orana*, March 1999, p. 33

Grey, Stephen, 'Going Native', *Overland*, no. 170, Autumn 2003, pp. 34–42

Healy, JJ, 'The Lemurian Nineties', *Australian Literary Studies*, vol. 8, no. 3, 1978, pp. 307–316

Jose, Arthur, 'Alias Henri Grien', *Forum*, 31 January 1923

Jose, Arthur, 'A Lordly Impostor', *Cornhill Magazine*, ser. 3, no. 65, October 1928, p. 79

Lawson, Henry, 'De Rougemont, Us and Some Digressions', *La Trobe Library Journal*, vol. 7, no. 28, October 1981, pp. 95–97

Longman, Peter, 'Making A Splash', *Theatres Trust Newsletter*, Theatres Trust, London, September 2002, reproduced online at <www.arthurlloyd.co.uk/Archive/Jan2003/Hippodromes.htm>, viewed November 2005

Musgrove, Harry, 'Stage Secrets', *Table Talk*, 21 October 1926

Sampson, David, *Australian Aborigines in Victorian Britain*, adapted from a lecture given to the Science Museum, London, June 2001, Fathom Knowledge Network, viewed October 2005, <www.fathom.com/feature/122435>

Spennemann, Dirk HR, *Louis Becke (1859– 1913): a biography*, The Johnstone Centre, Charles Sturt University, Albury, 2000, viewed November 2005, <http://life.csu.edu.au/LouisBecke/Bio.html>

Stilgoe, Ralph, 'The Naming of Como', *Sutherland Shire Historical Society Inc. Quarterly Bulletin*, May 1997, pp. 427–428

Newspapers

The Age (Melbourne) – September/October 1898; March 1901

The Argus (Melbourne) – January 1898; September/October 1898; March 1901

The Bulletin (Sydney) – September/October 1898

The Coolgardie Miner (WA) – September/October 1898

The Daily Chronicle (London) – September/October/November 1898

Daily Mail (London) – September/October 1898; July, September 1906

Daily News (London) – 15 August 1896; 4 October 1898

The Daily News (Perth, WA) – 19, 24 April 1914

The Daily Telegraph (London) – August 1898

The Daily Telegraph (Sydney) – September/October 1898

The Echo (Sydney) – 14 January 1890

The Evening News (London) – September/October 1898

The Evening News (Sydney) – January 1897; September/October 1898; February/March 1901

The Evening Post (Wellington, NZ) – October 1898

Figaro (London) – September 1898

The Herald (Melbourne) – 11 June 1921

The Home News for Australia – September/October 1898

The Illustrated Home News (London) — 15 March 1902

The London Morning — 20 October 1898

Nelson Evening Mail (NZ) — September/October 1898

The New York Times — September/October 1898

The Otago Witness (NZ) — October/November 1898

St. James Gazette — September 1898

The South Australian Register (Adelaide) — February 1922

The Star (Lyttelton, NZ) — 5, 25, 31 October 1898

The Sunday Times (WA) — January 1914

The Sydney Mail — September/October 1898

The Sydney Morning Herald — 18 September 1879; January 1897; September/October 1898; March 1901

The Times (London) — September/October 1898; 14, 17 January 1899; July 1906; 11, 13, 15 June 1921; 8 September 1921; 3 May 1929; 13 February 1946; 6 September 1950, 26 August 1969

The Washington Post — 2 October 1898; 11 May 1902; 1 February 1920

West Australian Times (WA) — January 1870

The Western Mail (WA) — October 1898; 4 January 1920

The Westminster Budget — August 1898

Westminster Gazette — September 1898

Periodicals

Punch (London) — September/October 1898

Review of Reviews (London) — vol. 18 (1898) pp. 263—64; 488

The Speaker (London) — September/October 1898

The Strand Magazine (London) — September/October 1898

The Wide World Magazine — vol. 1, no. 1, April 1898 to vol. 3, no. 14, April 1899; July 1921; February 1937

Notes

1 My retelling of all encounters between Louis De Rougemont and Captain Charles Milward is based on an account by Milward in his own unpublished journal, as transcribed by his daughter, Monica Milward Barnett. Material from the journal is copyright Monica Milward Barnett.

2 R Pound, *The Strand Magazine: 1891–1950*, Heinemann, London, 1966, p. 63.

3 As estimated by Ernest Favenc in *The History of Australian Exploration from 1788–1888*, Turner & Henderson, Sydney, 1888.

4 Golconda is an ancient Indian city once fabled for its precious diamonds whose name became synonymous with any rich source.

5 Charles Darwin, *The Voyage of the Beagle* (Harvard Classics vol. xxix), P. F. Collier & Son, New York, 1909–14, chapter xx, p. 16.

6 Legend has it Favenc stumbled across Louis Becke one morning spinning his South Sea yarns in a Sydney hotel, Pfahlerts. He later introduced a stuttering Becke to his editor at *The Bulletin*, JF Archibald, providing the catalyst for the adventurer's writing career.

7 Moresby had named the territory's principal city, Port Moresby, in honour of his father (and by happy extension, himself).

8 Woodes Rogers, *A Cruising Voyage Round the World*, Bell and Lintot, London, 1712.

9 Stradling, who declined the opportunity to go down with his ship, was rescued from drowning along with the remaining crew by a Spanish fleet, only to be clapped in irons and thrown into a Lima jail.

10 'A Convict's Letter: Extract of a Letter from a Young Man at Port Jackson to Mr. Thomas Olds, 9 April 1790', quoted in Alan Atkinson, *The Europeans in Australia: a history*, Oxford University Press, Melbourne, 1997, vol. 1, p. 125.

11 De Foigny was the first to dub the inhabitants of the little-known land 'Australians'.

12 *The Sydney Morning Herald*, 16 September 1898.

13 Samuel Johnson, *Rasselas, Prince of Abyssinia*, 1759, E. and S. Harding, London, 1796.

14 Psalmanazar was an adaptation of the name of the Assyrian King of the Old Testament, Shalmaneser III (2 Kings 17:3).

15 Dr Isaac Watts was an eighteenth-century English writer of religious verse, catechism and hymns.

16 Albert Calvert was the son of notorious mythomane John Calvert, who had claimed to be both the heir to the Baltimore peerage and the first white man to discover gold in Australia.

17 In 1896, a report from London in *The Coolgardie Miner* observed that most West Australians in the City had 'several miles of gold reefs to dispose of'.

18 *The Daily Telegraph*, Sydney, 26 November 1898.

19 John Blackwood, quoted in Finkelstein, David, *The House of Blackwood: Author–publisher relations in the Victorian era*, Pennsylvania State University Press, University Park, PA, 2002, p. 54

20 William Blackwood, quoted in Finkelstein, op. cit. p. 57.

21 William Blackwood, quoted in Finkelstein, op. cit. p. 59.

22 J Speke, *Journal of the Discovery of the Source of the Nile*, Dent, London & Dutton, New York, 1969 (originally published by Blackwood, Edinburgh, 1863), p. 15.

23 Quoted in W Peasley, *In the Hands of Providence: the desert journeys of David Carnegie*, St George Press, Perth, 1995, p. 184.

24 This and following quotes from *Table Talk*, 21 October 1926.

25 *The Daily News* (Perth, WA), 22 April 1914.

26 Quoted in Kay Forrest, *The Challenge and the Chance: the colonisation and settlement of north west Australia 1861–1914*, Hesperian Press, Victoria Park, WA, 1996, pp. 104.

27 *The Sunday Times* (Perth), 26 July 1914.

28 Quoted in N Keesing. *History of the Australian Gold Rushes by Those Who Were There*, O'Neil, Hawthorn, Victoria, 1971, p. 277.

29 Material relating to Rochaix's investigation into Henri Grien's case is based on information reported in *The Evening News* (Sydney), 28 September 1898.

30 Gould had met Grien as De Rougemont with Fitzgerald at his home in London and considered him 'a second Defoe'. Gould also reported Grien had set his son afloat on a stream at the back of his house on a boat he constructed of a mat and some sticks. Said Gould, 'The quick way in which he did it, and the safety of the frail craft, seemed to me marvellous; he must have had a lot of experience to do it.'

31 Quoted in M Cannon, *Life in the Cities*, Currey O'Neil Ross, South Yarra, Victoria, 1983.

32 *The Echo* (Sydney), 14 January 1890.

33 This and following quotes from Henry Lawson, 'De Rougemont and Us and Some Digressions', *La Trobe Library Journal*, vol. 7, no. 28, October 1981.

34 *The Sunday Times* (Perth), 26 July 1914.

35 O Sitwell, *Sober Truth: A collection of nineteenth-century episodes, fantastic, grotesque and mysterious*, Macdonald, London, 1930.
36 *The West Australian*, 4 January 1920.
37 *The Times*, 8 September 1921.

Index